In print @ ___

W9-BCG-948

JB
as is

Jung's Psychology
and its
Social
Meaning

BOOKS BY IRA PROGOFF

At a Journal Workshop:
The Basic Text and Guide for Using the *Intensive Journal* Process

The Practice of Process Meditation:
The *Intensive Journal* Way to Spiritual Experience

Life-Study:
Experiencing Creative Lives by the *Intensive Journal* Method

The Well and the Cathedral

The White Robed Monk

The Star/Cross

The Death and Rebirth of Psychology

Depth Psychology and Modern Man

The Symbolic and the Real

Jung's Psychology and Its Social Meaning

Jung, Synchronicity and Human Destiny

The Image of an Oracle

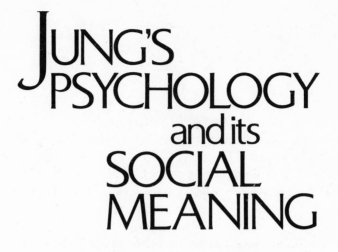

JUNG'S PSYCHOLOGY
and its
SOCIAL
MEANING

A Comprehensive Statement of
C. G. Jung's Psychological Theories
and an Interpretation of their Significance
for the Social Sciences

Ira Progoff

DIALOGUE HOUSE LIBRARY/NEW YORK

Published by
Dialogue House Library
80 East 11th Street
New York, New York 10003

Copyright © 1953, 1981 by Ira Progoff

Intensive Journal® is a registered trademark of
Dr. Ira Progoff and is used under license by
Dialogue House Associates, Inc.

All rights reserved. Except for brief excerpts
quoted in reviews, no part of this publication
may be reproduced, stored in a retrieval
system or transmitted in any form or by any
means, electronic, mechanical, photocopy-
ing, recording or otherwise without written
permission of the publisher.

Library of Congress Catalog Card Number: 85-25406

ISBN 0-87941-014-0

Printed in the United States of America

Third Edition 1985

CONTENTS

INTRODUCTION TO THE
THIRD EDITION

The world is rich with many dimensions of reality. One
aspect of truth is revealed to us through scientific experi-
mentation; another through intellectual analysis; another
through the creations of art, literature and music. All of
these are valid areas of experience and have played a vital
role in the enlargement of the modern view of life. But
there is another experience of reality which is much more
fundamental, for it functions as the source of supply on
which all areas of consciousness depend and without which
all our achievements in the world of knowledge would not
even be possible. It is so deeply-rooted, and so intimately a
part of mental life, however, that mankind has seldom been
able to disengage itself from it and see it with objectivity.
Within our cultural era, it is only now, when the personality has been rent asunder by one historical crisis after another, that it has become possible to analyze the hidden
workings of the mind. Intimate contents of the soul which
would have been kept inviolate in any other period have
been laid bare in our age through many a tormented autobiography, both in literature and the mental clinic, and it is
these that have opened the road to our new insights.

We are now able for the first time in Western civilization
to understand scientifically a dimension of reality which,
though unrecognized, has always had the greatest importance in human life. We are like people who have been

looking at a motion picture film thinking that the images on the screen are real things when suddenly we realize that they are only projections and that there is a projection machine hidden behind us. When we learn this, we want to know how the machine operates and whence it draws the images which it throws upon the screen. We want to find the source of the pictures; and with regard to the human mind, we want to find the source of the symbols which come to us in dreams and fantasies, in the arts and in religious visions. We want to understand the peculiar projection apparatus that is operating deep within the personality, and we want to understand the processes by which sometimes strange, sometimes exceedingly powerful symbols mold the contents of our conscious lives.

One of the great paradoxes which we must learn to comprehend is the fact that it is precisely when we feel most conscious and at our highest point of rationality that nonconscious forces penetrate the area of awareness and either becloud or dominate consciousness. On the personal level, it is then that we experience moods, hear voices, or have fantasies; on the historical level, a whole nation of apparently modern, reasonable human beings may be seized by a "mass psychosis," as occurred in the case of Nazism. As long as we have not mastered the unconscious side of mental life, we must be at its mercy. This uncomfortable fact hangs over us like a sword on a slim thread, a constant threat to the vaunted achievements of our scientifically rational world. We are only too well aware that, in our present situation, all the accomplishments of our civilization can easily be swept away if one nation equipped with modern technology is caught in the grip of a destructive symbol.

On the other hand, we must realize the significance of the equally important fact that the same forces which drive men to insanity can also be the source of the most creative inspirations. The reasons behind this great ambiguity in human nature will occupy us in many of the pages which follow. I would only remark here that what is often called "the unconscious" should not be thought of as pathological. Like all things, the human mind follows the principle inherent in its own essence; and, as we find it to be through all of Nature, this principle is that it realize itself, integrate itself, become whole in relation to its potentialities. An inner purpose is therefore contained within the seed of personality, and this we shall find to be a most important element in the dimension of reality which we are studying. It manifests itself in a great variety of events in personal life and in history, coming forth in mental phenomena which appear equally in primitive religions, ancient philosophies, and the depths of the modern mind. All of these are to be understood in terms of a natural process which leads toward wholeness, toward an inner integration and the expression of an inherent meaningfulness. In this context, the basic symbols of mankind can be seen to be living experiences of something natural and universal in man. Myths and religious beliefs need no longer be dismissed as "illusions." They are in themselves expressions of a valid aspect of reality, and each of the varied myths by which men live in history is a small participation in a larger, pervading truth.

The tremendous value of the work of C. G. Jung is that he has developed specific methods and tools with which to understand and amplify the dimension of reality which comes to us from beneath the conscious threshold. His accomplishment is essentially that of the pioneer in science, and his work should therefore be considered not as something complete in itself, but as a fertile new approach with broad possibilities. Because his concepts have grown out of his deep concern for the spiritual problems of our time, Jung is in a position to make a most valuable contribution not only to psychological, but to social fields of study. In this regard one of the main purposes of this book is to facilitate the process of integrating Jung's concepts into the mainstream of contemporary thought. The first step is merely to make his ideas available in a form in which they can be grasped clearly and handled intellectually. Unfortunately, Jung's own writings do not do this; they present overpowering difficulties to the beginner and in the past have materially retarded the acceptance of his ideas. Anyone who would deal seriously with Jung's thought must, of course, ultimately read Jung's own words, but there is a great value in being able to see his way of thinking as a whole, and especially in comprehending the social implications which Jung does not himself develop in great detail. My aim, however, is not merely to summarize Jung's ideas, but to present them in terms of an interpretation which will make it possible for them to be analyzed, mulled over, criticized, appreciated, and most important, *worked with* as hypotheses in related fields of psychological and *social study*.

This volume was first published in 1953. It had originally been written as a doctoral dissertation in the field of the social history of ideas. Most of it was worked on in the years just before and just after 1950. But that now seems to have been a long time ago. At that time it was not possible to carry out a doctoral study of Jung's work under the auspices of a university psychology department. At least, not any that I knew of. The situation is quite different today, especially because of events that have taken place in society. At that time, however, the atmosphere of opinion was severely turned against Jung. The prevailing attitude was antagonism and ridicule. Not only were his conceptions rejected out of hand, but the very subject matter of his writings was held to be irrelevant to psychological science.

Since that time many changes have occurred. Existential psychology in various versions has introduced a larger philosophical awareness in what had previously been an anti-philosophical profession. A variety of so-called "Humanistic" or "Third Force" psychologies centered around the writings of Abraham Maslow, Carl Rogers and Karl Menninger have made both the basic point that an experience of meaning in life is essential for psychological health and the further point that a major task of psychology is to draw forth the potentials of individual persons.

By acknowledging these two points, the psychological establishment, both in the universities and in the therapeutic professions, has increasingly accepted the point of view for which Jung has been energetically attacked in the past. It seems that the shifting of directions which I predicted in the Epilogue to the original edition of this book has actually come to pass. Jung is no longer a lone figure. His approach has now reached into the heart of the psychological field. That this has taken place gives new significance to the work that depth psychology can do and it opens new dimensions for the study of society and history.

The fact that this book is now called forth once again is in itself an indication of the reversal of thought that has taken place. For this is a book that takes Jung very seriously indeed. It proceeds upon a twofold conviction. The first is that there are more basic, seminal concepts about the nature of man and the development of his life in society to be drawn from Jung's hypotheses than from any of the other foundational authors in the field of depth psychology. This is not to negate the others but it is seeking a framework of thought that is large and deep and open-ended for the study of human life. Jung's work provides a broad and profound starting point. It takes us to deep waters where we can learn to dive and to swim.

The second is that the necessities of the present cultural crisis make it essential that Jung's concepts be brought into a form that is intellectually accessible to those who are working in the social sciences and the humanities. To contribute to this so that Jung's work can be assimilated into the thought of our time was a primary purpose in writing this book.

The first point mentioned above regarding the seminal value of Jung's work takes me back to the nineteen-forties when my main concern was to find a psychological conception that could be of real help in understanding society. I was soon brought to the conclusion that psychoanalysis is neither an appropriate nor an adequate tool for the study of culture. It was in vogue at the time, but it seemed clear to me that its emphasis on diagnosis could only lead to frustration. A psychology circumscribed by pathology can not lead to constructively dynamic social experiences. Realizing this, I became convinced that the various Freudian styles of psychology could eventually lead only to a dead end and great disappointment. When that happened, to whom could we turn for a depth understanding of society? Was there any psychologist who had a direct perception of the historical dimension of personality?

When I surveyed the field, I found that there was very little from which to choose if I kept that criterion strongly in mind.

Alfred Adler, to be sure, possessed a sensitive and profound awareness of social feeling. He certainly was much more sympathetic to social injustice than Jung was. But he had studied neither the historical nor the philosophical nor the aesthetic aspects of personality as deeply as Jung. Otto Rank brought a much larger knowledge of the history of culture and of the humanities than any of the other depth psychologists, but the situation of his life and his early death had prevented him from fulfilling the promise of his exceedingly wise intuitions.

There was nowhere to turn. And since I had already had the experience of realizing that the psyche of man has both a depth dimension and a time dimension, a dimension of time that is inwardly experienced, I could not be satisfied with any approach to man that did not also have this understanding. I searched among all the psychological writings that I could, and I was left with the observation that Jung was the only one who had taken any significant steps in developing an historical dimension of psychological depth. I was forced to the conclusion that there was no one but Jung from whom to choose. He had taken the field in this most fundamental area of study simply by default.

It then became a question for me of what would be the most fruitful context in which to pursue my study of Jung. The field of academic psychology was not a viable possibility at that time. Rather, it seemed much more appropriate to study Jung in the field of the history of ideas and on the edges of social psychology. Since that was all that was possible, that was what I did.

In hindsight, with my present perspective I am grateful for the circumstances that forced me to conduct my original studies of Jung's work in the field of the history of ideas. It had a fortunate outcome. It forced me to carry out my interpretation of Jung without the confinements of a narrow field of psychological specialization. This would actually have been inappropriate considering the nature of Jung's subject matter. I was left free to study his work in the larger context of the history of philosophy, social theory, and the study of culture. The fact that I did this eventually gave my study a degree of objectivity and an historical perspective that Jung himself profoundly appreciated. It was in fact, perhaps paradoxically, one of the factors that opened a doorway of communication between us.

Because of it, when I first went to visit Jung, I was able to say to him—half-apologetically as I recall at the time—that I had not studied him nor written about him as a member of his own school of thought, but rather as an outsider. I had studied him, I said, as though he were some historical figure long since dead, as though he were Plato, or Spinoza, or Hume, and as though there were no special school of thought surrounding him with devotion. I had read his books, interpreted and reconstructed his ideas with the same detachment that I would have shown to any of those worthies.

I remember that when I said this to Professor Jung on first meeting him, I was fearful that it would erect a block between us. It had quite the opposite effect, however. It established a solid intellectual basis of communication, and it opened the possibility for the long series of conversations that took place between us during the subsequent years.

Jung's response to my statement was that he felt hemmed in and narrowed by being thought of as the founder of a special school of thought. The essence of his work, he said, was that he felt that all serious thinkers are continuators of certain historical lines of thought in their culture at the same time that each is a mediator in a special way to the future. Thus he thought of himself, he said, not only as standing on the shoulders of authors in the past, but as seriously working with and carrying further certain problems and lines of investigation that had been the concern of those thinkers of the past to whom he felt a particular inner connection. His goal and conception of himself was not that he become like a flag, a rallying point and an object of loyalty, but rather that he be thought of finally as one who had carried forward certain lines of investigation in western thought in such a way that others would find it valuable to use his work in extending their own.

With this as the background, I felt free to tell Professor Jung something of what had transpired when I underwent my doctoral examination in defense of my dissertation on his work. I told him that when I gave the basic speech before the faculty committee presenting the main thesis, I began it by declaiming dramatically, "Just as Karl Marx said he was not a Marxian, so is C. G. Jung not a Jungian."

We both laughed at that. But suddenly Jung became

very serious. He paused and, in a manner that I later found to be characteristic of him, he went abruptly into a mood of deep reflection. "Yes," he said slowly, "I am not a Jungian." And then he added heavily as though speaking more to himself than to me, giving the impression that he was decisively resolving something within his own mind as he spoke, "I am not a Jungian," he repeated softly, "and I could never be."

The reader can readily understand how meaningful that statement was to me in 1953. I thought about it at length afterwards and I made it a point in our subsequent conversations to draw Dr. Jung on to elaborate his feelings in that direction whenever it was possible and appropriate for me to do so.

By the time the original manuscript of this volume was written, Jung had already published the books in which he articulated the main body of his thought. There had been, however, over the years a development in this thought that reached beyond the basic subject matter of depth psychology and opened large areas of hypothesis and speculation. But Jung had carefully kept this side of his intellectual life in the background, feeling that it was difficult enough for him to gain consideration for his basic concepts without complicating things still further.

When he was just past seventy-five years of age, however, Jung suffered an illness from which he did not think he would recover. When he did recover, he took the attitude that all the additional years that would follow in his life from that point onward were a free gift, an extra bonus of lifetime. And it must be for a reason, he thought. He interpreted it as a sign that he was being granted an extra quota of years in order that he might be enabled to give full expression to all the insights and concepts that had been developing within him at the deepest and even esoteric levels of his work.

Those extra years were thus to Jung a token of great

affirmation which life itself had given him. They carried also for him a heavy sense of responsibility. He felt that the task of stating these ultimate and deepest concepts and securing for them their proper audience was now placed squarely on his shoulders. Perhaps paradoxically, but feeling this burden placed upon him, made it possible for Jung also to experience during those years a great sense of spiritual release. Those later years freed him much more fully from the bonds of conventionality that had been the heritage of his Swiss burgher background. There were fundamental, even transcendent concepts to be formulated during these extra years, and Jung gave himself to it fully. It was as though an implicit bargain had been made.

As a result, the last decade in Jung's life was a period of remarkable productivity. Working at high capacity virtually to the time of his death at age 86, Jung was able to crystallize some of his most original lines of thought. In particular, where he had been following hypotheses which he had felt were too far from established attitudes to be published earlier, his new freedom gave him a new surge of fresh insight as well as the power of courageous statement. Some of the books that Jung published during the last years of his life are among the most pioneering and valuable of all. They do not alter the basic core of his thinking, but they add dimensions which indicate that, if Jung had been able to begin at the point where his old age forced him to stop, he would have made a further contribution of the greatest magnitude.

Among Jung's publications that add an important dimension to his work is his study of *Synchronicity* as "an acausal connecting principle." Synchronicity is a hypothesis of far-reaching implications, the significance of which is yet to be appreciated. It opens a line of thought by which the inner movements of change can be understood where change involves the inner process of the psyche and the destiny factors of human existence. As such, Synchronicity is not an alternative to Causality. It is a balance that complements Causality as an explanatory principle, giving an additional perspective with which to understand the permutations of life. In the years that followed the writing of this volume, drawing on some of my conversations with Jung in his later years, I wrote a special monograph on Synchronicity.*

Other writings from Jung's last period have this in common with Synchronicity: they merit, and often require, special studies in order to draw out their multiple levels of meaning. This is true especially of *Answer to Job,* a short book of major significance in which Jung in a personal way, without reserve or inhibition, expresses the inner dialogue he had conducted with God on his understanding of how God has lived out His life-drama in western civilization. This is a book also that requires special studies, theological, psychological, and existential; and it is bound to have many of these in the coming years.

Jung's later publications, *Aion, Mysterium Conjunctionis,* and the enlarged edition of the early book, *The Psychology of the Unconscious,* now reprinted as *Symbols of Transformation,* contain amplifications and extensions of his work in which he has articulated his furthest explorations into the depth of man. Sections of those books hold a major position in the total corpus of Jung's lifework. They will eventually be of great importance in helping us ascertain the "ultimate" directions toward which Jung's thought was tending. Many further studies, and many, many additional doctoral dissertations will be called for to interpret and clarify the writings of Jung's last years.

From several points of view, the work of Jung's last de-

* Ira Progoff, *Jung, Synchronicity and Human Destiny,* Julian Press, Press, New York, 1973, Dell Paperback, 1974. It is scheduled to be reissued by Dialogue House Library, N.Y.

cade culminates all that he had done before. It merits the most careful intellectual consideration as well as the most solemn meditation. While it was the culmination for Jung, it may also be the starting point for each of us. That was indeed Jung's purpose. The reader who wishes to explore further in the direction of Jung's later work may find some leads in the chapters that deal with Jung in my book *The Death and Rebirth of Psychology.*

One volume by Jung which was published after his death is different from all the others. That is his partial autobiography, *Memories, Dreams, Reflections,* which presents, if not a large percentage of Jung's Life experience, at least a representative portion of it. It is a book that is full of suggestive leads and stimulation. It will reward the closest attention. It is essential in understanding Jung's life and work.

His autobiography stands by itself in a very special way. It is Jung himself. It is not Jung himself talking about this or that concept or theory. But it is just Jung himself. This is the inner content that all the theorizings and all the explorations are about. The raw material is expressed in Jung's autobiography. For this reason, if there is any book to recommend as the companion, balance, and addition to the present one, it is *Memories, Dreams, Reflections.* This candid volume permits us and enables us to see what was happening inside Jung while he was on his lonely journey. All that we read in this study of his work must be set over against the private inner experiences that are described there. And not only Jung's experiences. Our own inner experiences as well. For it is the inner experiences of each of us that hold the key to our understanding of man both as an individual person and as a human being in history.

This last point is of great significance. The life of each person is unique, but the experiences through which we each pass as we reach toward our own wholeness have a great deal in common. There is much that we share, and yet we are each individual in our experience of life.

After my study of Jung's work, including the original publication of this volume, my attention continued to be drawn to the duality of human life in modern civilization, the fact that we have so much in common while each life is individual. Eventually I developed a method by which persons can work out in a tangible way the continuity of their lives, can place themselves in relation to it, while they develop the particular aspects of their lives that come to the fore at each moment of time. To do this is called Life-Positioning by the *Intensive Journal* process using the method of Journal Feedback. The method draws on the work of the great depth psychologists, particularly Jung and the later work of Otto Rank, as well as on the concepts of Henri Bergson, Jan Christian Smuts and Martin Buber.

In recent years it has been possible for me to take the *Intensive Journal* process out into society where individuals, regardless of their cultural background or their psychological point of view, have been able to use it to place themselves in the continuity of their own experiences, to see what their life is trying to become and to help it on its way. The *Intensive Journal* process seeks to fulfill on the practical level of individual life a main goal toward which Jung was moving as he worked on the conceptual level of inner experience. Of particular importance to me has been the way that Jung renewed the age-old metaphor of the seed, applying it in the context of modern depth psychology, making it possible not only for individuals to identify their own seed but to have access to it for psychological work that evokes the potentials latent there and develops them further. Of great value also in this regard has been Jung's understanding of the energic forces and the modes of perception that become available to us at the archetypal levels of human life. His insights in this area have many applications and extensions, as will become apparent when we discuss the body of Jung's thought in the pages that follow.

I have felt free to use Jung's large perspective, particularly his conception of the depth of the human psyche and its relation to time, in the work that I did after the period when I concentrated my attention on studying his system of thought. Eventually I came to the realization that in order to create a method by which each individual, as person, can position himself or herself in the movement of life, an open-ended point of view is necessary. It cannot be limited to any one framework of thought, but each person must be free to follow where his experiences lead. The *Intensive Journal* process begins with particular conceptions which serve to set it in motion. But then it is free to move in accordance with each individual life, to unfold what is in the depth of each person, to balance and/or express it. The special value of the *Intensive Journal* process on the practical level is that it makes it possible for each individual to experience the wholeness of his life as a totality in motion moving toward a future that is being formed in the openness of the present moment. It provides a method by which a person can work within his own life, combining an active sense of time with a perspective of the depth of symbolism, and finding in the combination of time and depth a key to the meaning of each individual life.

Jung's broad and deep view of life has made a large contribution to the quality of consciousness that is continuing to unfold in modern civilization. Thanks to persons like him at the start of the twentieth century, the future is now open-ended. Seeing what Jung has developed both as hypotheses and as a framework of thought, we can form from his work the perspectives of consciousness by which the difficulties in our time can eventually be overcome.

Part 1

THE BASIC CORE OF
JUNG'S PSYCHOLOGY

I

THE HISTORICAL SITUATION

In his work on the declining days of Rome,[1] the great Swiss historian, Jacob Burckhardt, describes how the people surrendered themselves to every exotic doctrine and foreign religious sect that they could find. They were searching everywhere because their traditional beliefs no longer seemed sacred and true to them and they needed to find a new meaning for their lives.

The similarity between our own time and that old Roman situation is all too easy to see. Ours also is a restless age in which old values have fallen into disuse while new values have yet to be found. Well aware that our old traditions are no longer strong, we live in a time of searching, eager for new insights that will have the power of guiding and inspiring. But a very practical problem besets us. Where are the tools of thought that can be adequate for our task? Where shall we find principles of knowledge capable of interpreting to us all the aspects and implications of our situation, our past, our present, our potentialities? Many thoughtful and sensitive men have seen this to be the problem, and most are agreed that the conceptions of life which we inherited from

[1] Jacob Burckhardt, *The Age of Constantine the Great*, trans. by Moses Hadas, Pantheon, New York, 1949. First edition 1852.

3

the nineteenth century lack the breadth and depth to meet a need as large as ours. New doctrines, new wisdom, a point of view with larger vistas, are necessary to overcome the spiritual malaise so reminiscent of declining Rome. Certainly these are difficult to find, and we can be sure that the answer will not come from just one field alone. It is a vast search and must ultimately involve every school of thought that is alert to the responsibilities of our critical age. It calls for a far-reaching discussion, and to this the following pages are offered as one small contribution with the special purpose of bringing the work of C. G. Jung into sharper focus in relation to the problems of our time.

Jung's subject of study is the psychic life of man. As a psychiatrist, his main interest is in the development of personality, but he realized at an early point in his work that he would not be able to understand his material unless he studied man on a canvas large enough to include the history of the human race as a whole, particularly its varieties of mythology, religion and culture. He therefore made it his principle to consider all forms of psychic phenomena as belonging within a single context. As a result, we find in Jung's writings that the problems of individual psychology, society, history and philosophy are treated not separately but in close inter-relation. They are all focused around his central problem, which is to study the infinite varieties of psychic phenomena in the life of man. Without stressing the question of methodology, but simply by following a procedure that expresses his special insight into his subject matter, Jung has developed an inherently unitary approach. His work is one of the leading instances of a holistic point of view applied to the study of man, and it is by virtue of this unifying aspect of his thought that Jung's psychology makes its contribution to the social sciences.

The first step in introducing Jung's ideas into the larger discussions of our time is, necessarily, to explain what they mean and what they imply, and to formulate them plainly so that they will be easier to examine. This is essentially our intention in the present volume: to give a clear understanding of the fundamental concepts in Jung's psychological studies and to indicate their significance for the interpretation of society and history. Because of a variety of factors which we shall discuss a little later on, a very large area of misunderstanding has clouded Jung's work practically since the publication of his *Psychology of the Unconscious* in 1912. The main reason for this is probably to be found in the fact that it is exceedingly easy to misinterpret Jung's individual theories unless their position in the larger context and structure of his thought is thoroughly understood. It is very important to grasp Jung's work as a whole and to keep in mind the way in which each of his specific doctrines and researches expresses his fundamental orientation to psychic phenomena.

Before starting, however, we should like to give the reader a small warning. Jung's work has to be understand as a unity, but Jung himself is not at all a systematic thinker, at least not in the usual intellectual meaning of the term. Although it is absolutely essential to understand the structure of his thought, it is wrong to think of Jung as a system-maker. As an individual, he is, in fact, just the contrary of a systematic person. He is altogether opposed, as a matter of principle, to the building of closed, logically air-tight, intellectual systems. He has a highly anti-systematic temperament, which has come to the fore not only in the development of his ideas, but even in the way he has presented them in his writings. The non-systematic character of Jung's books has certainly contributed not a little to hindering the general acceptance of his ideas. In his work he follows his interests and hunches, develops a hypothesis, works with it, changes it, develops another, returns to the first, alters it, and so on, as the play of his mind responds to his empirical evidence. What has emerged from all of this is essentially not a system but a point of view. And yet it is a point of view with an inherent inner unity centering around the solid core of fundamental doctrine that has been basic to all of Jung's thought since the early 1920's. Our aim is to present this solid core succinctly and yet clarified as fully as possible, so that the reader can feel the spirit of Jung's approach and can see the logical relationships between his assumptions and the conclusions, or hypotheses, to which he comes.

The first part of our study is devoted to Jung's psychological ideas, to presenting them and clarifying them. In the second part, we carry these ideas over from the mainly psychological area to apply them to the study of society and of history. We have to keep in mind that, in doing this, we are taking Jung's concepts into a field that is different from the one in which they originated. Jung is, fundamentally, not a sociologist and not an historian. His subject matter is primarily psychic phenomena as they occur in the *individual personality;* but his interpretation of individuality has the very special quality of being constructed directly in terms of an historical perspective. His conception of personality is inherently unitary, drawing together culture, religion and history within the single context of the human psyche. Actually,

Jung deals with social questions only because he feels forced to do so. The largeness of the requirements which he sets for real pychological understanding makes it nec ssary for him to be more than a psychologist. In a sense, Jung's work is like a river that overflows its regular channel; he cannot contain himself within his own psychological field, but spills over with far-reaching implications for the adjacent areas of the social sciences. "Spills over" is the proper phrase because it is so clear that it is against his natural inclination that Jung goes at all beyond his proper psychological field. He has frequently remarked that he would much prefer not to have to deal with social situations; but his understanding of the historical foundations of individual personality, and especially of the psychological confusions in the present era, forces him to do so. He realized long ago that the man who would understand human beings must "put away his academic gown, say good-bye to the study, and wander with human heart through the world. There, in the horrors of the prison, the asylum and the hospital, in the drinking-shops, brothels and gambling hells, in the salons of the elegant, in the exchanges, socialist meetings, churches, religious revivals and sectarian ecstacies, through love and hate, through the experience of passion in every form in his own body, he would reap richer stores of knowledge than text-books a foot thick could give him. Then would he know how to doctor the sick with real knowledge of the human soul." [2]

To do these things and to visit these places is altogether necessary, but they are not to be the taste of the respectable Swiss burgher mentality which is definitely a part of Jung's

[2] C. G. Jung, *Two Essays on Analytical Psychology*, trans. by H. G. and C. F. Baynes, Dodd, Mead, New York, 1928, pp. 2, 3.

background. It is really despite himself that he developed his insights into history and culture, and this is one reason for our opinion that eventually Jung's social concepts will be developed further by others than Jung himself has been able, or inclined, to take them. We may well expect that new insights will be brought forth which will develop the larger aspects of Jung's thought, and ultimately go beyond the range even of Jung's original perspective. It is indeed our hope—and it would be a lasting testimonial to the value of his work—that independent studies, taking their stimulus from Jung and developing the historical and philosophical side of his work, will in time branch out into wider fields.

In discussing Jung, we must always be aware of the pioneering quality of his mind. Where his concepts are rough or unclear, it is generally because they are not final formulations, but the first statements of a new approach to psychic phenomena. The characteristic of his work is that he opens new areas of thought and investigation not only for himself in the field of his own interests, but, almost inadvertently, for others, with concepts that break ground throughout the social sciences. Several important social thinkers have already taken notice of this quality in Jung's thought and have begun to explore those of his ideas which are relevant for their work. They now use only bits and pieces of Jung's concepts, but that in itself is a highly significant step, for it indicates that a process is just beginning which will ultimately integrate Jung's perspective into the social thought of our time.

JUNG'S SIGNIFICANCE FOR SOCIAL THEORY

There are very fundamental and objective reasons that make it a virtual certainty that Jung's thought will have an increasing importance in the social discussions of the coming years. The outstanding intellectual need of our time is to get beyond the limitations of the nineteenth-century conception of human nature. It left us too restricted a view of life with its rationalistic economic man and its biological and historical determinisms. In so far as there are developments of thought that can be said to be characteristic of the twentieth century, the most powerful and impelling force behind them is the effort to break free of the nineteenth century and find a larger vision of reality. The signs have, indeed, been apparent for many years. Freud's conception of the unconscious was one of the first signals that the break was coming. It was the first intellectual tool with strength enough to overthrow the old rationalistic psychology; but Freud himself did not have the final answers. He missed up on two main points: he did not understand history, and he did not understand religion.

One of the main weaknesses of rationalistic thought was that it had failed to penetrate to the roots of human motivations in history; it was content to speak of superficial factors, such as "desire" and "self-interest." Thinkers like Thorstein Veblen, who studied the "social habits of thought," tried to get beneath consciousness; but they did not have the psychological tools that would enable them to do so. The conception of the unconscious could have brought the answer, but Freud's biological and essentially anti-social formulation of it prevented him from comprehending history, and so the field has remained open and waiting for someone to throw the light of Depth Psychology on social and historical forces.

The fact that the limitations of Freud's point of view have become more generally apparent in recent years is fundamentally because his biological conception of man no longer seems adequate. The need is not only to get beyond rationalism and to reach the historical forces underlying consciousness, but to understand the unconscious in terms of its meaningfulness and in terms of its implications for man's spiritual life. The view of the unconscious in materialistic terms is still rooted in the concepts of the nineteenth century and is limited by their narrowness. The great need is for an understanding of the unconscious that makes all the dimensions of psychic reality available to man and does not limit him to his conscious and rational experiences. Instead of misconceiving of religion as an "illusion," new vistas could then be opened for spiritual experience. Such a conception might even ultimately bring about a creative synthesis at the point where religious philosophy and depth psychology come together.

Jung's work is oriented to meet each of these needs. His understanding of the unconscious undercuts and goes far beyond the rationalistic conception of consciousness. His interpretation of the psyche is inherently historical and is based on a social rather than a biological conception of man. Most important, without offering any one-sided metaphysical theories, he avoids a materialistic position and prepares the field psychologically for a deeper penetration of reality while interpreting the meaning of religious experience. In prophesying who are the people for whom Jung's thought will be important in the future, perhaps we can summarize it this way: if a social thinker is dissatisfied with the rational-istic psychologies that have developed out of nineteenth-century thought; if he feels that a depth psychological per-spective is necessary for an adequate insight into history, if he believes that this depth must be conceived in an historical and social rather than a biological sense; and if, further, he feels that the unconscious must be understood as opening on a larger realm of spiritual and psychological meanings, then he must of necessity turn to Jung. It is not, of course, that Jung has the full and final answers. Far from it. What he has done is only to open a field. It is simply that of the original developers of psychoanalytic theory, Jung is the only one who has dealt systematically with both the dark side of man and the integrative spiritual faculties of the human being. Because of this, he stands out as a beacon and rallying point for those who believe that the answer to modern problems must include an understanding of the depth layers of the unconscious from an historical point of view, together with a dynamic conception of the spiritual nature of man.

In the effort to obtain a larger view of reality, and espe-cially of its psychic aspects, Jung has made an effort to place himself outside the *gestalt* of the Western mind in order to gain access to the insights of other peoples and other world-views. He feels the need of a larger perspective than the occidental philosophies of Christendom have heretofore de-veloped. With this purpose, and just because he is aware of the limitations of his own European personality and of the needs of his Western patients, Jung has gone to the ancient religions and philosophies of the Orient to translate their way of thinking about psychic processes into terms that can fit the Western orientation. One of the most fertile and challenging contributions that Jung has to offer comes from the fact that he constructs his interpretation of psychic phenomena out of the age-old material of cultures that are distant from the modern mind both in time and in place. It is essentially an effort to blend the subtlety of the East with the practicality of the West and to convert the wisdom of the ancient and oriental religions into a form in which they can be used by the modern sciences of man.

Of course, Jung is not alone in his desire to build a universalistic point of view by bridging the psychologies of Orient and Occident. He believes, in fact, that the journeys of Western thought to the ancient East constitute a major cultural trend that is bound to increase in coming years. It is, in part, a balancing process by which the Western mind seeks to complement the excessively objective orientation toward life which it has developed in modern times. In another sense, too, the eagerness of the West to taste the exotic Oriental doctrines is a recurrence of the situation that Burckhardt observed in ancient Rome. Out of the fact that traditional religions are waning and that the old social values are losing their acceptance as truth, there has grown the tendency to look outside of Western civilization for new answers, and it is not surprising that they should be found in the most ancient philosophies of all. The historian, Arnold Toynbee, has also noticed this phenomenon and has stated that it is a characteristic of all civilizations in their declining days that they look to foreign lands for their new philosophies of life. If this is so, it means that when Jung turns toward the East to return with psychological insights for the West, he is expressing an historical tendency that will ultimately be of major importance.

From the points that have been mentioned so far, we can see that Jung's psychology does not involve just psychology *per se*, but the totality of the personal and historical lives of Western Europeans. His purpose is to go beyond the academic side of psychology and come to grips with the actual problems of individuals as their lives are lived now in the turmoil of history. In this sense, there is a general existentialist quality in Jung's thought, if we understand the word "existentialist" in its most fundamental connotation. It begins with the meaninglessness of the individual's existence as it is lived in this declining period of Western civilization, and works toward the experiencing of the meaning of life out of the struggle of personal being. Jung's psychological view of life requires the confrontation of the world—cosmic and social—by the individual who has struggled with the psychic contents that are within himself to find his own essential nature. This is the same emphasis that is found in the oriental philosophies, where the burden is placed on the individual human being in the belief that each person must struggle through to find the light for himself. In the present situation of western culture, the effect of such a view is to stress the separation between the modern man and his cultural symbols. The modern personality is forced to live *in search*, in search of itself, psychologically, spiritually, and historically. Jung's work thus reaches its central problem at the point where all the pressures of modern civilization converge and exert their impact on the individual's existence. It is this focus of study that has attracted the attention of such varied social thinkers as Lewis Mumford, Paul Tillich and Arnold Toynbee. They have taken up Jung's ideas in connection with specific interests of their own, and from a cursory look at their work, the reader can get some preliminary impression of the kind and range of problems that Jung's thought touches in the social sciences.

MUMFORD, TILLICH AND TOYNBEE

The work of Lewis Mumford is particularly interesting for its affinity with Jung's point of view. In his writings, Mumford does not display a detailed familiarity with Jung's concepts, but from time to time he makes the kind of reference that brings an idea of Jung's right to the fore of his thinking. Mumford's own work has a social orientation, and it is through the study of history that he comes to see the crucial importance of psychology and religion for the understanding of the modern age. Like Jung, Mumford takes a unitary point of view, since he is interested in the study of man as a whole, but he comes from a direction that is just the opposite of Jung's. Jung comes to historical problems from a psychological starting point and Mumford is just the reverse; but their thought converges on their common subject matter, which is the understanding of human life in terms of the full depth of personality and in terms of the historical largeness of time.

Mumford shares with Jung the basic idea that our modern historical problems are fundamentally psychological and religious. In particular, he realizes that there is a great significance in Jung's dictum that the psychological disharmonies of our time are really aspects of the weakening of traditional religious symbols. Like Jung, Mumford is not bound by any of the old faiths, and so he is not one of those who dutifully call for a "return" to the traditional, as though that were even possible any more. Rather, he looks for a deeper scientific understanding of what is involved psychologically and historically in the collapse of traditional symbols. At this point, Mumford seems to be mulling over some of Jung's other concepts—not within their Jungian context, to be sure —but with an effort to extract their implications. He turns to Jung's larger view of the nature of religious symbols, of the force of faith in history, of the consequences of the break-up of systems of faith, the weakening of symbols, and especially the colorless objectification of reality resulting from the "withdrawal of projections" in the modern secular worldview. Further, Mumford points to Jung's insight that even on a large historical scale, what is pressed out of consciousness may nevertheless exert its force in the unconscious, so that when beliefs in gods are thrust aside, they may return as a possession by devils within the mind, haunting individuals, and driving masses of people to acts of historical madness. The place of the irrational in our scientific civilization, the nature of the primitive and archaic elements in the modern mind, the flux in faiths as an historical phenomenon—these are problems which Mumford has seen and on which Jung's perspective throws a special light.[3]

The work of the Protestant theologian, Paul Tillich, is also an effort to apply this general point of view in solving a similar range of problems. Basing his studies on a firm but flexible interpretation of Christianity, Tillich realizes that an adequate religious position requires both psychological un-

[3] See especially, Lewis Mumford, *The Conduct of Life*, Harcourt, Brace, New York, 1951.

derstanding and an historical perspective. He thus sees the spiritual flux of the modern cultural situation not only as the central problem of our time, but as the confluence for the various sciences of man. As a theologian and social thinker, Tillich comes from quite a different direction than Jung, but curiously enough he shares Jung's opinion that the foundation of Depth Psychology is an essentially religious experience. Further than that, Tillich follows Jung's analysis of the psychology of the modern Protestant individual and agrees that the deadening of the traditional religious images and the effort to rationalize religious beliefs has resulted not only in a weakening of the core of religious life but in a thinning out of the resources of the individual personality.

Tillich's analysis of the nature of our secular culture and the meaning of its appearance at this point in history has much in common with Jung's social theories and is exceedingly fruitful for understanding the spiritual and psychological aspects of modern culture. As a theologian, too, he is especially interested in the question of grace, of the psychological bases of faith and of true inspiration. Here Tillich's thought is altogether in the spirit of Jung, as he realizes that inspiration is essentially a kind of possession, since every religious prophet must be in the grip either of a god—or of a demon. Inspiration is possession from above—or possession from below; and when it is the latter, to speak of a psychosis or to speak of a demonic possession is equally correct. Tillich's work as a whole constitutes an extremely significant contribution because he is a theologian who sees that Depth Psychology is the dynamic foundation of an authentic spiritual life, and that all spiritual and psychological factors must be understood historically in their cultural significance.

His work is an effort to deal with spiritual and social questions in an integrated way, and while Tillich has already drawn on Jung at various points, there is much that can fruitfully be done in further relating their ideas.[4]

From still a third direction, we find that the historian, Arnold Toynbee, is turning with increasing interest to Jung's formulations. The large canvas on which Toynbee sketches the life and death of civilizations has provided many people with a means of finding a perspective for themselves in the modern world situation. There is special significance, therefore, in Toynbee's opinion that the study of the history of civilizations requires a Depth Psychological dimension, and especially in the fact that he regards the concepts of C. G. Jung as being the closest in spirit to his own approach.

The theories of Jung and Toynbee meet on one of the most fundamental problems in the interpretation of society: the understanding of what constitutes the real continuity in history. To a thinker of Toynbee's acuity it is apparent that while the outer structure of a civilization breaks apart when it "dies," something yet lives on. Even the outer products of a culture can remain in existence only as long as they correspond to something that is alive within the human beings of the age. Fundamentally, then, the real continuity in history does not consist in the external forms of a civilization nor in the surface flow of events, but rather in the forces that are psychologically active in the depths of the people. While civilizations pass away, the propagation of peoples goes on; time accumulates within the human race even while the outward

---

[4] See Paul Tillich, *The Protestant Era*, U. of Chicago Press, Chicago, 1948, particularly Introduction and Chapters 4, 8, 9.

manifestations disappear. In these terms, Jung's historical conception of the unconscious is highly suggestive to Toynbee, as it must be to anyone who sincerely tries to understand the variations of history from a universalistic point of view.

When we regard the unconscious as a crucial concept for the study of history, the questions of the nature of the individual and of the particular bit of consciousness that goes with individuality must be asked in a new light. Because of his determination to maintain a large view of history, Toynbee has always found that the problem of relating the uniqueness of the individual personality to the life-stage of the historical civilization in which it appears is as important as it is difficult. In his most recently published book, he takes a position that is a paraphrase of Jung's. "The collective unconscious," Toynbee says, "underlies a consciousness that rides on it like a cockleshell floating precariously on a bottomless and shoreless ocean." He comes finally to the view that it is in the human psyche, vast though it be and strange to fathom, that we must look for the secrets of history.

As far as we can judge from his present writings, it would seem that even in the days when his theories had a rationalistic cast, Toynbee knew that this would be the direction in which the answer would be found. Speaking in retrospect some years ago, he said that his major problem of finding the mythologic clue to history would have been much easier if he had known of Jung's work at an earlier date. As we shall see in our later discussion, the relation of myth to history remains at the heart of a dark and potentially most fertile area of social study. It comes at the point where the psychology of the unconscious and the study of the history of civilizations converge. On one level the interpretation of mythology gives the key to the inner history of a people, the intimate symbols of group life that exert a force beyond the consciousness of the individual; on another, more subtle level, when its symbols are deeply understood, mythology has within it the power to bring at least a shaded insight into the meanings of the historical process itself. Toynbee is sensitive to these issues and to the importance of Jung's contribution. One may hope that in his volumes still to come these ideas will lead him beyond his present theological position and will result in a deepening of the psychological aspects of his imposing historical work.[5]

MISCONCEPTIONS REGARDING JUNG'S WORK

Neither Mumford, Tillich, nor Toynbee, of course, deals with Jung's work as a whole, but only with those of his ideas which are particularly stimulating to them in their own studies. Each of them comes to the study of society from a different direction, and each is interested in a somewhat different aspect of Jung's work. This is quite characteristic of the way in which Jung's ideas have been utilized by social thinkers. They are taken up piecemeal, here and there, wherever they have reached fertile ground in independent minds. In the main, however, Jung's psychological theories have not yet been treated in the integrated way that can bring out the full scope of their implications for the social sciences, and that is the lack which we would remedy with the present study.

The main reason that Jung's work has not been ade-

[5] See Arnold Toynbee, *Civilization on Trial*, Oxford U. Press, New York, 1948, Essays 1 and 13.

quately appreciated so far is that its coming to maturity was a very uneven process, impeded by many disputes and personal misunderstandings. In developing his ideas, Jung made temporary stops at other schools of thought, frequently taking over their terminology and giving it his own meaning. He would always make his new definitions clear, but when such changes are attempted, a gap that cannot be bridged inevitably remains. The accustomed meanings of terms tend to linger on, and even if they do not actually outlive the new definitions, they weaken them by an imperceptible process of forgetting and blending—of which even the innovator can be guilty. One of the main factors contributing to the general misinterpretation of Jung's ideas is his retention of old terms with new meanings, and then, occasionally, changing their meanings still again as his thought has continued to grow. Jung himself has contributed in no small measure to the frequent misconstructions set upon his writings; but fundamentally all such difficulties must be understood as the result of working in so new a field. A mind that is rushing on for new hypotheses cannot always stop to look behind and make sure that its definitions are covered. It must remain for those who come after to retrieve what has been lost, to clarify what has been done unsystematically, to draw together loose ends. Also, if in the course of its development a line of thought moves from one field to another, there is no reason to expect that everyone will at once be aware of the changes that take place. Much of the value of Jung's thought has so far been missed because he has not yet been understood in his proper position in the history of thought; but that is something that can now be remedied.

In general parlance, Jung is still classified as part of the great triumvirate: Freud, Adler and Jung. He is thought of as one who modified Freud but remained a psychoanalyst, and this, of course, is altogether misleading. If Jung were still a psychoanalyst, it would be relatively simple to interpret his ideas—but then there would be much less to them. In the psychology textbooks and in the surveys of psychoanalytical thought, he is still referred to as a "deviant" from Freud. When he is mentioned in such books, however, the discussion is generally limited to those doctrines that fit within a strictly psychoanalytical framework; and with such a limited context, it is quite understandable that his contribution is dismissed as just an unorthodox reformulation of some Freudian ideas. It should be clear from what has already been said that to do this misses the main development of Jung's thought and fails to take into account just what is most valuable in his work. It is impossible to grasp the import of Jung's contribution as long as one thinks of him as merely a split-off from psychoanalysis. He represents an altogether separate and independent line of thought based upon fundamentally different postulates. The later development of Jung's thought goes far beyond the principles of psychoanalysis and draws upon a much wider variety of intellectual materials. This becomes clear when we look at the background of his life and work. We find that his roots reach not only to thinkers other than Freud, but his most fundamental concepts are derived from an altogether different intellectual direction.

THE GENESIS OF JUNG'S THOUGHT

Jung was born in a small town near Basle, Switzerland in July of 1875. The son of a Protestant minister, he comes of a

Swiss family with a wide cultural background. Both medical doctors and ministers are to be found in Jung's family tree, just as both physician and pastor are expressed in his work.[6]

In Jung's conception of his personal development, he places great importance on his Swiss background. He feels that he has, in some way, participated in the Swiss neutrality in international affairs so as to be able to take a mediatory position in the world of thought, independent of the usual European intellectual creeds, transcending and combining the philosophies of Orient and Occident. Jung thinks of Switzerland as being somewhat beyond the problems that beset the other European countries. Placed right in the midst of Europe, the Swiss are close enough to take part in European culture and to understand the lives of other Europeans; and yet their independent character and their non-involvement in recent European wars have given them a vantage point above the turmoils of European history. To Jung, the geographically central position of Switzerland is significant of its being a mid-point in the realm of knowledge as well, and in terms of his personal philosophy, this means to him that it is destined to play a leading role in the integration of world thought. Two factors, then, his pride in a strong family cultural background, and his consciousness of the mediatory function of being a Swiss, combine to give Jung his sense of special fitness for his task. Such ideas, of course, are subjective factors, but their importance is not to be ignored if we would understand the character of the man and his work.

As a young man, Jung thought he would perhaps become a paleontologist or an archaeologist, for he was fascinated by

[6] This brief account of Jung's development is based on a summary of various published and private papers and conversations.

the early forms of things. He went, however, into the study of medicine and received his M.D. degree in 1900. Throughout his medical studies, he had continued his reading in philosophy, and when it came time to decide on a field of specialization, he chose psychiatry in the belief that this was the area in which medicine and philosophy would come together. While he was still studying at the hospital, he came upon a case that had a great influence on his thought. It was a case that made a tremendous impression on him personally, and set the main problems for his further studies for years to come. The patient was a fifteen-and-a-half-year-old girl who displayed two completely separate personalities. In her waking life she was a very commonplace type of troubled individual, but under hypnosis she became a lady of the world with a grand manner and a knowledge of many things. To Jung, at that point in his education, there was something especially strange and challenging in this, and from then on he focused his research on the unconscious phenomena of the psychoses.

We should keep in mind that at that time psychiatry had not yet formulated definite concepts for discerning the unconscious processes. Jung cast about for a starting point, and it occurred to him from his earlier studies in philosophy that Schopenhauer's conception of the will might be of relevance. He thought that the separate personality which came to the surface under hypnosis might in some way be an expression of the will—"will" here being understood in its old sense (which Jung later discarded) as the basic force in the world, the non-reasoning, ever-continuing, pulsating force of life. There is in Schopenhauer a definite conception of unconscious elements in human personality, of drives and desires exerting pressures beyond the control of rationality. Jung felt that Schopenhauer held the clue to the problem, or at least that he provided the tools of thought with which the problem could finally be solved. He could not, however, accept the conception of the will as purely non-rational and as completely devoid of meaning. Eduard von Hartmann, whose *Philosophy of the Unconscious* had achieved popularity by that time, offered a conception that seemed more accurate. He spoke of the will in nature as being propelled by an inner purpose which nevertheless is not conscious. According to this view, there is in the world a teleological principle which is unconscious of its own purposes and yet drives all the life forces in the direction of its aims. The combination of teleology and unconsciousness appealed to Jung, but he did not yet settle down content with any answers. He continued to mull over the Schopenhauer-Hartmann line of thought and went about his psychiatric studies.

At this point, also, Jung embarked on his association test experiments. These were exceedingly fruitful for him at this early stage of his research. His principle was essentially very simple. He would mention a word to the patient and ask him to reply with the first word that came to his mind. Working from a list, Jung would record and compare the reaction time for each of the responses. By relating the words that had the longest reaction time, and by interpreting the association words that were given, Jung found that he was able to piece together definite constellations of psychic material which were being hidden in the unconscious. He was thus combining in a very acute way and with clinical application the general idea of the unconscious which he had derived from Schopenhauer and Hartmann and the older idea of psychological association, which was quite common in both English and German thought at that time. These experiments had been carried through in considerable detail before he heard of the work that Freud was doing.

In 1900 Jung read Freud's *Interpretation of Dreams* for the first time and felt that he did not understand it. It was the first volume by Freud that he had seen. All he could do then was to set the book aside and continue with his experiments and studies. In 1903 he read *The Interpretation of Dreams* again, and this time he had altogether different results. On the basis of his association test experiments, he felt now that he could agree altogether with Freud's theory of repression and, moreover, that he was now in a position to verify the basic conception of the unconscious in great detail. He was uncertain about the question of sexual trauma and about the importance that Freud gave to sex in the genesis of neurosis. At that point, however, the problem of sex did not seem to Jung to be nearly as important as the more fundamental and far-reaching conception of the unconscious in general. He put it aside as something which he did not yet understand.

When his book on the association test was published, Jung was brought into closer contact with those interested in the Freudian line of work. He associated himself with Freud's position from that time on, and he defended Freud's views in various professional conventions at a time when it was highly unpopular to do so. Not until 1907 did he finally meet Freud, and then he was altogether impressed by him. He found Freud a most unusual individual, a man of remarkable abilities, who was wholly possessed by the idea of his discoveries. Nevertheless, Jung could still not bring himself to take sexuality as seriously as Freud did. He began, even, to wonder whether there was some unconscious reason for which the sexual factor had so strong a fascination to Freud that it seemed about to dominate and unbalance his scientific work.

In 1909, Freud and Jung were invited to lecture at Clark University in the United States. The trip, which they made together, gave them an opportunity to become more fully acquainted with one another. They analyzed each other's dreams and discussed their common interests at great length. The exchanges that took place then seem to have had a great effect on Jung, and he appears to have felt then that there were weaknesses in Freud's position that he would never be able to accept. It was at that time that he began to question and study Freud in a more critical spirit, but without making any formal break. He remained identified with the psychoanalytical movement, but to answer his growing doubts he began to develop his own line of research, not knowing where it would lead. He followed his independent studies for some years, and it was only when he published his results in *The Psychology of the Unconscious* in 1912 that the distinctness and newness of his approach become apparent. From then on he had to cut his own path. All in all, then, though Jung was publicly identified with Freud's point of view for almost a decade, it was only for a very few years that he can be considered to have been under Freud's direct influence.

The turning point in Jung's development seems to have been his return from his trip to America in 1909. He felt convinced then that he had caught sight of basic weaknesses in Freud's approach. At this time, also, Jung seems to have undergone a period of personal uncertainty and intellectual doubt resulting from the fact that he had to withdraw the reliance he had begun to place in Freud. Jung felt himself to be an outsider now, unable to accept Freud's formulations and yet without a set of adequate postulates of his own. He was groping for a new lead when he decided that he would have to take up again on his own a detailed and concentrated study of symbols.[7] He felt better equipped this time, however, because now he had the benefit of his experience in working with Freud's material.

Jung returned then to Schopenhauer and Hartmann and took up again the notion of the will as the basic force in life. He undertook to work with the conception developed by Hartmann of an underlying unconscious principle in the world, a principle that is also teleological in the sense that it carries its purposes within itself and manifests them out of its own nature. When he applied this idea now, however, he gave it a more specifically psychological interpretation than he had before. He understood the life-force of will now as libido, as raw, instinctual energy which comes up within the human personality from the unconscious to consciousness. In applying here a psychological formulation of energy, Jung was using an idea which came from Freud—and also from Pierre Janet.[8] He added to it the thought that when libido

[7] In his thoroughly revised German edition of *The Psychology of the Unconscious* Jung looks back at his precarious personal situation during those formative years. See his "Vorrede" to *Symbole der Wandlung*, vierte umgearbeitete Auflage von *Wandlungen und Symbole der Libido*, Rascher, Zurich, 1952.

[8] In 1902-3, Jung was in France studying under Pierre Janet. It is difficult to assess the full extent of Janet's influence on Jung, but it has certainly not been inconsiderable. It is regrettable that while Janet has made a very large contribution to depth psychological thought in general, his contribution has seldom received adequate recognition in the United States.

comes up from the unconscious, it comes up in the form of symbols. He concentrated, then, on analyzing the formations and transformations of libido as symbolism in the unconscious, and it was his first research in this direction which led to the publication of his book, *The Psychology of the Unconscious,* in 1912.

APPROACHES TO SYMBOLISM

During this period, Jung centered his main work on his effort to develop a method of interpreting symbols. Once he had become convinced of the inadequacy of those interpretations which reduce dreams and myths to their sexual content, he kept himself open for any point of view that had the possibility of providing a new clue. His studies led him into many diverse fields at this time, and it would be misleading to isolate any particular doctrine as being the sole root of his present approach to symbolism. Some main sources, however, are apparent.

The work of J. J. Bachofen, a Swiss also from Basle, who wrote in the mid-nineteenth century, was very important to him. Bachofen's interpretations of ancient symbols were being widely read in Germany during the early part of the twentieth century. His works, of great power and originality, were a culmination of the romantic interest in mythology, but with their vast scholarship and penetration, their implications went beyond the scope of romantic thought. Bachofen is remembered today—especially in the English-speaking countries, where he is only superficially known—mainly for his thesis that the rule of society by women was the original condition of civilization. His contribution is, of course, much larger than that. He undertook an analysis of the full range of cultural factors, dividing them into two types: those founded on the rule of women and those founded on the rule of men. He interpreted the symbols of myths and religions in such a manner as to draw out their inner relatedness to their cultures and particularly to their type of society. In his way he set out to demonstrate the relationships between the matriarchal and patriarchal cultures in terms of the histories of various nations.

Many people have been interested in aspects of Bachofen's work and have applied them to fit their special points of view. The nineteenth-century Marxists found Bachofen's thesis to their taste because, in undercutting the idea that the patriarchal family is a natural or divine institution, it lent support to the Marxist conception that the family, as an essentially historical phenomenon, is variable and may be changed. Freud and his followers are also generally very much indebted to Bachofen, not for his thesis as such, but for his approach and method in treating symbolical material. Bachofen's writings played an important role in preparing the minds not only of the psychoanalysts, but also of the public, for the significance that was to be attached to dream and mythic materials.[9]

In relation to Jung's development, Bachofen's very large contribution was to show that symbols have to be interpreted with reference to their historical meaning. Bachofen has been called, not without reason, the "historian of pre-history" because of his contention that it is possible to reconstruct the nature of a society with very limited recorded materials as

[9] For a recent acute use of Bachofen's work to undercut Freud's central analysis of Oedipus Rex, see Erich Fromm, *The Forgotten Language*, Rinehart, New York, 1951, Ch. VII.

long as one is able to understand the meaning of the symbols that are used in its myths, sagas, religious rituals, dramas, or other cultural materials. Transferred into psychological terms, such a point of view would mean that in the interpretation of symbol formation in individuals, the symbolic meanings must be interpreted with an understanding of their historical and cultural frames of reference. Bachofen also worked with the idea that there is a continuity in the psychic development of each nation, and that the various phases of its cultural life continue to be expressed in the symbolism both of individual and group experience. When Jung reformulated his conception of the unconscious, he enlarged it to include historical symbols, a proposition which his empirical researches verified. We shall discuss later the various aspects of the "collective unconscious" as Jung has come to understand it, but at this point we should merely mention that the analyses of J. J. Bachofen were an important contribution to this idea.

While there can be little question about Bachofen's importance for Jung's intellectual growth, it is extremely hazardous to say at what particular point or in what degree the two lines of thought actually converged. Bachofen's writings were in the air in Switzerland; everyone within a certain cultured class knew about them and spoke about them. Bachofen was in a sense the epitome and fullest development of the interpretation of mythology which had been going on at a very intense rate and with strong philosophical support for about a century. Much of this was contained in him, and if one finds in Jung little specific reference, for example, to the later mythological philosophy of Schelling, we can assume that this general orientation to myth and reality nevertheless does come to him through his interest in Bachofen's work.

One of the most important influences on Jung's thought throughout this period was Friedrich Nietzsche. It is true, of course, that Nietzsche had been an important factor in the development of the orientation underlying psychoanalysis as a whole. But for Jung, Nietzsche had a special importance. Nietzsche was not merely a philosopher to him, but a "phenomenon" of the utmost significance for the interpretation of psychic events. The meaning of this will become more apparent later when Jung's psychological concepts have been described. The general point, however, is that Jung regards Nietzsche's falling off into insanity as being intimately related to the other basic fact in Nietzsche's life, that Zarathustra had "come" to him, had "possessed" him, a few years before. Jung interprets the sayings of Zarathustra as the product of a separate personality split-off from the real Friedrich Nietzsche, living and speaking as an independent individual. When the split became too great, when the dissociation had sundered the connection with reality, the delicate tension collapsed, and both Nietzsche and Zarathustra were lost to the world.

The thing that interested Jung so in Nietzsche's psychic life was that this was exactly the psychic situation that he had observed in the first case he had handled as a psychiatrist: the case of the fifteen-and-a-half-year-old girl who had manifested under hypnosis a personality altogether different from her personality in daily life. This was the case that had started him off on his researches, for he had wanted to know whether it was a piece of the Life-Will that had split off, or how such an unconscious manifestation could otherwise be explained. The analysis of the girl patient had been broken off before he could accumulate sufficient material to study her adequately. When he realized that the same condition had been present in the great philosopher and that there was plenty of material available to analyze, it was naturally a very important discovery for him.

After he had made it clear that he had taken an approach that was independent of Freud's position, Jung steadily proceeded to round out the full lines of his thought. He reached the point where he had a conception of the unconscious, of energy, and of psychic processes relating the unconscious to consciousness. What he needed then was a clearer understanding of symbols and of the process of symbol formation in relation to personality as a whole. With regard to the cultural understanding of symbols, Bachofen had given him one key by demonstrating the relationships between the historical life of a people and its psychic experiences. Nietzsche— studied now as a philosopher rather than as a psychic phenomenon—reinforced Jung's approach to myth by pointing out that myth has a "style of thought" all its own. Jung then undertook to interpret myths of all kinds. He carried over, however, one main technique from his psychiatric practise. When he read a myth, he would take special care to regard it as though he were listening to the anamnesis of a patient. He would take the attitude that in a myth, a group—a collective psyche as it were—was going back over its memories to its distant group past, or was relating something that corresponded to a dream experience. This point of view was an expression of his basic orientation as a medical doctor and of his determined effort to maintain the methodology of a psychiatrist even while he was being led to a field that was manifestly larger than psychiatry itself. In another sense, however, when looked at more closely, we can see that while Jung was taking a psychiatric standpoint, he was also following the method of Bachofen. That is to say, Bachofen had held that a mythology is essentially an autobiography of a people, and that an interpreter who knows how can read the history—that is, the memories—of a nation in its myths. Jung was thus following both a psychiatric and an ethnological methodology in his approach to symbols—though he was apparently not altogether aware at the time that both points of view were present in his work.

Through this double procedure he came to his conclusion that a basic similarity underlies the contents of myths and of dream and other fantasy material produced by the individual. Freud, we know, had already reached a similar conclusion, not only in his interpretations of myths like that of Oedipus to explain psychic mechanisms, but also in his tendency to equate the psychology of primitives with that of modern neurotics. The difference, however, was that Freud proceeded on a biological, primarily sexual basis, while Jung was now interpreting the unconscious symbol formations of individuals from a cultural point of view. Since he was dealing with the historical aspects of symbols, Jung was now in a position to observe patterns of symbolism which transcended the individual case. He came to the conclusion that there are certain recurring universal types, or motifs, which are expressed in a multitude of historical forms, varying from ancient and primitive myths to the dreams of modern individuals, but present in essence in all of them. He worked out his basic approach to symbols with the underlying premise that mythologic thought in general is to be described in terms of the same characteristics as the unconscious, and that the symbolic manifestations of the unconscious, from myth to dream, may be studied under a common frame of reference.

From the Swiss Bachofen, Jung learned to interpret symbols with an ethnological perspective, and it was from still another scholar of Basle, Jacob Burckhardt, that he assimilated an historical point of view which could be applied to the modern situation. During Jung's youth, Burckhardt was one of the outstanding men of culture in Basle, virtually a cultural institution in himself. Jung would watch him pass by every day going to his place at the university. Burckhardt's writings were read and studied as a matter of course; it was part of being a citizen of Basle. Jung absorbed Burckhardt's historical orientation, then, not because he was a close student of society during his early years, but because Burckhardt's work and insights were part of the cultural atmosphere. Without consciously taking over any specific doctrines, the historical way of thinking about all human phenomena became part of his underlying outlook, and later on it was a natural step for him to apply an historical point of view to the analysis of psychic phenomena. In this sense, Jung's work must be interpreted as being related to the great Burckhardt tradition, and as constituting an approach to the historical life of man made from the special point of view of Jung's psychological field of study.

As an historian, Burckhardt's aim was to interpret the inner structure of those sensitive periods of transition, such as the Renaissance or the declining years of Rome, periods of rapid flux in the socially accepted meanings of life. He felt that such periods of transition are especially significant for understanding the forces active in history because it is then that the greatest intensities of change are expressed. Burckhardt founded his work on the idea that the dynamics of man's inner life, his beliefs and his passions, comprise the materials for the life and death of societies. He maintained a psychological focus while studying the ever-changing contexts of historical cultures, feeling that an insight into the dynamics of history depends on penetrating the deepest beliefs by which individuals live in any given culture. In his study of the latter days of Rome, Burckhardt analyzed in detail the varieties of beliefs by which individuals tried to find a framework of meaning for their lives. Through his descriptions there emerges the clear idea that the psychological qualities of individuals involve something more than the peculiarities of individual behavior. The individual expresses in his personality the characteristics of his culture as a whole, and particularly the qualities and problems of the particular historical phase in which he lives. The individual contains something of his culture and its history within him, and because of this there is always a double aspect to the study of man. On the one hand, the psychological qualities of individuals constitute the basic materials for the study of historical periods; on the other hand, the cultural context, when it is understood with a large sense of time, provides the fundamental perspective for an insight into the breadth and meaningfulness of personality. Burckhardt followed the first of these points of view, while Jung followed, essentially, the latter. The two together constitute the point of convergence at which the historical study of society and the psychological analysis of the unconscious meet.

SOCIAL THEORY AND THE UNCONSCIOUS

This convergence represents today the most important aspect of the holistic study of man as a social psychological being. Much social and historical work other than Burckhardt's has been pointing toward the conclusion that it is necessary to understand the hidden, or unconscious, motivations in history. It expresses a problem that has been growing for a century and a half in the social sciences. While the development throughout the nineteenth century was quite generally in the direction of historical, or at least of evolutionary, thought, psychological questions were allowed to remain in static terms. Those systems of thought which did have an historical point of view were mainly oriented toward economic or toward social issues; when it came to psychological questions, they did not develop an historical perspective. That is to say, while a thinker like Marx adopted an historical point of view when approaching economic, or social, or political questions, he assumed the main psychological motivations as given, and as remaining the same through all the vicissitudes of history. In having this static psychological conception at the base of his historical analyses, Marx took the position most characteristic of eighteenth- and nineteenth-century social thought, with its hedonistic and utilitarian assumptions. As the impact of Kantian epistemology was felt on the social sciences, however, it was realized that the categories which Kant had understood as the basis of knowledge were essentially social and variable in history. In Europe this line of analysis was worked out by Wilhelm Dilthey and in America by Thorstein Veblen. Dilthey's work in this regard is essentially an expansion of the epistemological area of study, and his historical studies tend to remain on an abstract and conceptual level; Veblen, on the other hand, developed his studies in his independent, rather esoteric way, and gave his ideas a specifically sociological application.

From a variety of directions, other social theorists have realized that it is necessary to be able to analyze the psychological points of view animating individuals in different societies. In addition to Dilthey and Veblen, the writings of Fustel de Coulanges, Emile Durkheim, Georg Simmel, and Max Weber in Europe, and William Sumner and Charles H. Cooley in America point in this direction. It is clear to them that the development of cultures in history moves on a level that underlies consciousness, so that the crucial problem in social study is really the need to understand the contents and forces in the deeper levels of the human being. In their effort to do this, they make use of such general concepts as "folkways," "collective representations," "institutions," and "social habits of thought," but these are manifestly inadequate for the detailed insights that are necessary. The historical study of society requires the additional dimension which the analysis of the symbols and processes of the unconscious alone can give; and for this, the logical step is to move in the direction of Depth Psychology, as a general approach, and to seek analytical tools that will understand the unconscious as the psychological base underlying society.

One main difficulty, however, has prevented this step from being taken. As the theory of the unconscious came to be developed by Freud and his followers of the psychoanalytical school, it had an altogether individualistic frame of reference. While Freud believed that he was developing his material empirically both from a clinical and an anthropological point of view, it was only his clinical material that could be considered to be adequate in any degree. His use of cultural data left social scientists gasping because of its misconceptions. He worked from a static, non-historical point of view and dealt with social material not in order to understand it sociologically or historically, but in order to reduce it to his biological (i.e., instinctual) frame of reference. This is just the opposite of the kind of approach that is required if the concept of the unconscious is to be developed as a fruitful category for the study of history. It has to be formulated in an inherently historical way so as to relate the depth levels of unconscious motivation directly and intrinsically to the social nature of human life.

THE SIGNIFICANCE OF JUNG'S THEORIES AS OPPOSED TO FREUD'S

This is the point at which C. G. Jung becomes important for the social scientist. Once we come to the conclusion that the integrated study of man requires a combination of the social-historical point of view and an investigation into the psychology of the unconscious, Jung's views must necessarily become the starting-point of discussion. His conception of the unconscious is specifically sociological, and his analysis of the phenomena of the unconscious is set in the context of history. Jung's studies are just the opposite of Freud's in this regard, since Freud's biological starting-point leads to concepts which, by their very nature, are inapplicable to the study of society. This is not generally conceded by followers of Freud, but a close analysis of the many efforts to apply Freudian psychological concepts to social studies reveals generally that all they have done is to graft Freudian phrases onto what is essentially either a Marxian or a Darwinian social theory. It is a very misleading practise born of the careless use of psychiatric and social terminologies without a substantial principle to relate them. Many competent social scientists have grown impatient with the whole idea of applying the psychology of the unconscious to social studies because of the confused and undisciplined excesses of Freudian excursions into social theory. For this reason, it is exceedingly important to realize that Jung's concepts are precisely the opposite of Freud's in this regard, and that the criticisms merited by the Freudian application to sociology are not at all applicable to Jung. This will become more apparent in the later chapters of the book. Now, merely to establish the negative side of this point, a cursory analysis of Freudian theory will be sufficient.

THE FREUDIAN POINT OF VIEW

In terms of its general psychological theory, Freud's work presents a combination of the Hormic driving forces and the Hedonistic pleasure-pain theory, seasoned with a light sprinkling of Schopenhauerean and Nietzschean philosophy. The first of these is expressed in the concept of libido, or sexual energy, which Freud developed very much as the motor power of personality. The second supplies the "mechanisms" by which raw libido forms itself into definite psychological characteristics. The combination is similar to that developed by William McDougall, who has given the strongest statement of so-called "Instinct" psychology. McDougall originally began to build his system as a substitute for mechanistic Hedonism, but in the end he too had to rely on a self-interest theory, although he camouflaged it transparently under the phrase, "the self-regarding instinct." Instinctual energy, though it is the dynamic element in Freud's theories, could not be carried through in psychological analyses without recourse to a calculus of pleasure-pain. Freud's formulations varied after his early writings, but Hedonism is very definitely one of the intellectual roots of his ideas.

Freud's basic conception of the human being is that it begins its life as an amorphous mass of energy, is gradually shaped into an individual by contacts with the outer world, and that it always bears the marks of its infantile sexual experiences. It is a conception that has many affinities with the French Sensationist philosophy, particularly in the sense that it stresses both the formlessness of the individual at birth and the importance of contact with the environment. Freud makes the important addition, however, that the individual is activated even in his original amorphous state by a powerful internal force of energy which impels him toward the outer world.

The reception with which these impulses are met determines the development of the personality. When they are well received, the instinctual drives are gratified; when the needs are not fulfilled, the energic impulses are repressed below consciousness, where they linger and exert pressure until they come out again either in their own or in some other form. Freud conceives of the unconscious as the subterranean cellar of consciousness, where the individual stores those thoughts or urges that he wishes to keep darkly hidden, things that have been in consciousness and have been forced out of it, or ideas so dreadfully feared that they must be kept from entering consciousness at all costs. Even while they are repressed in the depths of the person, such energic impulses continue to press with their full force to be admitted to consciousness. If they cannot enter in their present shape, they may be converted into some representative form, attaching to themselves an equivalent amount of libidinal energy. If they cannot come to the surface even this way in the course of conscious life, they may wait and present themselves when consciousness is relaxed, as in sleep. It is in this context that dreams are significant to Freud, and in these terms, too, that he developed his methodology for interpreting the strange symbolism not only of dreams, but of all expressions of the unconscious.

In developing his views of personality Freud frequently called on the social sciences for his illustrations. The very significant point stands out, however, that none of his concepts is inherently historical or sociological. All his conceptions are, rather, cast in biological terms, and are based upon viewing the individual in a biological frame of reference. We see this clearly in Freud's conception of the "id," in his analysis of the stages of sexuality, and in the fact that both the "ego" and the "super-ego," as he derives them, are based on biological premises. The theories of infantile sexuality and the Oedipus Complex, with the many constructions derived from them, grow out of the view of the human being in biological terms. The most basic concept of all, the unconscious, through its close relation to sexuality, is virtually defined in terms of biologically oriented mechanisms.

These points are important to observe because they indicate that Freud comes to the question of the unconscious with the very opposite of a social or historical approach. Our discussion has indicated that the logical tendency of social thought as expressed in the work of such men as Burckhardt or Veblen is to point toward the study of the unconscious as underlying the social categories of consciousness which develop in history. As the problems raised here are historical, we may well assume that they will have to be answered ultimately in cultural terms. It is quite understandable that, as a medical man by training, habit and interest, Freud did not approach his work with a social orientation. What is crucial, however, is whether his underlying concepts were so constructed as to be applicable at all in the analysis of social phenomena. The non-sociological nature of Freud's interpretation of the unconscious is indicated by the fact that the core of his theory of personality involves a counter-posing of biology and society as opposites. Raw, instinctual energy presses upward and outward seeking expression in the world; the restraints of society press it back down, inhibiting the natural spontaneity of sexuality. Freud sees the human being as caught in the midst of this tension between his natural urges and the prohibitions of custom. His view, then, is that the basis of conflict within the individual grows out of the very fact that the individual lives in a society. Freud does not take the essentially sociological perspective of seeing society as the necessary condition for the development of individuality. Instead, he regards society as a restraining and inhibiting factor which fetters the individual and stunts his growth. We can see the remnants of Rousseauist romanticism in Freud's work.

FREUD'S APPROACH TO SOCIETY

With this background, we can follow the logical consistency which leads Freud to focus the basic issues of society and psychology on a single "primal" situation. As he views it, the individual is a "cell" of the social aggregate,[10] and each person carries in his structure, at least potentially, the essential characteristics found in all the rest. More particularly, Freud follows a reductive, that is, an analytical methodology which leads him to go backward in time to the "cause," or at least to the first appearance of a psychological condition. Since he holds that there is a virtual equivalence between the nature of society and individual psychology, it follows that the "cause" of any psychological condition is to be found ultimately in its original appearance for mankind as a whole. These two lines of thought in Freud are underscored and drawn together by his supposition that all human beings carry deep within themselves certain psychological characteristics which constitute generically recurring traits of the race. Ultimately, then, all psychological problems may be drawn back to archaic man for their derivation, and the problem of the "origin" of society and of the psychological nature of man becomes one and the same.

Freud's description of the "primal crime" carries the limitations of the anthropological knowledge available to him at the time he wrote. In the final analysis, however, it does not depend on ethnological materials but on his interpretation of certain psychological phenomena which he claims to have observed in modern man as well as in the primitives. Freud's position, stated simply, is that in the beginning there was the "primal horde," in which the despotic father ruled his sons with an iron hand and kept his women for himself. Finally,

[10] Sigmund Freud, *Group Psychology and the Analysis of the Ego*, trans. by James Strachey, The International Psychoanalytical Press, London, 1922, pp. 6-12.

the sons were driven to revolt, kill the father and eat him; at last in repentance and to expiate their sin, they developed religious rituals and laws in which they included the veneration of the father under various symbols, together with rigid taboos against incest. All this involves, of course, a highly hypothetical situation, but Freud takes the position that it did actually happen and that it occurs again and again in the unconscious of all human beings because it is inherent in the psychological structure of the race.[11] We may criticize such a theory from many points of view: for its dubious accuracy on the question of the "origins" of society, for its misinterpretation of the symbolic material on which the analysis is based, and for its assumptions regarding the Oedipal pattern of patricide and incest. However, at this point, we may content ourselves with simply asking what such a doctrine signifies for the relation between the analysis of the unconscious and the study of society.

In the study of social institutions, the fundamental point stands out that consciously held attitudes are underlain by psychic contents in the unconscious. Two large problems emerge from this: one is the nature of the unconscious, what it involves and what its extent is; the other question has to do with the contents of the unconscious, how they are evolved and what they signify. Freud pointed his analyses at both of these questions, but he approached the unconscious from the special point of view of the medical doctor diagnosing the illnesses of personality. He did frame some of his studies in terms of at least putative social situations, but Freud's approach is not inherently sociological. His analysis of the "primal" group, for example, goes far into the past, but it is nevertheless not historical. There is no sense of continuity, no linkage in terms of group historical movement to lead, under any historical pattern, from the primal to more recent situations. It would seem to be in the very nature of Freud's preconceptions that he expects the same psychological facts to prevail if one stops to analyze at any point along the flow of time in society. In discussing the individual, Freud does take a generic approach; but his treatment of society is altogether without a developmental point of view. His underlying conception of the unconscious is that it is potentially the same for all men, regardless of the historical situation, because the original experiences with the parents are inherent in the nature of man. This is the basis on which Freud interchanges the analysis of modern dreams and primitive customs in his interpretations of neurosis.

The purpose of Freud's work, fundamentally, was not to analyze the individual personality in terms of society or within an historical setting—though he did attempt to do this—but rather to find the biological roots of neurosis. His stress on sexuality grows out of the fact that his first studies developed in the medical area of psychiatric diagnosis, and therefore they necessarily have a biological orientation. The consequences, however, are that when Freud or those who follow him approach social questions, their concepts are structured so that they lead to psychiatric diagnoses of society rather than to essentially psycho-historical analyses. Recent works have shown a tendency to classify groups as varied as the Navahos and the Nazis by means of the same psychiatric concepts. Such categories are designed for the interpretation of mental disorders in individuals, and they can be highly misleading when applied to social institutions or to large historical movements, where the issues of psychiatric diagnosis are not involved at all. The most fundamental criticism is that, in the psychiatric approach to society, the unconscious is conceived in biological terms. This makes such an approach unhistorical, if not anti-historical, in its point of view, so that the most essential aspect of society—the time aspect— is left out.

As we understand the problem, then, the main criterion for the application of Depth Psychology to the analysis of society is that the unconscious must be conceived of as inherently historical. Freud takes a first step in this direction and then is cut short by the limitations of his biological orientation. From one point of view his Oedipus theories can be interpreted as an effort to derive psychological principles from the analysis of an imputed "primordial" nature of man. Going back in time, however, should make his method historical and pre-eminently social. The significant thing is that, after reaching a point where a social interpretation of his material is indicated, Freud explicitly refuses to take the step, saying it would take him beyond his proper field. He sets a rigid limit to his area of study, and it is therefore from his own writings that we can see the point at which his work ceases to be relevant for social-historical research.

Freud articulated his position on this point by setting himself in contrast to the sociological approach to the unconscious attempted by LeBon. He quotes LeBon as saying, "Our conscious acts are the outcome of an unconscious substratum created in the mind by hereditary influences. The substratum consists of the innumerable common characteristics handed down from generation to generation which constitute the genius of a race." [12] If we read between the lines in Freud's comments on LeBon, we can see that he was indirectly addressing himself to the social historical interpretation of the unconscious, which C. G. Jung was beginning to develop at that time.[13] LeBon's work and Jung's, of course, were quite different both in their scope and in their methodology; but to Freud, they had the common quality of providing a contrast for him in stating that the individual should be understood with reference to the social and historical conditions out of which he emerges. In discussing LeBon, Freud was at the same time taking his position on the ideas which Jung had brought forward, and he attempted to dismiss them with the summary statement that such studies did not belong within the domain of psychoanalysis as he defined it. It is significant, however, that Freud grants the basic point, insisted on by LeBon and, in a more far-reaching way, by Jung. "We do not fail to recognize," he says, "that the ego's nucleus, which comprises the 'archaic inheritance' of the human mind, is unconscious.[14] He accepts the crucial concept that the sources of the individual are social and historical, but he turns away from the questions that it raises, preferring to focus on the purely individual aspect of the unconscious, the "unconscious repressed." Freud admits that it is the historical side of the unconscious that contains the "most deeply buried features" of the human being, but these, he says, lie

[12] Gustave LeBon, The Crowd, Fisher. Unwin, London, 1920, pp. 30-31. Quoted by Freud in Group Psychology.
[13] Jung indicated his first tendency toward an historical development of the unconscious in his Psychology of the Unconscious in 1912. Freud wrote his Group Psychology in 1921.
[14] Sigmund Freud, Group Psychology, p. 10, fn.

"outside the scope of psychoanalysis." It is worth pointing out that while some "followers" have extended Freud's concepts to work out psychiatric diagnoses of societies, Freud's own position—in so far as he has adhered to it—is more reasonable and more defensible. As a medical man his interest was in the individual case, and he therefore dealt with the unconscious on the level of its individual, personal manifestations, leaving its historical and social aspects as open questions.

Jung's research became most active just at the point where Freud felt he could go no further. He raises the question of whether it is really possible to understand personality without going first to the historical foundations which underlie it and are prior to it. Jung's question goes to the heart of Freud's position on the relation of the individual to society, and in this sense his work represents the step beyond Freud, breaking through the impasse created by Freud's extremely individualistic emphasis. On a point like this we can see the two-sidedness of Jung's relation to Freud. On the one hand, Jung drew upon a variety of sources to develop a point of view that was in radical contrast to Freud's with regard to the conception of the unconscious and the nature of man in general; and yet, on the other hand, he came to some of his most important and original answers while he was in the act of grappling with problems which arose while he was thinking within a Freudian frame of reference. Fundamentally, it was Jung's unorthodox questioning of the conception of the nature of individuality that led to his break with Freud.

JUNG AND THE SHIFTING OF DIRECTIONS

Any cursory comparison of Jung's work with that of Freud or with the Freudian schools indicates that the differences between them go much deeper than merely intellectual points of view or medical method. Freud's work is materialistic, biological in its orientation. He analyzes mental attitudes, follows them back to their origin, reduces them to the circumstances of their first appearance so far as he is able, and explains beliefs in terms of cause and effect. He takes a matter-of-fact attitude toward reality, is sceptical of all metaphysical concepts, and regards religion as an "illusion." His point of view is strictly that of the medical doctor who has applied his methodology to the mind. Jung, on the other hand, points to the reality of religious experience; considers that the biological side—at least in the usual narrow sense of the term—is less important than the historical and spiritual side of man; holds that a deterministic view of causality seldom applies to mental phenomena, and that a reductive and analytical approach should be replaced by one which synthesizes psychic contents and takes cognizance of the purposive nature of man. Jung deliberately takes an open attitude toward reality, holding that there is more to the universe than the materialist can know, and he relies on the inherent creativity of personality rather than on psychological "mechanisms" for his therapy. Such differences of viewpoint go deeper than mere intellectual considerations. They involve not only the primary assumptions as to the ways of study, but the most underlying presuppositions as to the nature of man and the world; and, for Freud and Jung as human beings, they involve basic divergences in their *a priori* attitudes toward life.

It is, of course, a well known fact and to be expected that every psychologist must express something of his own personal views in his scientific work. Freud, working with his analytical methodology, epitomizes—at least when compared with Jung—the point of view of the biological sciences. His roots are in the positivistic approach to science, and his faith, in keeping with modern scientism, is that rationality can conquer everything—even the dark unconscious. On the other side, Jung's point is that the use of analytical reason alone cannot heal the psyche and, more fundamentally, that it is just this attitude with its overemphasis on the rational side of consciousness that is at the root of the mental disaffections of modern times. In other words, the cure that has been proposed in the form of psychoanalysis is itself an aspect of the very same mental state as that out of which the sickness has come.

In his recommendation for therapy, then, Jung calls for the reorientation of consciousness so as to develop the intuitive faculties and to bring about a spiritually synthesizing experience rather than a merely analytical understanding. With regard to the general trend in modern attitudes, Jung is convinced that an equalizing movement is psychologically necessary to balance the overstress on the rational side of the psyche. He has already seen the signs of such a trend in the creation of animistic philosophies like that of Henri Bergson and especially in the widening interest in the ancient and oriental religions. Such developments necessarily take place slowly and, for the most part, beneath the surface of historical events, so that they are seldom easily perceptible. Their cumulative effect in history, however, is very great, and they may finally culminate in changes in the underlying point of view of a civilization. Historians like Burckhardt and Toynbee have observed that such alterations in fundamental points of view take place during the transitional periods between major phases of civilization, as, for example, the declining centuries of Rome. At that time, the secular, rationalistic point of view gave way to one of religious dimensions, and a whole new psychology emerged both for the society and the individual. In our own age, a corresponding development is taking place, and in Jung's view it is due to gain momentum steadily because it is a need created by the historical nature of modern consciousness. Jung's own work can well be understood as being an aspect of this large transition in the underlying point of view in modern times.

In general, Jung's significance for modern thought rests on the fact that he expresses a *shifting of directions* in the study of man. On the level of social theory, the study of the nature of consciousness in society indicates the larger field of the unconscious and the need for understanding the unconscious in historical terms. Jung's work is of crucial importance in this area since, in his pioneering way, he provides the point of view and tools of analysis that are necessary, at least to start. But his significance goes beyond social theory. His larger contribution is to the modern man's conception of himself, to the opening of new vistas of life experience through our insight into the contents and operation of the psyche. Whereas the prevailing temper has been mechanistic, analytical, and materialistic both in sociological and psychological studies, Jung proceeds with a point of view that follows the inherently creative purposiveness of psychic life. He is thus a transitional figure in the sense that his work epitomizes the shift from the rationalistic view of life to an outlook that encompasses a larger conception of reality. The spiritual side of life to Jung is not a mystery or a dogma, but a fact to be penetrated and to be lived. What he has done, then, is a significant beginning in the construction and application of a broader, more flexible approach to human problems. In the following pages our purpose is to clarify and interpret the many-sidedness of Jung's orientation, from its psychological and historical foundations to its social meanings. When it has been fully comprehended, we can look for its weaknesses and its implications, criticize it and enlarge it; and most important, we hope that understanding Jung in perspective will make it possible for his approach to be adapted more fruitfully by those who would carry it over to their special fields of work.

I I

THE PSYCHE AND THE LAYERS
OF CONSCIOUSNESS

THE MEANING OF THE COLLECTIVE UNCONSCIOUS

Jung's conception of the unconscious has been open to much misinterpretation mainly because he used a highly misleading terminology. In particular, the phrase "collective unconscious," one of Jung's pivotal terms, has led to a great deal of misunderstanding. Because of the word "collective," it has often been understood to mean a kind of communal unconscious, something like a "group mind." But that is very far from Jung's meaning. Actually, the significance of the word "collective" in his thinking is as a contrast to the word "personal," and Jung uses it to convey the idea that the human being contains psychic materials whose reality is *prior* to the fact of individuality. The "collective" refers to a level of psychic contents that is deeper than, prior to, and more fundamental than the individual personality. It is not collective at all in the ordinary sociological sense of something that is a joint possession. It is collective rather in the sense that as something generically present in *man*, it is collectively held by all men. Most essentially what Jung intends to convey by his concept is not that the unconscious is held in common as a collective inheritance, but rather that the unconscious contains materials which are held collectively by all men *be-*

53

cause they have a psychic reality which is *prior to personal experience.* This is to say, these materials are present *in potentia* because they are inherent in the psychic structure of the individual, from both a biological and an historical point of view, and in the course of the individual's life, depending on his experiences, some of them will be actualized and developed on the surface of the consciousness.

When we analyze the phrase "collective unconscious" closely, we realize that neither word really expresses the true spirit of Jung's thought as he finally developed it, and that both words have highly misleading connotations. The word "unconscious" is really at the heart of the confusion. Taken in itself, it is a negative word referring, simply, to the condition in which there is no consciousness. But that is not what Jung means to convey. His basic concept is that the psychic area which he designates as the "unconscious" is the source out of which all the materials of consciousness as a whole emerge. In this sense, the unconscious is a positive rather than a negative factor. It is amorphous to the degree that it is difficult to analyze by intellectual tools, but it is conceived as a definite entity with a creative role in the psyche: it supplies the fundamental symbols and other psychic contents that are brought to the surface in daily life. It is an affirmative factor in Jung's theory of personality, and a word like "unconscious," with its negative connotation of the absence of consciousness, is particularly misleading.

Jung's use of the term can largely be accounted for by the way in which his thought developed. Before he read Freud, as we have already seen, Jung had been interested in the work of Schopenhauer and Edouard von Hartmann, and from their writings he had derived a conception of the unconscious. With them, however, the unconscious was mainly a philosophical and principally epistemological idea. When Jung turned his attention to Freud, it was in the hope that, as a medical man, Freud would enable him to fill in the conception of the unconscious with empirical psychological facts. Working under the stimulus of Freud in the early days of psychoanalysis, Jung therefore took over Freud's definition of the unconscious and used it as a hypothesis for his own research. It happens that, as things worked out, Jung found himself changing Freud's formulation until he had a radically different concept, but the term remained. He had held it originally on the philosophical level as a fundamental idea that had given great stimulation to his intellectual development; and on the practical level, it was a term with which he had become accustomed to working. It was quite natural, then, that he should carry it over and continue to use it even after he had altogether redefined it and had reformulated it in terms of a much larger area of psychological contents.

It is an interesting fact that the term "unconscious" offers in itself a much better description of Freud's original formulation than it does of Jung's. Freud thought of the unconscious specifically in its relation to consciousness, as the underside of consciousness, embracing those psychic contents that the individual has hidden from consciousness or those that have reached the surface and have subsequently been forgotten. It is thus to Freud a negative concept, the negation of consciousness, and its use as a negative term is easily understandable. Jung, on the other hand, steadily broadened his formulation of the concept as his analyses of dreams and myths led him to the conclusion that the most important psychological factors exist *in potentia* prior to the individual's experience and are therefore prior to consciousness. He emerged finally with a new thought, but he continued to use the old term. Even with Jung's explicit redefinition, it was inevitable that confusion should result. The conception of the "collective unconscious" has continued to be discussed in psychological literature in terms of Freud's original theory, and this is not only misleading but altogether wrong, but for this Jung must himself accept a large part of the blame. His carrying over of an old term to describe an essentially new idea has often placed him in the awkward position of having to reply to his critics by saying that they do not understand what he is trying to say.

Of the two words in the term "collective unconscious," both are unclear and confusing. Jung intends the word "collective" merely to signify the opposite of personal and subjective. He intends the word "unconscious" to mean the large, amorphous, creative area deep within the person. In this sense, the phrase that Jung does occasionally use in his writings, "objective psychic" is considerably better than "collective unconscious," and perhaps, had he used it from the beginning, it might have spared him much unnecessary criticism and misunderstanding.

We should take into consideration the fact that the word for "unconscious" has somewhat different overtones in German from those it has in English. Even as Freud used the term, it carried with it something of that part of the German philosophical tradition in which the unconscious signifies a dynamic, demiurgic force in life, and Jung certainly retains the overtones of this way of thinking in an even more marked degree than Freud. Consequently, though Jung intends the term "unconscious" to be used scientifically as an analytical tool, his use of it suffers from an inherent ambiguity which must be kept in mind.

THE PSYCHE

In order to understand the full nature of Jung's conception of the unconscious, we have to place it in the context of his total theory of personality. Jung's basic unit of study is the "psyche." It is his way of referring to the totality of the psychologic structure of the human being. Jung hypothecates the "psyche" as a kind of non-physical space, since he conceives of it as the general area in which "psychic phenomena" occur. It is a kind of space that is within the personality. Jung speaks of the events that take place within it in terms that are analogous to, but not literally the same as movements in the physical world. He speaks of libido moving up or down, forward or backward, inward or outward in the psyche. Beyond this, the most important aspect of the psyche is that it is a reality in its own right, that it functions in terms of its own principles of operation, and that it can be understood only within its own terms. In describing the phenomena of the psyche, however, since his concepts are novel and unconventional, Jung often tries to make his meaning clear by using analogies drawn from the physical sciences. Sometimes this is helpful, and sometimes it is quite misleading. The reader will save himself much confusion, therefore, if he will keep in mind that when Jung discusses psychic processes *as if* they were physical processes, he is only using metaphors for the purpose of description.

The best way to understand the concept of the "psyche" is functionally as the framework and starting-point of Jung's thinking. It functions in his approach to man as a general category of the psychologic, which can be taken as a frame of reference for the study of the events that take place *within* the human being. Jung intends it as a completely neutral concept with no metaphysical connotations of any kind, neither the materialism of biology, nor the idealism of a "soul substance." The one philosophical system that does have a concept that corresponds to the way Jung defines the psyche is the Chinese Taoist. In the translations of their writings this is usually rendered as the "person," and it refers to the totality of the human personality as a kind of spaceless space, an inner cosmos.[1]

THE CONTENTS OF THE PSYCHE

Jung develops this idea from a functional point of view. He asks what moves in this "space," and his answer is "energy." He refers to the energy operating in the psyche as "psychic energy." As with physical energy, we cannot say *what* psychic energy is; we can only say *that* it is. Jung admits that he has been faced in the psychological sphere with the same dilemma that confronts the physical scientist, namely, the necessity of using for operational purposes a concept that cannot ultimately be defined. Used in this way, his idea of energy serves a purpose in Jung's thought very similar to the role it plays in Freud's; that is, it offers a comparative basis for the measurement of energic forces in at least approximately quantitative terms. The assumption is that, as a method of procedure, while we cannot say what energy is in itself, we can measure it in terms of the comparative intensities of its individual manifestations.

[1] E.g., the statement in the Tao Teh King, "The purpose of Tao is the regulation of the person."

In most of his writings Jung uses two terms interchange-ably to describe the energy which operates in the psyche: psychic energy and libido. In the latter case, borrowing a term from Freud, he redefines it with his own meaning. To Freud, libido meant instinctual energy, basically sexual in nature. To Jung, it signifies "the energy of the processes of life." [2]

The main difference between them is that Jung works with a larger and more flexible concept of energy. He treats it under two aspects: one is energy expressed on the cosmic level of life, energy as a whole; the other is energy mani-fested specifically in the psyche of man. On the wider plane, under its cosmic aspect, it corresponds somewhat to Henri Bergson's "élan vital," and in this sense, as Jung remarks, psychic energy becomes "a broader concept of vital energy which includes so-called psychic energy as a specific part." [3] It is the movements of this specific "part" of life energy that constitute the main subject matter of his studies.

THE PRINCIPLE OF OPPOSITES

Jung's analysis of energy in terms of movement leads to his concept of "psychic process," and his study of this then de-pends on the "principle of opposites." The principle of op-posites involves an underlying methodology for Jung. It is a kind of dialectical orientation; yet it is not a principle of logic in the Hegelian sense. It is based on the idea that all forms of life may be understood as a struggle of contending

[2] C. G. Jung, *Psychological Types*, trans. by H. G. Baynes, Harcourt, Brace, New York, 1923, p. 262.
[3] C. G. Jung, *Contributions to Analytical Psychology*, trans. by H. G. and C. F. Baynes, Harcourt, Brace, New York, 1928, p. 17.

forces, a moving, dynamic tension, a continual "running counter to." Nevertheless, it does not postulate any conception of the nature of Being as such, and it specifically avoids the assumption of a spiritual logic inherent in the world.

The principle of opposites is intended not as a literal description of reality, but as a *way of thinking* about the phenomena of the world as they appear from the point of view of the psyche. It is therefore not a principle of logic, but an approach to the world, growing out of the fact that the psyche draws its experiences of the world in terms of contrasts and opposites. Jung interprets the fact that the world views have been cast in these terms as an indication that the principle of opposites is a main characteristic of the psyche. The central experience of Hinduism, for example, is in the achievement of "freedom from the opposites"; in the Chinese philosophies, Yang and Yin, the mixing of male and female, is the underlying principle of the universe; and corresponding concepts are found in the Egyptian, the Zoroastrian, and the Judaic religions, in addition to the mythologies of many American Indian and primitive groups. Jung's favorite source for the intellectual formulation of this idea is in the pre-Socratic philosopher, Heraclitus. He frequently quotes Heraclitus' doctrine that life is a constant flux, a turmoil that never ceases:

> "From the living comes death, and from the dead, life; from the young, old age; and from the old, youth; from waking, sleep; and from sleep, waking; the stream of creation and decay never stands still. . . . Construction and destruction, destruction and construction—this is the norm which rules in every circle of natural life from the smallest to the greatest.

⁴ *Psychological Types*, p. 541.

Just as the cosmos itself emerged from the primal, so must it return once more into the same—a double process running its measured course through vast periods, a drama eternally re-enacted."

The main significance of such a statement to Jung is that it brings a sense of movement and a sense of time to the interpretation of the world. It is a cosmological principle; but he sees it, more fundamentally, as a psychological principle because of his basic idea that any concepts under which the universe may be understood by man must necessarily correspond to processes that are active in the psyche. The fact that the principle of opposites is found throughout mankind means, therefore, not that the cosmos operates in a way that is in accordance with it, but rather that it expresses some general principle of the psyche. Jung's point ultimately comes to the assertion that the cosmological views of mythology describe not the outer universe but the inner cosmos of the psyche. The basis, therefore, on which Jung adopts the "principle of opposites" as a way of thinking is that it corresponds to the psyche's way of operating, since it is a principle formulated in terms of conflicts, tensions, and irregular oscillations from one extreme to another.

PSYCHIC ENERGY

Every level of psychology, the modern individual and ancient mythology, is characterized by the see-sawing movement of opposites. Loves becomes hate; enthusiasm becomes depression; the sedate old man "has his fling"; the cynic finds rebirth; the sinner is converted. But the principle of opposites is much more fundamental in Jung's thinking than merely as a descriptive category for certain psychological phenomena. It is inherently related to the basic process by which life energies are created. His view is that the presence of opposites means a tension, and that human energies are called forth only because of the tensions created by the pressures of conflicting opposites. "Everything human is relative," Jung says, "because everything depends on a condition of inner antithesis; for everything subsists as a phenomenon of energy. Energy depends necessarily on a pre-existing antithesis, without which there could be no energy. There must always be present height and depth, heat and cold, etc., in order that the process of equalization—which is energy— can take place. All life is energy, and therefore depends on forces held in opposition." [5] The principle of opposites is therefore inherent in Jung's conception of the nature of the psyche, and it provides both a starting point and a methodology for his studies.

There are several important, but rather different, correlaries that follow from this idea. One is that the amount of energy generated and set loose varies directly with the depth and intensity of the internal conflict. Jung puts this in the form of the simple statement that, "the greater the tension between the pairs of opposites, the greater will be the energy that comes from them." [6] It gives him a basis for relating the principle of opposites to approximately quantitative valuations of energy, at least when they are taken relative to one another.

Taken further, Jung deduces that the permanence of any new attitude varies directly with the intensity of the conflict

[5] C. G. Jung, *Two Essays on Analytical Psychology*, trans. by H. G. and C. F. Baynes, Dodd, Mead, New York, 1928, p. 78.
[6] *Contributions*, p. 27.

of opposites out of which it was formed. "After violent oscillations at the beginning," he says, "the contradictions balance each other and gradually a new attitude develops, the
final stability of which is the greater in proportion to the
magnitude of the initial differences." [7]

The basis of these formulations is that, whether the psyche
is in conflict or at peace, the one constant and continuing factor is the movement of libido. Psychic energy is generated
through conflict within the person, and continues as the active
force within the psyche, being dissipated in activity and being recreated by newly emerging tensions. According to
Jung's conception, psychic energy moves in a variety of directions. It starts off one way, meets an obstacle, and re-
treats. It moves backward for a while, and finally goes off in
another direction. After a while this new movement meets a
difficulty and splits, the energies going off in two separate
directions. The movement of psychic energy has countless
variations in the life of each individual. As it splits, some
shoots off wildly in meaningless activity, while some goes
down into the unconscious and emerges in strange psychological forms. It is a constant process of starting and stopping,
of going forward and backward, this way and that. The libido is restless and a wanderer, an uncertain traveller, for-
ever seeking and seldom finding its destination.

PROGRESSION AND REGRESSION

Jung focuses his attention on the analysis of the movements of the energies in the psyche. Although the libido does
not follow any set pattern in its wanderings, it does operate
according to certain observable principles. These are the

[7] Ibid., pp. 27, 28.

psychic processes, the most basic of which Jung designates as 'progression" and "regression."

The "progression" phase of libido movement takes place when all is going well with the psyche and the psychic energies can move outward toward life in a creative and confident way. Jung refers to this as the "daily advance of the process of psychological adaptation." [8] While it is active, the individual experiences a "vital feeling," an exhilarated sense of well-being; the world seems good and pleasant. When the situation is reversed, when the progression movement of libido is detoured for any reason, "the vital feeling that was present before disappears, and in its place the psychic value of certain conscious contents increases in an unpleasant way; subjective contents and reactions press to the fore and the situation becomes full of affect and favorable for explosions." [9] The psychic phenomenon that now takes place involves a change in the direction of libido movement. The appearance of an obstacle that the flow of psychic energies cannot at once overcome causes the balance between the opposites to be broken apart. Since it was this balance that maintained the equilibrium of the psyche and permitted the forward movement of the libido to go on, the "breaking up of the pairs of opposites" means that the progression movement can no longer continue. "During the progression of the libido the pairs of opposites are united in the coordinated flow of psychical processes. Their working together makes possible the balanced regularity of these processes, which, without this reciprocal action, would be

[8] Ibid., p. 34.
[9] Ibid., p. 35.

one-sided and unbalanced." [10] But when the flow of libido is obstructed, this cooperation of the opposites is over. Something has intervened. The result is that instead of harmony within the psyche, there is discord and internal friction. The individual no longer feels free to go forward. "The obstacle dams up the river of life. Whenever such a damming up of libido occurs, the opposites, formerly united in the steady flow of life, fall apart and henceforth oppose one another." [11]

The conflict that now occurs generates additional energy, but it is energy that is not going anywhere. It is not being applied in the progressive adaptation of life. The energy, therefore, remains within the psyche, accumulating as it increases, and eventually it begins to move in the opposite direction, downward, deeper into the psyche. The libido is then in a "regression" movement and expends itself within itself. It moves down toward the unconscious, first at the surface levels, and then descends further downward into the lower layers of the psyche.

The "progression" movement of psychic energy is a movement up from the unconscious to consciousness and out into the external world; the "regression" movement goes down from consciousness steadily deeper into the unconscious. In order to grasp Jung's conception of this, we have to visualize energy as moving in a kind of psychic space which extends from consciousness at the surface, at the point of the individual's contact with his environment, downward into the person to layers of psychic contents that are prior to the individual's experience with the external world. In this sense, the

[10] Ibid., p. 35.
[11] *Psychological Types*, p. 114.

psyche is the totality of the area in which the psychic energies move about and in which psychic processes occur.

THE THREE LAYERS OF THE PSYCHE

Understanding the psyche in these terms as the background for all psychic phenomena, we can represent schematically the way Jung thinks of the various levels of consciousness. He conceives the psyche as having three layers. At the surface is consciousness; below it is the Personal Unconscious; and at the base is the Objective or Collective Unconscious. It is similar, in a general way, to a cross-sectional drawing of geologic rock formations. At the top is a thin layer of surface rock; below that a somewhat thicker layer of rock of another type; and underneath these two, a dark volcanic base that extends back to the very core of the earth itself (perhaps as the individual relates to the universal) and which occasionally erupts, shooting its materials up to the surface through the other two layers.

Jung conceives of the topmost layer as the thinnest and the most fragile of all. Consciousness contains the attitudes with which the individual approaches his immediate external environment. It contains the basic orientation with which he plays his role in society, and also it gives him his starting-point for rational and logical analyses.

Beneath this is the Personal Unconscious. Here are contained those psychic contents that have been repressed from consciousness, deliberately or unconsciously forgotten, and also those drives and desires that have not yet reached consciousness. The Personal Unconscious contains material that either has been in consciousness or may potentially be in consciousness. It is therefore material that is peculiar to the particular individual in whom it is found. It contains, as Jung has phrased it in one of his later formulations, "fantasies (including dreams) of a personal character, which go back unquestionably to personal experiences, things forgotten or repressed." [12] As he stated it at an earlier date, in the Personal Unconscious there are to be found "forgotten memories, suppressed painful ideas, apperceptions sometimes described as below the threshold, that is, sensory perceptions that were not strong enough to reach consciousness and, finally, contents that were not yet ripe for consciousness." [13]

This layer is placed in between consciousness and the larger area of the Collective Unconscious. In a sense, it is part of the unconscious proper, because what Jung here calls the Personal Unconscious is really just what Freud refers to as the Unconscious, or specifically, the Unconscious Repressed. Jung, however, places it in the larger context of the totality of the psyche, and the Personal Unconscious is to him only the "more or less superficial layer of the unconscious." [14]

The bottom level, which is also the largest and deepest area of the psyche, the Objective Unconscious, is the focus of most of Jung's studies of the psyche. He looks to it as the source of the materials that come into consciousness and as the point of contact between the individual and the greater-than-individual forces in life. The fundamental hypothesis on which Jung works is the idea that the potentialities

[12] C. G. Jung and Carl Kerenyi, *Essays on a Science of Mythology*, trans. by R. F. C. Hull, Bollingen Series XXII, Pantheon, New York, 1949, p. 102.
[13] *Two Essays*, pp. 67, 68.
[14] C. G. Jung, *The Integration of the Personality*, trans. by S. M. Dell, Farrar and Rinehart, New York, 1939, pp. 52, 53.

within the individual personality are not left unaffected by
the developments of history, and that what happens in time
leaves its mark not only on the psyche of the individual, but
also on the continuity of the human race.

THE CONTENTS OF THE UNCONSCIOUS

In one of his more recent essays, Jung has stated his
"methodological principle" for the study of the unconscious in
a succinct way that fits well in our discussion here. *"Contents
of an archetypal character,"* he says, *"are manifestations of
processes in the collective unconscious.* Hence, they do not
refer to anything that is or has been conscious, but to something *essentially unconscious.* In the last analysis, therefore,
it is impossible to say what they refer to. Every interpretation necessarily remains an 'as-if.' The ultimate core of
meaning may be circumscribed, but not described. Even so,
the bare circumscription denotes an essential step forward
in our knowledge of the pre-conscious structure of the psyche,
which was already in existence when there was as yet no
unity of personality." [15]

We can feel in this statement Jung's sense of the relation
between the structure of the psyche and the development of
man in time. As "consciousness comes out of the unconscious," so the materials of the unconscious are prior to
what comes into the surface layer of the psyche. When
psychic contents come up from the lower layers, they may become part of the conscious attitude of individual personality, but the first question is what these contents are in themselves. In this regard Jung has developed the concept of
"archetype," by which he means "forms or images of a col-

[15] *Essays on a Science of Mythology,* p. 104 (Jung's italics).

lective nature which occur practically all over the earth as constituents of myths and at the same time as autochthonous, individual products of unconscious origin." [16]

Archetypes are fundamental patterns of symbol formation which are observed to recur throughout mankind in the contents of the mythologies of all peoples. Jung has also used the term "primordial image" in this regard. By "primordial" he wishes to indicate that they have been expressed in the earliest days of the life-history of the human species. However, the important point in this is not simply that they are old; what is important to him is that they were present in very ancient days *because* they grow out of the nature of the psyche in its most rudimentary, pre-conscious form. Since the archetypes were present so far back in man's development, Jung infers that they have their basis in what is most fundamental in the structure of the psyche itself.

Actually, the fact that these images have been present in "primordial" times—as indicated by their presence in the most ancient myths—does not mean that they are produced only in the early stages of man's history. On the contrary, they may occur spontaneously in the most modern psychic phenomena, and the reason is that, since they are in the most basic layers of the psyche, they are present in all periods of history. Therefore, the importance of their being *primordial* images is that they may potentially be produced in all periods of history and in all social circumstances. Being the oldest, they may also be always the newest, since they occur in ever-new forms out of the ancient nature of the psyche.

It is important to stress the word "spontaneously" in de-

[16] C. G. Jung, *Psychology and Religion* (Terry Lectures—1937), Yale University Press, New Haven, 1938, p. 63.

scribing the occurrence of primordial images in later-than-primordial times. Jung's concept has often been misinterpreted as meaning "inherited ideas." The implication is that he believes that once these primordial images have occurred in human history, or in any racial group, they are then passed on to future generations as part of a "collective" inheritance. What he really means is not "inherited ideas" but "inherited pathways," that is to say, tendencies that are ingrained in the nature of the psyche and are inherited only in the sense that the structure of the psyche is inherited, carrying with it a tendency to express itself in certain specific ways. The primordial images are not always the same; they vary from culture to culture and from one historical situation to another. This is so just because their contents are not inherited; if they were "inherited ideas," the same symbols would always be expressed. What are inherited are the same *tendencies;* therefore, it is the *Underlying patterns of symbol formation* and not their specific details that are always the same.

The evidence for this is found in the similarity of symbolic content in myths, religions, fairy tales, sagas, poetry, and so on. Certain underlying and recurrent symbols are readily observed. We see, for example, the archetype of the eternal wonder child, as in Christ, the infant Hermes, Zeus, or Moses, and the symbols of William Blake and Meister Eckehart; or the archetype of the universal creative mother, as expressed by Mother Nature, the earth goddesses in the Greek and Roman religions, as well as the "Grandmother" of the American Indians and the "female principle" in its many incarnations in the Oriental religions; the archetype of the hero is represented in the many forms of hero-cycles in the Celtic mythology, the Scandinavian, the Hindu, Greek, American Indian, and so on. Jung refers to these as "motifs." There are a great number of them that can be identified through the study of comparative mythology and religion. Their importance, however, is not in the actual symbol. It is in what they represent or express of the deeper layers of the psyche. These motifs come to the surface of the psyche in a great variety of forms, and the problem is to get behind this variety into the unity of the motif, and thereby to inquire what the motif itself signifies. In this sense, Jung's method is to go *via historical material* to the universal patterns underlying the psyche. The social scientist, on the other hand, will find the reverse of this problem as most important; after the meaning of the motif has been grasped, he will want to know how the expressions of these motifs vary, and why they take just their particular manifestations in the course of history.

To maintain an accurate historical perspective, we should keep in mind that Jung came to his concept of the archetype through studying the phenomena of a particular historical situation. He was studying the dreams of modern Western Europeans a few years before and a few years after the first World War. He was studying, it should be observed, the dreams of individuals, and not of collectivities. What impressed him as a crucial phenomenon requiring explanation was that the dreams and other unconscious products which he analyzed had a tendency at certain points in the individual's condition to simulate the kind of symbols found in myths and religions with which the individuals themselves had no direct contact. This seemed to him a great stumbling block for psychological theory, and he finally interpreted it to mean that the inherited structure of the psyche contains the tendency to produce "primordial images" which vary in countless forms around certain basic motifs. Jung's conclusion, therefore, is that the individual may, under certain circumstances, bring to the surface these deeply rooted images out of the very base of the unconscious.

PSYCHIC PROCESSES AND THEIR ARCHETYPES

The underlying principle is that the inherited structure of the psyche carries with it certain necessary psychic processes, which take the form of spontaneously recurring patterns by which the psychic energies within the individual seek expression. These inherently-contained psychic processes come forth in the form of the archetypal motifs. Consequently, when Jung says, "Contents of an archetypal character are manifestations of processes in the collective unconscious," the key thought is that these contents do not exist in themselves as "inherited ideas," but *rather emerge as expressions of the psychic processes which are inherited because they are in the structural nature of the psyche.* These are generic to the nature of the human being as such, and therefore, they are expressed in the individual in dream and fantasy, just as they are expressed in the group *via* myth, collective delusion, and so on.

We can see here again how misleading the term "collective" unconscious is. In the above quotation, Jung uses it to describe psychic phenomena which occur in individuals as expressions of psychic processes inherent in man. They are more pervasive than the individualized products of the Personal Unconscious, but they are not restricted to collective or group phenomena. When, therefore, the individual expresses something from the collective unconscious, it is primordial because it comes out of the inherent nature of man.

It is worthwhile to note the attitude that Jung takes toward the study of the unconscious. At the opening of his lectures on *Psychology and Religion* delivered in 1937 at Yale University, he remarked rather slyly, "Nothwithstanding the fact that I have often been called a philosopher, I am an empiricist and adhere to the phenomenological point of view." [17] Speaking to an American audience, he was at pains to stress his intellectual kinship to William James' kind of Pragmatism. As Jung uses the word "phenomenological," it has a very general meaning and may possibly mean to him the European equivalent of James' Pragmatism. Nevertheless, Jung has frequently reiterated, even in his most recent publications, that he works from the "phenomenological point of view," and his statement must therefore be taken seriously.

It is part of his basic methodology, as indicated in the statement cited above, that he treats the contents of the unconscious merely as "manifestations." They come to the surface, and there they are to be observed. Nothing else is to be presumed about them. We would, very likely, be carrying intellectual derivations too far if we attributed Jung's psychology to a substructure of Kantian epistemology, but it is a fact that there is a point in Jung's thought where he has a close affinity to Kant, particularly on the question of what the psychological investigator is in a position to assume about the nature of psychic reality.[18] On the question of reality in general, Jung agrees with Kant that we are not able finally

[17] Ibid., p. 1.
[18] See in particular, *Psychological Types*, pp. 55-62.

to know the thing-in-itself. Within the experience of the individual, however, things may be "psychologically real," in the sense that they involve great intensities of psychic energy, and thereby great emotional affect. The symbols that are activated in the psyche operate within the personality of the individual as real things; that is, they have a force and power of their own. Jung goes even further. Psychic phenomena have in themselves a specific empirical existence and are to be taken as an area of reality within their own terms. Just as external objects are considered to subsist within the frame of reference of the physical world, so, in an equivalent sense, psychic phenomena constitute the realities of the psyche. We should treat the manifestations of the psyche, Jung says, with the same respect as to their legitimacy that we give to the phenomena of nature. The unconscious "affects us just as we affect it. In this sense, the world of the unconscious is commensurate with the world of outer experience." [19]

We may say that the manifestations have a power and authenticity of their own; but on the question of what they *are in themselves*, Jung states that we must remain silent. Ultimately, we cannot define what the contents of the unconscious are. We can observe them *as phenomena* appearing in the experience of individuals. We can analyze them, describe them, and interpret the nature of the phenomena in which they appear; but ultimately we cannot reduce the contents of the unconscious to the terms of consciousness. We cannot, in a word, rationalize the unconscious. We may study its phenomena empirically, and in the area of mystery which remains, we can, perhaps, intuit or experience their mean-

[19] *Two Essays*, p. 198.

ings; but all scientific study on this subject must proceed with the strict limitation kept in mind that the unconscious cannot be reduced to the terms of consciousness.

The principle involves something more than the methodological limitation that we cannot know the ultimate nature of the unconscious. Consciousness and the unconscious are each expressed in different terms. While the contents of consciousness come from the unconscious, there is a qualitative change that occurs. Consciousness proceeds in terms of analysis and differentiation, in terms of special attention to "the most minute details." The unconscious, on the other hand, has an opposite way of thinking. Non-analytical, undifferentiated, it takes its symbols as they are, and does not break them down as consciousness does. This means that the basic categories and ways of procedure are different in consciousness from those that prevail in the unconscious. Therefore, Jung says, we must "always make sure that we do not foist conscious psychology upon the unconscious. . . . Its mode of thinking is altogether different from what we understand by 'thinking.' It merely fashions an image that answers to the conscious situation. . . . The only thing it is not is a product of rationalistic reflection." [20]

One of Jung's most fundamental and far-reaching principles on this question is that "nothing produced by the human mind is completely outside our psychic range." [21] Whenever a psychic content comes to the surface, no matter in how strange a form and no matter how obscure its meaning may be, he assumes that the mere fact of its presence indicates that it expresses something that is active in the psyche. In

[20] Ibid., p. 95.
[21] The Integration of the Personality, p. 8.

interpreting the phenomena of schizophrenia in particular, there is often the problem of dealing with symbolism that is altogether strange to consciousness. "A psychosis," in Jung's terms, however, "implies a condition in which certain mental activities appear spontaneously out of the unconscious." [22] These contents, brought out of the lower areas of the psyche, are understood as psychic remainders out of the historical past, as contents which have never been integrated into consciousness, and which have been brought up autonomously in the course of a condition of disequilibrium in the psyche. Material that contains archetypal symbols may very well be drawn up to the surface in such situations, but actually, the more "primordial" a root image the symbol is, the more difficult it is to interpret. Archetypal images that appear in a psychotic are particularly strange because they come to the surface of the psyche without any relation to their original historical context.

Archetypes have a double aspect. On the one hand, they are the symbols that represent psychic processes generic to the human species. In this sense, they express universal tendencies in man. On the other hand, the psychic processes do not possess any symbolic content until they are expressed in the lives of specific historical individuals. In themselves the archetypes are only tendencies, only potentialities, and an archetype does not become meaningful until it goes out into the world and takes part in life according to its nature and according to the time in history in which it occurs. As Jung phrases it, the archetypes "draw the stuff of experience into their shape, presenting themselves in facts, rather than pre-

" Ibid., p. 7.

senting facts. They clothe themselves in facts, as it were." [23] What we come in contact with, then, in the lives of historical individuals, are not archetypes as such, but archetypes manifested, that is individualized, in the facts of the world.

ARCHETYPES AND HISTORY

At this point, we can begin to see how the conception of man with which Jung is working sets the basis for an approach to the problem of the dynamic inter-relation of the individual psyche with the underlying forces of history. Archetypes come to the fore again and again in history, always taking different forms, and always presuming at each moment of history that the particular form in which they find themselves is the only one that is "true" and "eternal." Every attitude that is expressed in consciousness is an historical manifestation of an archetype with a long history in the human psyche. Even the conscious attitude expressed by modern science is subject to this principle, despite its air of pure rationality. "Whether its endeavors were called Euthemerism, or Christian Apologetics, or Enlightenment in the narrow sense, or Positivism, there was always a myth hiding behind it, in new and disconcerting garb, which then, following the ancient and venerable pattern, gave itself out as ultimate truth. In reality, we can never legitimately cut loose from our archetypal foundations unless we are prepared to pay the price of a neurosis, any more than we can rid ourselves of our body and its organs without committing suicide." [24]

[23] *Psychological Types*, p. 379.
[24] *Essays on a Science of Mythology*, pp. 105, 106.

It is necessary to remark in commenting on this passage that when tracing the manifestation of an archetype in history there is a great deal of careful thought required if one is to avoid bringing the wrong phenomena together under the heading of a single archetype. When it comes to the application that Jung has made of his concepts to actual historical study, there is a great deal left to be desired and to which the social scientist will object, as in the above passage. However, the main point is that the *concept of the archetype in history opens a way* for the unified study of the phenomena of the psyche and the phenomena of history.

On the question of the necessity for keeping the conscious attitude in close touch with the historical bases of the unconscious—and especially with one's historical archetypes—Jung is particularly eloquent. One of his major contentions regarding the "diagnosis" of the condition of modern man is that consciousness has been overstressed to the point where an unbalanced situation has developed in the psyche. The modern attitude, Jung asserts, "entirely forgets that it carries the whole living past in the lower stories of the skyscraper of rational consciousness. Without the lower stories it is as though our mind is suspended in mid-air. No wonder it gets nervous." [25] "The more powerful and independent consciousness becomes, and with it the conscious will, the more is the unconscious forced into the background" until "consciousness gets so far out of touch with [the archetypes] as to make collapse inevitable." [26]

In these terms, the disorders of personality experienced by

[25] *Psychology and Religion*, p. 41.
[26] C. G. Jung and R. Wilhelm, *The Secret of the Golden Flower*, trans. by C. F. Baynes, Kegan Paul, London, 1931, pp. 85, 86.

individuals in any given historical situation are an expression of forces that are more than individual. The occurrence of neurosis in an individual may be interpreted as a manifestation of a more general breakdown characteristic of that period of history as a whole. Or, more fundamentally, a personal disorder may be understood as a situation within the psyche in which a disharmony has developed between psychic contents that are more than personal in their nature. Psychic phenomena that involve the archetypes have to be understood in this way, and to interpret them in terms of their individual expressions may be very misleading. Jung's position on this point, growing out of his conception of the Objective Psychic and the historical nature of man, places him in opposition to the mainstream of studies of individual personality—particularly in a position that is the opposite of the Freudian point of view—and yet he would appear to be on very strong ground.

"Individuality," Jung says in the book that marks a turning point in his thought, "belongs to those conditional actualities which are greatly overrated theoretically on account of their practical significance. It does not belong to those overwhelmingly clear and therefore universally obtrusive general facts upon which a science must primarily be founded. The individual content of consciousness is therefore the most unfavorable object imaginable for psychology, because it has veiled the universally valid until it has become unrecognizable. The essence of consciousness is the process of adaptation which takes place in the most minute details. On the other hand, the unconscious is the generally diffused, which not only binds the individuals among themselves to the race, but also unites them backwards with the peoples of the past and their psychology. Thus the unconscious, surpassing the individual in its generality, is, in the first place, the object of a true psychology." [27]

[27] *The Psychology of the Unconscious*, trans. by B. M. Hinkle, Dodd, Mead, New York, 1916, 1949, p. 199.

I I I

PERSONS WITHIN THE PERSON

THE AUTONOMOUS COMPLEXES

We have spoken of Progression and Regression as the forward and backward movement of energy in the psyche. We have now to ask what kind of psychic contents become attached to these movements, and in what form they are brought together.

Jung has described the psyche as being based on a tension of opposites. Consciousness balances the unconscious in a "reciprocal relativity," each side of the psyche actually being dependent on its opposite. Psychic energy emerges out of this tension. The varying intensities of energy expressed in psychic movements are determined by the degree of conflict between opposites. The main characteristic of a tension in the psyche is that its force is exerted beyond the control of the individual. It is autonomous in the sense that it sets energy free independent of the guidance of consciousness. The very fact of its existence as a conflict in the psyche indicates that it is something that consciousness cannot subdue. Energic forces set free by these conflicts, therefore, may operate under their own power and live, as it were, a life of their own within the personality.

Such quantities of released energy have an attracting power that gathers various psychic contents together around them

into a "constellation" or "complex." These complexes, acting
under their own power, break away from the totality of the
personality. As Jung interprets it, "the tendency to split
means that parts of the psyche detach themselves from consciousness to such an extent that they not only appear foreign
but also lead an autonomous life of their own." [1] This means
not only that they go out of the control of consciousness, but
that they may operate in consciousness within their own
terms. They become "autonomous partial systems," and they
function like small personalities within the total personality.
In itself, this is not necessarily an abnormal condition. Such
psychic "splits" are actually necessary if the individual is to
specialize the direction of his energies so as to accomplish
some particular work. The "autonomous complex" provides,
very often, the "flavor" and distinctiveness of an individual's
personality. It becomes a danger point only when, operating
as a "partial system," it goes too far out of relation to the rest
of the psyche, and a condition of unbalance results.

Jung took his clue for the interpretation of "psychic splits"
from the way they are symbolized in the products of the unconscious. He found that in dreams these complexes are expressed as other individuals. According to the type of complex they represent, he has found them to be portrayed by
the figure of a man or a woman, in certain cases by figures that
the individual has never seen before, but invariably the autonomous complexes appear in personified form. He infers, then, that the unconscious is itself providing the key to
their interpretation for, in giving them "the character of per-

[1] C. G. Jung, "Factors Determining Human Behavior" *Harvard
Tercentenary Conference on Arts and Sciences*, Harvard University
Press, 1937, pp. 57, 58.

sons," it indicates that the complexes function as individualities within the psyche.[2]

The nature of the complexes depends on their function in the total operation of the psyche. Their symbolical representation in dreams tends to portray this function in the kind of figures which represent the complex, and in the kind of action that takes place in the dream. In particular this is true of the Persona, of the Shadow, of the Animus and the Anima. These are original concepts that Jung has developed in order to describe the main types of autonomous complex in terms of their function and personification in the psyche.

THE PERSONA

By the Persona Jung means the mask that the individual must wear in his daily intercourse in society. In this sense, life is always a masquerade to some degree. His idea here is that the individual is never able to meet his fellow human beings with the totality of his personality, his combined consciousness and unconscious. He cannot present all of these at once to other people because he himself does not have them all in control at a given time. What happens is that in particular social relationships the individual develops specific parts of his personality according to the situation and according to the other individuals with whom he is in contact. It comes about, then, that the individual has many personalities, many sides to his life, in proportion to the number of differing life situations in which he finds himself. Up to this point, Jung's concept of the Persona is very similar to what William James described in his *Psychology* as a multiplicity of selves in the person. The individual is a child to his

[2] *The Secret of the Golden Flower*, pp. 108, 109.

mother, a student to his teacher, a lover to his wife, an em-
ployee to his employer, and a boss to those who work under
him. In some situations his Persona will show affection, in
others sternness, in others meekness—and they may be more
or less inconsistent with each other, depending on the unity
in his social relationships and the degree of integration that
has taken place in his psyche.

Underneath the surface of consciousness and separated
from the part of the personality that comes in contact with
other individuals, there is the flux and conflict of the deeper
levels of the psyche. In order to shield these from the im-
pacts of daily social contacts, an outer shell is developed.
Jung chose the term "Persona" because in Latin it originally
meant a mask. It referred to the mask worn by actors on the
ancient stage, and as Jung understands it, the Persona masks
the inner life of the individual when he comes forth into the
stage-play of social life. Society actually requires that an individual have a category into which he can be fitted. Is he a
doctor, lawyer, working man? Is he amiable, harsh, reliable?
Society requires these easy classifications, and the individual
in his turn seeks to create a mask to make such a satisfactory
classification possible. The mask then becomes the conscious
ideal of his personality, by which he seeks to represent himself in his social relations on the most favorable terms.

The Persona, taking different forms within each individual, becomes identified with the Ego. It specifically does not
refer to the Self, that is, it does not relate to the personality
as a whole, but instead, the Persona becomes identified with
that small part of consciousness that is the Ego. In this regard, Jung speaks of an "Ego-complex." "By Ego," he says,
"I understand a complex of representations which consti-

tutes the centrum of my field of consciousness and appears
to possess a very high degree of continuity and identity." His
thought is that the Ego is not so much a psychic fact as it is an
actual "condition of consciousness, since a psychic content is
conscious to me in so far as it is related to my Ego-complex." [3]
As it functions in the psyche, the Ego is the focus or mid-
point of consciousness and has available a sum of psychic
energy around which is constellated a variety of psychic contents, mainly in the form of conscious attitudes. It is this
Ego-complex that reacts to the experiences of the individual's life in terms of consciousness, and it is this also with
which the Persona is identified.

In dreams, or in other unconscious symbol formations, the
Persona tends to be represented by a figure that embodies
similar qualities. It may be represented by a stern old man
or woman, a clown, a vagabond, and so on. What is most important about the Persona is that it represents the conscious
attitude, and as such it is placed in the psyche as an opposite
to the unconscious. Because of this, the contents of the Persona are apt to be in a constantly tense relationship with the
unconscious. Any extreme in the Persona will be balanced by
an extreme in the unconscious. An individual, for example,
who builds a conscious mask that is overly pious or "moral"
is bound to suffer from pressures by the unconscious in the
opposite direction. As Jung remarks, "Whoever builds up
too good a Persona has to pay for it in irritability." [4]

To take another example, an individual who decides that
he wants to appear to other people in the mask of one who
takes a "scientific" attitude toward all things may create such

[3] *Psychological Types*, p. 540.
[4] *Two Essays*, p. 209.

a Persona successfully, only to be reminded by the unconscious that "high rests upon low." As it personifies the conscious attitude, the Persona must rest solidly on the unconscious, or else it will not be secure, and it may easily come into a condition in which it is particularly vulnerable to the conflict of opposites within the psyche. In such a situation, "an opposite is forced up from within; it is exactly as though the unconscious suppressed the Ego with a force equal to that which drew the Ego into the Persona." [5] We are then brought to the problem of the collapse of the Persona and the conditions of its re-establishment. This is always a crisis in the life of the individual, and it involves several other questions which will be discussed a little later on.

THE SHADOW

There is a tendency for the Ego to develop what it feels to be the strong side of its personality and to integrate this into its dominant conscious attitudes and into its Persona-mask. As the strong qualities are intensified in consciousness, the weaker, unadapted side falls back into the unconscious. There it gathers together into a constellation, and when an appropriate psychic condition has sent a sum of libido into the unconscious, it comes up as an autonomous complex. This complex contains the weaker side of the personality, its dark side, so to say, and its autonomous actions have a tendency to lead the conscious personality into trouble. Jung gives it the general name of "Shadow" to signify the rather sinister role it plays in the psyche. It shoots up into consciousness without warning, coming into the individual's ex-

─────────────

[5] Ibid., p. 210.

perience as sudden moods or urges leading the individual to do things of which his conscious attitude does not approve. It may lead the individual to commit blunders that he cannot explain or excuse. It is as though a separate individual were in the personality deliberately doing things wrong against the wishes of the conscious Ego. The expression that a person is "not himself" conveys the meaning of this. There is an autonomous personality at work in the psyche in the form of a "partial system," which intrudes into consciousness and takes over parts of consciousness at inopportune moments. That it acts as an individual person is altogether appropriate for its meaning, since in its expression in the unconscious it appears as a dark, sinister person, or an awkward, clumsy, incompetent individual, or some other personality type to suit the case.

It is very important, but often difficult, to distinguish the Shadow from the Ego and the Persona. There is often an overlapping and intermingling, which may involve many difficulties for the individual if the two are not effectively differentiated from one another. Under the impact of conflicting urges from the Persona in consciousness and from the Shadow in the unconscious, it is crucial for the individual to be able to tell which represents the strong side of his personality and which the weaker. On his ability to distinguish these two correctly may depend his success in making his adaptation to life.

Particularly in the condition of neurosis, when the libido has turned back into the psyche and a twilight of unconsciousness covers the greater part of the personality, the Shadow portion is enlarged. Its role in the personality becomes greater, and the individual is subject to much more "inexcusable" error-making in this situation than when the psychic opposites are back in balance.

One very common occurrence which Jung describes is the projection of the Shadow into other people. We do not realize certain faults and weaknesses that are present in ourselves, but we ascribe them to the other person, in whom they may or may not be present. It is the old question, referred to by Jesus, of first taking the beam out of one's own eye. "We still attribute to the 'other fellow,' " Jung says, "all the evil and inferior qualities that we do not like to recognize in ourselves. That is why we have to criticize and attack him." [6] We may note that this is one way to approach the psychological side of the "scapegoat" problem, which is such a perplexing and ubiquitous phenomenon in history. It has been noted by many writers—though Jung does not approach this problem—that the Nazis attributed to the Jews many personality traits of which they themselves were much more guilty. We may find in this at least a partial clue to some of the ingredients that go to make up the scapegoat.

Jung has made a very interesting application of the concept of the Shadow in some remarks on the nature of Freud's theories and the public reaction to them. The loud cry of protest that went up when Freud presented his analysis of sexuality indicates the strength with which men will battle anyone who calls their Shadow side to account. They deny that they have this Shadow side, and they make all sorts of counter-accusations. Freud, of course, realized this within the context of his own system and took the attitude that the attacks on his theories were proof that he had truth on his side.

[6] C. G. Jung, *Modern Man in Search of a Soul*, trans. by W. S. Dell and C. F. Baynes, Harcourt, Brace, New York, 1933, p. 163.

While the extent of the first protest against his ideas does not, of course, prove these ideas to be true, it does indicate that Freud's darts had hit the mark, and this has been further borne out by the fact that after the first extremely loud rejection they have become so widely and inordinately popular.

In his analysis of the personal side of the unconscious in its relation to sexual drives, Freud was putting his focus on the weaker side, the underside, of personality. "The end-product of the Freudian method," Jung says, "is a detailed elaboration of man's shadow side . . . It is no wonder that there arose on all sides the most violent opposition to Freud and his school . . . by those who believe in illusion on principle. But I maintain that there are not a few among the opponents of the method of explanation who have no illusions as to man's shadow-side, and who yet object to a biased portrayal of man from the shadow-side alone. After all, the essential thing is not the shadow, but the body which casts it.

"The horror which we feel for Freudian interpretations is entirely due to our own barbaric or childish naïveté, which believes that there can be heights without corresponding depths and which blinds us to the really 'final' truth that, carried to extremes, opposites meet. Our mistake would lie in supposing that what is radiant no longer exists because it has been explained from the shadow-side." [7]

We have, then, in the Persona the well-adapted side of consciousness, and in the Shadow the unadapted side. These are the two main autonomous complexes and appear as opposites to each other with respect to consciousness and the Ego.

[7] Ibid., pp. 46, 47.

ANIMA AND ANIMUS

Jung distinguishes another set of figures which represent autonomous complexes referring each to one side of the sexual adaptation. The "Anima" and the "Animus" represent the opposite of the dominant attitude in consciousness. The male, for example, develops a conscious attitude which contains qualities of the kind that are generally regarded as masculine. In his business or professional life he expresses a certain masculinity of manner and orientation. By the same token, the female, in developing her conscious attributes and her relationships to other people, does this in what is socially regarded as the "feminine" way. On the other side, while masculine and feminine qualities are developed to characterize the conscious attitudes respectively of the male and the female, the unconscious, maladapted side takes on just the opposite aspect. As the balancing element in the psyche, there is in each man a feminine side, and in each woman a masculine side. In the man the feminine side is personified in the unconscious by the Anima; and in the woman the masculine side is personified by the Animus.

Jung claims that there is a biological basis for these sexual opposites within the personality. In each man there is a majority of male genes and a minority of female genes; and the opposite holds true for women. The Anima corresponds to the female minority in men; and the Animus corresponds to the male minority in women.

It is a matter of common observation that there is a "womanish" element in men, which expresses itself more or less noticeably according to the time in the life-history of the individual. In the male, the Anima expresses itself in daily life through inexplicable moods of a petty, nasty, "catty" spirit; and "in the same way that the Anima produces moods," Jung says, "the Animus produces opinions," arbitrary, belligerent, hair-splitting opinions.[8] What is involved is the assertion of the undeveloped side of the personality. The feminine side of personality is always present in a man, and the masculine side is always present in a woman. Neither is expressed generally in a dominant, but rather in an inferior way. When a woman engages in activities that simulate the activities of men—as some of the extremes of the Suffragette movement—the result is an inferior man, so to speak. Therefore, Jung has pointed out that when usually masculine traits are expressed in women they come out in a maladapted form. When the feminine side comes to the fore in a man, it does so in moods by which the unconscious overtakes the conscious attitude and introduces unpleasant effects.

When symbolized in dreams, the Anima appears to a man in the figure of a woman, generally either a woman with a blank face or no face at all, or a woman whom the man may not recognize in terms of his conscious experience. When the Animus appears in dreams to a woman it takes the form usually of a plurality of men. In both cases, the appearance of figures personifying the Anima or the Animus indicates that archetypal figures in the unconscious have been activated.

The main point to keep in mind is that these complexes in the unconscious are associated with the weak and unadapted side of the personality. The first form in which the negative

[8] *Two Essays*, pp. 226, 227. For an advanced discussion of the issues involved in the Anima and Animus concept, see, C. G. Jung, *Aion*, Rascher, Zurich, 1951, Part I, Ch. 3.

elements are expressed is the Shadow. The nature of the Shadow-side is that it is the direct opposite of the qualities identified with the Ego. It is negative in a specifically personal sense, and it is therefore operative only on the level of the Personal Unconscious. In the course of the individual's life, however, there is a tendency for the sum of energy attached to the Shadow to be increased as psychic contents of a more than personal nature constellate around the Shadow figure. This means that the Shadow is now covering a larger area of the psyche and is now involving material that is not merely personal but archetypal in nature. When this takes place, the Shadow can no longer be confined to the Personal Unconscious, where it can more easily be controlled. Its center shifts to the deeper level of the unconscious, and as this happens the complex becomes invested with increasing sums of psychic energy and psychic affect until a transformation in the complex takes place. On the basis of the images with which this change is represented in dreams and fantasies, Jung has concluded that when the Shadow is brought into the lower levels of the unconscious and collective psychic contents are added to it, it can no longer be expressed by a figure of the same sex as the Ego. Having gone more deeply into the unconscious, it must turn completely into the opposite of consciousness. The Shadow side of a man, previously expressed by a masculine figure, is now represented by the image of a woman; and the Shadow of a woman now comes out of the unconscious in the form of one or more male figures. The Shadow, in short, changes into an Anima or Animus.[9]

* Aion, p. 24-26.

The concomitant of this transformation is an increase in the unpleasant side-effects which accompany the unconscious complexes. In particular, there is a more marked intrusion of unwanted psychic contents into consciousness. It signifies that a crucial period has begun in the development of the individual. It means that unconscious contents which had previously been dormant will now be filled with energy, that the unconscious as a whole will now play a more overtly active role in the psyche, and that the tension between consciousness and the unconscious will increase markedly. There is both a negative and an affirmative side to such a situation. On the one hand, the individual will now suffer through a period of unconscious intrusions into consciousness, a period of disturbances in the normal habits of life and of other inner tensions, which reflect the weakening of the conscious position. On the other hand, the emergence of the Anima or Animus as an autonomous factor means that the creative readjustment of the psyche can now be begun. The Anima figure tends in time to become identified with the unconscious as a whole. As contents in the unconscious are activated, they are therefore able to be projected by means of the Anima or Animus figures. The first effects are unpleasant, but the larger aspects involve the process by which the unconscious is brought to terms with consciousness. The integration of the personality can be accomplished only *via* the Anima or the Animus, since they are the autonomous personification of the unconscious in the male and female. Much more important than their negative side-effects, is the affirmative role which they play in the process of individuation around which Jung has based his psychotherapy. We shall discuss this in greater detail in a subsequent section.

PARTIAL SYSTEMS AS "POSSESSIONS"

The autonomous complexes that have been discussed up to this point correspond to basic processes in the psychic life of the individual. They are personified in the unconscious according to the role that they play in the development of the personality. Jung recognizes that many complexes can be interpreted as being composed of material that either has been in consciousness or is being repressed from consciousness. In this sense, the autonomous complexes could be interpreted along Freudian lines as being based on the unconscious repression of sexual forces. As Jung sees it, however, "this explanation is by no means valid for all cases, because there can evolve spontaneously out of the unconscious, contents which the conscious cannot assimilate." [10] In other words, in addition to complexes formed out of suppressed sexuality, there are complexes which come directly from the unconscious and refer not to external experiences, but to inherent psychic processes. In some cases, where the libido has regressed into the objective layers of the unconscious, archetypes may be reactivated and become the nucleus for an autonomous complex. Then the contents that come to the surface are apt to be strange and unusual when viewed in the light of conscious experience. In the case of a weakly balanced psyche, the overpowering effect of an autonomous complex based on an archetype is a leading symptom of psychosis. In certain types, the meaning of insanity is that a strange unconscious content has become the basis of an "autonomous partial system" and has taken control of the personality.

[10] *The Secret of the Golden Flower*, p. 108.

Jung describes the psychosis of Nietzsche as a most significant instance of an autonomous complex based on an archetype (the God Archetype) becoming attached to a very large
sum of libido and causing a disastrous dissociation of personality. The passage in which he discusses this is worth quoting
at length:

"Nietzsche was no atheist, but his God was dead. The result
was that Nietzsche himself split and he felt himself forced to
call the other self 'Zarathustra' or, at other times 'Dionysos.'
In his fatal illness he signed his letters 'Zagreus,' the dismem-
bered Dionysos of the Thracians. The tragedy of Zarathustra
is that, because his God died, Nietzsche himself became a
God; and this happened because he was no atheist. He was too
positive a nature to content himself with a negative creed.
For such a man it seems to be dangerous to make the statement that God is dead. He becomes instantly a victim of 'in-
flation.' Since the idea of God represents an important, even
overwhelming, psychical intensity, it is, in a way, safer to
believe that such an autonomous intensity is a non-ego, perhaps an altogether different or superhuman entity . . . Con-
fronted with such a belief man must needs feel small, just
about his own size. But if he declares the 'tremendum' to be
dead, then he should find out at once where this considerable
energy, which was once invested in an existence as great as
God, has disappeared to . . . If it does not appear under the
disguise of a new name, then it will most certainly return in
the mentality of the one from whom the death declaration has
been issued. Since it is a matter of tremendous energy, the
result will be an equally important psychological disturbance
in the form of a dissociation of personality. The disruption
can produce a dual or a multiple personality. It is as if one
single person could not carry the total amount of energy,
so that parts of the personality which were hitherto functional units instantly break asunder and assume the dignity
and importance of autonomous personalities.

Happily enough for the rest of mankind, there are not many individuals as sensitive and as religious as Nietzsche. If dull people lose the idea of God, nothing happens—not immediately and personally at least. But socially the masses begin to breed mental epidemics, of which we have now a fair number." [11]

We can see from this the great power of the autonomous complexes both in individual personality and in social movements. They may result in "possessions" which can take over the entire personality. They may form "autonomous partial systems" within the psyche, deriving their energic base either from the conflict of the opposites of consciousness, or from the activation of archetypal images. In either case, the "greater the energy, the stronger will be the constellating, attracting power." This then "splits off from consciousness as an independent complex to lead a separate existence in the unconscious, where it can be neither corrected nor interfered with by the conscious mind." [12] Such elements may be a source of great strength. They may be the "genius" of an individual; and they may also be the demon that "possesses" him. When a man is possessed by such a demon, it may truthfully be said that he is not himself.

The reason that the power of such a demon can be so complete is that when the autonomous complex comes out of the unconscious and identifies with the Ego, the individual does not distinguish it from his conscious attitude. He may feel himself vaguely to be in the grip of a "mood" or something similar, but it does not occur to him that it is not actually "himself" who controls his personality. The failure to dis-

[11] *Psychology and Religion*, pp. 103-105.
[12] *Modern Man in Search of a Soul*, p. 36.

tinguish between the unconscious complexes and the conscious personality is a source of great danger. Before the elements of the psyche can be harmonized they must be marked off and defined so that what is unconscious is not confused with what is conscious. When we accept the theory that the complexes are autonomous forces operating as separate individualities in the psyche, we have the further problem of finding the identity of each of them. We have to identify them in the person, describe them, and understand their functioning in order to be able to control and manipulate them in achieving the integration of the personality. The degree of success in using the process of individuation as a therapy depends on a correct insight into the elements which make up the autonomous partial systems, and it is for this purpose that Jung has developed his theory of personality types.

I V

INTROVERT, EXTRAVERT AND
PSYCHOLOGICAL TYPES

THE CONTEXT OF THE THEORY OF TYPES

The terms "introvert" and "extravert," which Jung developed, have become part of everyday speech. In the process of being popularized, however, they have come to be used in a loose and generalized way that deprives them of the specific analytical insights which belong with the conception of "psychological types." The meaning of the terms "introvert" and "extravert" depends on the context of Jung's theory of "types," and their significance can be grasped adequately only when they are understood in terms of the total structure of Jung's thought.

Contrary to the simple tests that appear in the "psychology" columns of the newspapers, the theory of types is not a convenient way to classify people into neat little pigeonholes. It is not a basis for saying to each in his turn: you're an extravert; you're an introvert; you're a thinking type; you're a feeling type; and so on. There are psychologists who look for a set of handy categories which they can use to explain people away and then file them in a tidy compartment of their minds. Jung offers no such principle. Instead, he has developed a rather involved system by which to focus, in a tentative and hypothetical way, on the more important factors in the personality of the individual.

The reason why Jung worked out his theory of types may already have occurred to the reader from what has already been presented up to now. In tracing the progression and regression of the libido in terms of the autonomous complexes, one question had to be deliberately avoided: what are the raw materials out of which the complexes are made? Why is it that one individual in the same environment develops a Persona of one type, while another Persona is developed in an altogether different way? In other words, while we have been dealing up to this point with the psychic processes, we now have to ask what the specific psychic contents of these processes are.

The thinking by which Jung develops the theory of types runs somewhat as follows. His study of the individual has to focus on the movement of libidinal energy in the psyche and on its manifestations in psychic phenomena. That is the basic material with which he works. If we follow the expression of libido as the individual makes his adjustment to experience, we find that certain aspects of this movement tend to follow similar patterns within particular individuals. To this extent, it can be said that there are necessary steps in the expression of libido, and this provides certain criteria with which to study the development of the personality in daily life. It does not give any absolute standard of measurement; but it does provide a starting point on which at least to construct some hypotheses. Jung's theory of "psychological types" must be kept within this limiting context; it is an effort merely to find something to work with in tackling the problem of individual differences.

THE FOUR FUNCTIONS

The first point at which the individual meets the outside world is through the senses. He must first establish "the fact that something is there." Jung terms this "Sensation."

The individual must go further than mere sensation, to the point where he can understand the meaning of the things with which his senses have come in contact. He must assimilate them into consciousness. This second step, which "gives the interpretation of that which is perceived," Jung calls "Thinking."

After the object has been given a meaning, it must be evaluated. The individual judges whether the new sensation is pleasant or unpleasant in terms of his psychic orientation. The function which "establishes the value of the object" Jung calls "Feeling."

Finally, there is an aspect of experience which eludes consciousness. There are things that the individual knows directly, intuitively, we should say; these are the implications and overtones of experience which cannot be known in any other way. The "immediate awareness of relationships" Jung calls "Intuition." [1]

The libido has thus made four stops. At each point, psychic energy was expressed in a different way toward experience, and yet in a necessary way. Each one of the four phenomena which occurred when the libido met the object of experience must occur in some degree in every experience the individual has in life. Each is an expression of libido, and Jung terms them the four "functions" of the psyche.

[1] For these four definitions, see "Psychological Factors Determining Human Behavior," pp. 60, 61.

"By psychological function," Jung says, "I understand a certain form of psychic activity that remains theoretically the same under varying circumstances. From the energic standpoint a function is a phenomenal form of libido which theoretically remains constant in much the same way as physical force can be considered as the form or momentary manifestation of physical energy." [2]

RATIONAL AND NON-RATIONAL FUNCTIONS

There are, thus, four psychological functions in which libido is constantly expressed: Sensation, Thinking, Feeling and Intuition. Of these, Jung terms two "rational" and two "non-rational." He terms thinking and feeling as "rational functions" because they involve a deliberate attitude and action on the part of the individual toward the object. In thinking, the individual interprets the object; in feeling he judges it. Jung therefore describes them as "rational," in the sense that they are purposive functions from the individual's point of view. In sensation, the relation is more passive; the object is only experienced by the individual. In intuition, the very nature of the process is that the individual does not purposively or rationally seek to understand the object; it "comes to him," as the saying is. Sensation and intuition are, therefore, termed the two "non-rational" functions in man.

Jung postulates it as a matter of his own experience and observation that there is, in general, a compensatory relation within each pair of functions. In the rational set, thinking and feeling act as opposites and tend to balance each other, while sensation and intuition are in the same relationship in

[2] *Psychological Types*, p. 547.

the non-rational set. Consequently, if we set the four functions down on paper so that they would form a circle in terms of these relationships, thinking would be opposite feeling, and sensation would be opposite intuition.

THE PURPOSE OF THE FUNCTION-COMPASS

At this point, the conception of the four functions can begin to be useful. Jung likes to think of them as a compass which he can use as a guide in interpreting a psychological condition. Certainly the psyche is enough of a wilderness when we approach it, not knowing where to begin or what to look for first. Jung intends the compass of the four functions to give a sense of direction and to serve as a means of orientating the study of personality. It is certainly a flexible compass, for it can be used with any one of the four points taken as "north," according to the psychological qualities of the individual. The function-compass may be set to fit the dominant function of the individual to whom it is being applied.

The main point to keep in mind in the theory of types is that all four of the functions are experienced by every individual to some degree, and although one is more highly developed in each individual than the others, the other three remain. Each individual, according to his nature, tends to specialize in one of the functions. It may be any one of the four; but whichever one it is, whether rational or non-rational, the individual raises it to a conscious level in keeping with other aspects of his psychological development. Most important is the fact that the individual uses his leading or dominant function not merely as a means of experiencing the world, but as the basis around which he organizes his personality. The individual uses the dominant function as a focus for orientating and for building his psychic life. If, for example, it is his nature to make thinking his dominant function, he does not merely use his thinking process as a means of interpreting experience; everyone uses "thinking" for this purpose. But, as a "thinking type" he makes of thinking more than a means; it is to him a goal in itself. Thinking becomes his "nature"; he approaches life in its terms, and other people come to classify him in their minds in terms of the characteristics that follow from the dominant use of the thinking process. An individual can have any one of the four functions dominant in his psyche, and he then orientates his personality around it. Whichever one is dominant for him is "north" on his particular function-compass. The other functions move around correspondingly. The dominant function is at the peak of the individual's consciousness, since it is the most highly developed in his psyche. If thinking is dominant, it is fully in consciousness under normal conditions and feeling is in the unconscious; the other two functions waver in between, depending on other factors in the psyche. If sensation is dominant, it is conscious while intuition is unconscious. The following diagrams illustrate the way the function-compass looks for each individual, depending on his dominant function.

The function-compass is, of course, only a conceptual representation of the situation in the psyche. Actually there is a great deal of variation and all the functions overlap. The value of the compass is that it gives a starting-point for thinking about the functions, and it is a way of visualizing how the opposites balance one another and maintain their constant inter-relationship.

INTUITION COMPASS

SENSATION COMPASS

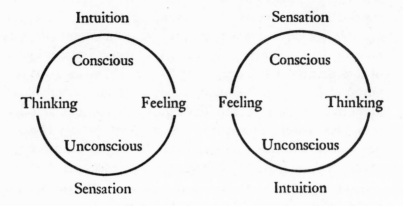

THINKING COMPASS

FEELING COMPASS

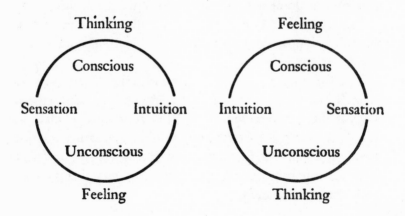

DIFFERENTIATION AND THE DOMINANT FUNCTION

The main characteristic of the dominant function, which-ever it happens to be, is that it is well developed in the field of consciousness. It becomes this way only by virtue of the fact that unconsciously the individual favors it over the other functions. It receives a greater intensity of psychic energy and is able to rise from the unconscious to consciousness. Once on the higher level, its manner of operation is trans-formed. It is clearer, in sharper focus, and its contents are more finely differentiated. The explanation is difficult to give, but it seems that while the function was in the uncon-scious, there was a tendency for its contents to have a gener-alized, uncertain nature, and to appear indirectly or in sym-bols, as is characteristic of the unconscious. While a function is below in the unconscious, it has a tendency to be amal-gamated, and to fuse its contents in an undifferentiated way. There is a tendency, for example, for thinking to be mixed with feeling in such a way that neither feeling nor thinking can be clear or efficient, since each is contaminated by its op-posite and cannot operate with clarity in its own terms. As Jung phrases it, "Just so far as a function is wholly or mainly unconscious is it also undifferentiated, i.e., it is not only fused together in its parts, but also merged with other functions." [3]

When the function is carried up by the forward movement of libido into the realm of consciousness, it is separated from its opposite (differentiated, in Jung's terms) and becomes keen, aware, specialized and increasingly competent as it be-comes increasingly differentiated. In coming into conscious-ness it has left its inferior aspects behind. It is free to develop

[3] Ibid., p. 539.

itself in its own terms and, depending on outer circumstances, the conscious ego is inclined to give the dominant function full freedom to do this. In due course, the Ego and the dominant function may be fused, and the entire Persona—that is, the conscious appearance that is displayed to the outside world—may come to be nothing more than the dominant function. We see this very often in the case of men who make their professions their whole lives.

In moving out of the unconscious, the dominant function leaves behind the characteristics of the unconscious. If, however, it ever returns to the unconscious because of a change in the equilibrium of the psyche, it recovers all the impediments it once owned. It is only while it is in the field of the conscious that it is gifted with strong abilities and is able to lead the personality. This process of differentiation is indeed important to the psyche. "Differentiation consists in the separation of the selected functions from other functions, and in the separation of its individual parts from each other. Without differentiation direction is impossible, since the direction of a function is dependent upon the isolation and exclusion of the irrelevant. Through fusion with what is irrelevant, direction becomes impossible; only a differentiated function proves itself capable of direction." [4]

In primitive societies, the specializations of life are less rigid, and the less intense development of consciousness permits a fairly low degree of differentiation to be sufficient. It is possible in a society with a moderately low degree of differentiation for the individual to have all four of the functions in consciousness, though one will necessarily be more highly developed than the others. In modern times, however,

[4] Ibid., pp. 539, 540.

a man who wishes to build a socially acceptable Persona needs to specialize in one of the functions at the expense of the others. "The very conditions of society force a man to apply himself first and foremost to the differentiation of that function with which he is either most gifted by nature, or which provides his most effective means for social success. Very frequently, indeed as a general rule, a man identifies himself more or less completely with the most favored, hence the most developed, function. It is this circumstance which gives rise to psychological types." [5]

THE INFERIOR FUNCTION AND THE SHADOW SIDE

In specializing in this way under the press of modern social competition, the individual must make a particular effort to suppress his weaker functions. He deliberately cuts them out of consciousness so that he can concentrate on the strongest function, that is, the function on which he can "capitalize." In doing this, however, he creates a very dangerous situation within his psyche, a situation of unbalance. Originally, the differentiated function rose from the unconscious to consciousness because it received a greater supply of psychic energy. As its development is intensified now, it receives increasing quantities of libido until finally it begins to be overcharged. This energy has to come from somewhere, and necessarily it is withdrawn from the other functions, especially from the opposite of the dominant function. At first nothing unfavorable happens, and the condition may continue for some time, especially if the other functions have some degree of consciousness. But as the draining of libido continues, the weakest function drops below the threshold

[5] Ibid., p. 564.

of consciousness and goes steadily deeper into the unconscious. Whatever energy content it retains then ceases to belong to itself alone, but is transferred to the unconscious,
where it activates dormant elements.

Now the danger signals begin to reach consciousness.
Strange manifestations of the unconscious burst in on the
conscious attitude which the dominant function maintains in
the Persona. Moods and weaknesses of every sort break
through the conscious veneer. The weakest and least adapted
function is taken over by the Shadow complex and becomes
identified with the negative, unpleasant side of the personality. The opposite of the conscious attitude reaches the surface, breaking in on consciousness as an autonomous "partial
system." Based on the opposite of the dominant function,
the complex operates with a power of its own, and acts to
embarrass the Ego by foolish and tactless errors. When a
group of psychic contents possesses enough libido to move up
from the unconscious and disturb consciousness in this way,
a neurosis is in full swing. The individual realizes that something is amiss, that his weaker side is taking over his personality. He strains all the harder to assert his dominant function, but in doing this, he only intensifies the one-sidedness
and worsens his condition. Jung has often observed that when
"the patient seeks to compensate the unconsciously disturb-
ing influence by means of special performance of the directed
function . . . the chase continues even, on occasion, to the
point of nervous collapse." [6]

The condition of neurosis which develops in this way indicates the dangerous effects of the over-differentiation of any

[6] Ibid., pp. 370, 371.

function. The very quality which is the strength of a psychological type may turn out to be its weakness if it is carried to the point of over-balance.

INTROVERSION AND EXTRAVERSION

Up to this point, our discussion of types has been in terms only of the psychological functions. We have noted four types, one for each of the dominant functions. The dominant function develops as an aspect of the progression movement of the libido, and the conscious attitude it creates decays when a regression movement sets in. There is, however, another type of libido movement. "The libido moves not only forward and backward, but also outward and inward." [7]

This additional direction of the libido adds a new aspect to the psyche. When we discuss the forward movement of the libido, we must specify whether it is a forward movement *inward* or a forward movement *outward*. That is to say, the progression movement of the libido may be directed out into the environment, toward concrete objects of the objective world; or it may be directed inward down into the person. Similarly, the regression movement of libido can be a retreat to the inner world, or a retreat from the inner world to the world of objects.

Jung describes the general direction of the libido movement under the terms Introversion and Extraversion. The movement toward the outer world is Extraversion; the movement toward the inner world is Introversion. Every person has both tendencies in his nature. Just as everyone goes through a time when the libido moves forward and a time

[7] *Contributions to Analytical Psychology*, p. 45.

when the libido regresses, so everyone must experience movements in an outward direction and in an inward direction. Jung's analysis here, however, is based on his observation that there is a tendency for the conscious personality to concentrate on either one of the directions. Regardless of his other psychological qualities, the individual seems, at least to his neighbors, to be "by nature" an open, friendly, casual, externalizing personality, that is, an extravert; or else he seems to be reserved and withdrawn and preconcerned, and they think of him as "by nature" an introvert. It is these common sense observations, made by people in their daily relations, that led to the easy acceptance of Jung's two terms.

The reason a person gives the impression of being either an introvert or an extravert is that his dominant function has come to be associated with that particular type of libido movement. In each personality there are parts that are extraverted and parts that are introverted. It depends on which function—dominant or inferior—and also on which autonomous complex the libido has become identified with. An individual who is a thinking type may be extraverted in his dominant function, but introverted in his inferior function of feeling. Introversion or extraversion in itself means nothing; it is merely a direction of libido movement. But everything depends on what is being moved.

Jung himself remarked that the terms introvert and extravert by themselves mean as little as when "Molière's *bourgeois gentilhomme* discovered that he ordinarily spoke in prose. These distinctions attain meaning and value only when we realize all the other characteristics that go with the type." [8]

Modern Man in Search of a Soul, p. 28.

LIBIDO MOVEMENT AND THE VARIETY OF TYPES

There is really no such person as an introvert or an extravert *per se*. The syndicated newspaper strips which ask, "Are you an introvert? Are you an extravert?" are asking impossible questions. They have taken the words from Jung and missed the meaning. There are, however, extravert types who have identified extraversion with their dominant function, with thinking, feeling, sensation, or intuition, as the case may be. There are, thus, extravert thinking types, extravert feeling types, and so on. Similarly, for those who have identified their introverted libido movement with their dominant function, there are introverted thinking types, introverted feeling types, and so on. All in all, Jung has named two psychological types for each of the four functions, one for each of the directions of libido movement. Of these eight general psychological types, however—though many of their characteristics are definite and specific—there are really as many variations as the discerning eye can find. The eight psychological types serve the same purpose as the function-compasses; they are guiding principles, tools of analysis, to help the psychologist orient himself. Moreover, the introversion-extraversion concept gives the function-compass a second dimension, considering the individual's relation to the outer world in terms of his dominant and inferior functions.

Jung has made some interesting observations on the personality traits that tend to be found among the various psychological types. He has contrasted Immanuel Kant, the introverted thinking type, with Charles Darwin, the extraverted thinking type. One can readily see the basis of difference here. Both have differentiated thinking as their dominant function, but one turned thinking outward and the other turned thinking inward. "Darwin ranges over the wide fields of objective facts, while Kant restricts himself to a critique of knowledge in general." [9] Jung remarked also, on how prevalent the feeling type is among women, though, of course, not exclusively. The extraverted feeling woman is the easy-going, companionable mother and wife, while the introverted feeling type is devoted to her family in a quiet way. Jung points out that she is the type of whom it may be said that "still water runs deep," and then he adds, "They are mostly silent, inaccessible and hard to understand; often they hide behind a childish or banal mask and not infrequently their temperament is melancholic." [10]

Of the introverted intuitive type Jung says, "Had this type not existed, there would have been no prophets in Israel." But many an eccentric may also be discovered among those who have a strongly introverted intuition function.

SIGNIFICANCE OF THE TYPE THEORY

The important point to keep in mind is that the characteristics of the types are not, in themselves, of primary significance. Jung was not interested in building up a descriptive typology with definite qualities assigned to each of the eight types, neatly defined and categorized. That would be pedantic and artificial. He merely sought some clues with which to approach the psychic processes of the individual. The infinite varieties of individual differences are the external result of the combinations of libido movement and

[9] *Psychological Types*, p. 484.
[10] Ibid., p. 492.
[11] Ibid., p. 307.

psychological function. The specific value of Jung's concepts is that they do not operate on the surface. When, for example, Jung describes a man as an extraverted feeling type, he is not calling him a name. He is describing the nature of the libido movement in the individual and the psychological function to which this movement is attached, in so far as these facts are observable from the analysis of conscious and unconscious contents. In understanding Jung's theories on types, it is not important to remember the names of the types or their superficial qualities. What is important is to be aware of the dual nature of libido movement, inward and outward, forward and backward, and the way these movements are related to the dominant and inferior functions, to the creation and destruction of the conscious attitude.

The theory of types is inextricably connected with the principle of opposites. In the function-compass, the opposite of the dominant function remains in the unconscious, or is the first function to return to the unconscious when the conscious attitude grows weak. This balancing includes the introvert-extravert concept. If the person is an extraverted feeling type, the dominant function is feeling and the inferior function is its opposite, the other of the two rational functions, thinking. The feeling function is expressed in an extraverted way; the thinking function in an introverted way. When both are conscious and under control, there is no danger. But when the weaker thinking function slides back into the unconscious, it slides back into the Shadow side, and in such a condition, the thinking function tends to be especially tactless. If the conscious attitude breaks down—if the Persona can no longer hold itself together in society—the introverted thinking attitude may very possibly take over the personality of the extraverted feeling type—but in a weak, inferior form.

We should keep in mind that the dominant function and its corresponding type are aspects of the libido in its progression phase; in regression the libido leaves the psyche open to the incompetence of the inferior function and also to the weird and overwhelming effects of the reactivated unconscious contents. "The superior function is always the expression of the conscious personality, its aim, its will, and its achievement, while the inferior functions belong to the things that happen to one. Not that they merely beget blunders, e.g., *lapsus linguae* and *lapsus calami*, but they may also breed half or three-quarter resolves, since the inferior functions also possess a slight degree of consciousness. The extraverted feeling type is a classical example of this, for he enjoys an excellent feeling rapport with his entourage, yet occasionally opinions of an incomparable tactlessness will just happen to him. These opinions have their source in his inferior or unconscious thinking, which is only partly subject to control and is insufficiently related to the object; to a large extent, therefore, it can operate without consideration of responsibility." [12]

As a descriptive analysis, Jung's theory of psychological types is very interesting. As a series of concepts to be used for classifying individuals, it can be the basis for a great variety of "tests" to be worked out and graded and reduced to charts and statistics. But the real value of the type analysis for Jung is that it gives him some tools to work with. The concept of "type" means nothing in itself. There is no such thing as a pure type, and it doesn't matter at all. The balanc-

[12] Ibid., pp. 426, 427.

ing of the principle of opposites and the ever wandering libido, inward and outward, backwards and frontwards, while the conscious and unconscious press each other in a never ending tension, is the basis for the study of the psyche. The difficulty has been in finding a way to think of those movements in specific terms without losing the essential sense of psychic dynamics. Jung offered his theory of psychological types as an effort to meet this need.[13]

[13] *Modern Man in Search of a Soul*, p. 108.

V

THE FUNCTION AND MEANING
OF NEUROSIS

Jung tells the story of one of his patients, a business man about forty-five years of age. "It was a question of the typical self-made man who had worked his way up in the world from the bottom. He had been very successful and founded an immense business. He had succeeded in gradually organizing the business so as to be able to retire from the management. Two years before I saw him he had indeed retired." [1]

The man had left his business and gone to his estate for the peace and leisure he had planned. But he experienced no happiness. Instead, "he had a complete nervous collapse. A healthy man, of uncommon physical strength and abounding energy, he was reduced to the condition of a peevish child. There was an end to all the splendid prospects. He fell from one state of anxiety into another, and tormented himself almost to death with fantastic worries. He then consulted a famous specialist who immediately and correctly judged that there was nothing wrong with the man but idleness. The patient saw the sense of this and returned to his former work. To his great disappointment, however, no interest in his business could be aroused. Neither patience nor resolution were of any use. His energy could not by any means be forced

[1] *Two Essays on Analytical Psychology*, pp. 50-52.

back into the business. Then his condition became worse than before. All that had formerly been living, creative energy in him was now turned back against himself with terrible, destroying force. His creative genius rose up, as it were, in revolt against him; and just as he had formerly built up great organizations in the world, so now did his demon create a subtle system of hypochondriacal illusion that all but annihilated him. When I saw him he was already a hopeless moral ruin.

"I tried to make clear to him that such a gigantic energy might indeed be withdrawn from business, but the question remained, where should it go? The finest horses, the swiftest cars and the most entertaining parties failed in this case to allure the energy; although it might be quite rational to think that a man who had devoted his whole life to serious work had a natural right to enjoy himself. Yes, if fate could be brought under human control, it would certainly be so— first work, then well-earned leisure. But fate takes an irrational course, and inconveniently enough, the energy of life demands a channel congenial to itself; otherwise it is simply dammed up and becomes destructive. My line of argument met with no response, as indeed was to be expected. A case so far advanced as this can only be cared for till death. It cannot be cured."

PSYCHOLOGICAL MEANING OF FATE

There is something of "fate" expressed in a neurosis. Certainly, Jung feels it so. It is not fate in a metaphysical sense, but rather that the necessary principles of the individual's life tend to come to the fore ultimately in the course of a lifetime. What is decided consciously by the individual is subject to veto by the deeper, more fundamental nature of the personality. The best laid plans go astray, not only because of a capricious external world, but because there is an inner necessity in each person. Just as the acorn has a purpose concealed within it, so has the personality. Ultimately, the attitudes of consciousness must express what is essential and latent in the seed—or else there is danger. If we are to talk of "fate" in human life—in Jung's sense—it is simply this, that the fundamentals of the unconscious set the limits within which conscious attitudes can develop. When a man goes beyond that limit, he commences to build without a foundation, and in time his structure must collapse. The plans of the retiring business man were perfectly rational; but they did not grow from the nature of his unconscious. They were arbitrary thoughts in the nature of those "good ideas" that do not work out in practise because they involve only the surface of events. The unconscious ultimately tends to overthrow conscious elements that are contrary to its requirements.

In the case of the business man, considering the unwitting error he had made, it was an evil "fate." But it does not need to be so. In fact, Jung points to many situations in which it is just the reverse. Many biographies tell of individuals who started out on conscious paths that were inadequate compared to the potentialities of their unconscious. Soon their unused energies dammed up and made themselves known to consciousness through the disturbances of neurosis. The individual was thus hindered in the work he had consciously chosen for himself, but his attention was called to the unconscious resources he was ignoring. The world of literature has many such instances, cases of men who started in the practi-

cal world of affairs and were drawn back by "failure" to the
art in which their true talents lay. One thinks immediately
of Honoré de Balzac, who tried to make his name in business
and in the Paris Court, but whose ambitions only gained
him a collection of debts which pressured him to produce his
prolific contribution to world literature. Nietzsche, too, tormented by a neurosis that recurred in most painful ways,
often confessed that, without it, he would hardly have written at all.

Jung's contention is that there is an important sense in
which the unconscious is to be understood as a messenger of
fate, calling the individual back to himself when the one-
sidedness of consciousness leads him astray. Inevitably it re-
minds him of his limitations when he shoots too high; and
also it forces him to remember the potentialities he has yet to
express. It is the destiny a man has within himself, higher or
lower than he would like it to be, but firm in its demands
upon his actions. Whether it seems beneficent or cruel, the
individual can ignore it only at his own risk. When the unconscious needs to issue a sign of warning, it speaks through
a neurosis. If the true meaning of the painful experiences
is understood, and if the tension is drawn through to its
necessary conclusion so that it can be resolved, it will have
functioned as a reminder recalling the individual to his true
self. On the other hand, if the warnings of neurosis are
ignored, as they were by Jung's patient, the most serious results may follow.

TWOFOLD ASPECT OF NEUROSIS: CAUSE AND PURPOSE

As Jung sees it, there are two questions to ask of a neurosis:
from what has it developed? And where is it trying to lead

the individual? The first is a question of causes, the second a question of purpose. The tendency of psychoanalysis, as it has developed in Freudian terms, is to lay all stress on the first question. Freudian psychoanalysts have made it their aim to trace neurosis back *via* sexuality to the earliest period of childhood. Jung's point is that this has a very limited value to the individual who is seeking clarity out of the confusion of neurosis. The individual experiences his neurosis as a great personal crisis. He feels confused, at odds with himself, unhappy; "things go wrong" because his attention is split and, as failures accumulate, he may come to question his own integrity. Neurosis is a time of crisis in the here and now; as Jung phrases it, a crisis in the "present moment." To divert the attention backward to childhood in search of hidden secrets and frustrations may uncover interesting personal data, but it is a detour for the neurotic. He needs to find himself, as it were, in the Now.

Because this is so, it becomes most important to answer the question of what the meaning of the neurosis is; what it is trying to say. Jung tells about a patient who had developed his intellectual qualities ·out of proportion to the rest of his psyche. The unconscious had been disturbed by the disequilibrium that ·resulted, and the individual was caught in a conflict of opposites. At first Jung tried a thorough analysis, ferreting out the elements of the past, according to the method developed by Freud. Soon the individual reached a complete understanding of his neurosis; he knew its causes, manifestations, and so on. In short, as an intellectual, he had grasped it with his consciousness; but he could make no progress in curing it. The fact that he knew its causes simply had the effect of riveting him to the conditions. He knew his weakness lay in the undeveloped faculties of the unconscious, but they were weak and so he could do nothing with them.

"The conscious attitude of my patient is so over-balanced on the side of the intellect that nature herself rises against him and brings his whole world of conscious values to naught. But he cannot make them unintellectual and forthwith depend upon another function, as for instance feeling, for a quite simple reason: he has not got it. The unconscious has it." [2] The problem of the individual is to restore a balance within the psyche. By looking backward into the past, he may come upon a clue to restoring the equilibrium he had before the neurosis occurred. But that was an unhealthy balance, based on the predominance of consciousness. The very fact that it fell apart should indicate to him that it was not adequate and that additional factors in the psyche must be taken into consideration. Through the dissonances in consciousness which it makes manifest, the neurotic situation forces the individual to come into active relation to the larger areas of the psyche. Then the unconscious can not only no longer be ignored, but it becomes the most important element in the resolution of the neurosis. The unconscious alone can provide the psychic materials for new attitudes that may be integrated into consciousness. The mere analysis of past conditions of consciousness cannot make such new contents available, for the simple reason that analysis cannot, by itself, create anything new.

2 Ibid., p. 238.

NEUROSIS AS "INNER CLEAVAGE"

In this young intellectual patient, Jung finds the essence of what neurosis means whenever it occurs. The conflict between the conscious and the unconscious makes a battlefield of the psyche. "Neurosis is an inner cleavage—the state of being at war with oneself. Everything that accentuates this cleavage makes the patient worse and everything that mitigates it tends to heal the patient. What drives people to war with themselves is the intuition of the knowledge that they consist of two persons in opposition to one another. The conflict may be between the sensual and the spiritual man, or between the ego and the shadow. It is what Faust means when he says, 'Two souls dwell in my breast apart.' A neurosis is a dissociation of personality." [8]

The only solution lies in binding together the elements which have split apart. It is not a simple process. They are already together—they are close enough to fight each other. The individual must find a way to unite them so that both can be changed and become aspects of something greater than either. To raise the causes of the neurosis to consciousness is not enough. The contending principles must be actually fused into something greater than either one alone. A new attitude must be created, a completely new attitude in which the original elements will be hardly recognizable. It goes to the heart of the personality, and it necessarily involves the very meaning of life because it comes from a crisis in which the individual is torn between conflicting ways of living.

Jung's key lies in following the course of libido. He points

[8] *Modern Man in Search of a Soul*, p. 273.

out that in the case of the patient who had over-concentrated his psychic energy on his intellectual or thinking function, a corresponding amount of energy had been withdrawn from his other psychic functions. These dropped down into the unconscious, where they activated first elements of the Personal Unconscious, and then archetypes of the Objective Unconscious. Some of these became nuclei around which other elements gathered, so that autonomous complexes were formed in the unconscious. The greater the individual's emphasis on the thinking function, the greater became the strength of the complexes and the more frequently they were able to break into consciousness. These were the symptoms of the neurosis. They indicated that the libido was split, and that part of its energy was not moving forward to adapt to the environment, but was regressing inward.

The regression movement also performs a function of adaptation not to the external world, but to the inner world of the psyche. The regression movement has the purpose of adjusting the unbalance which must develop in the psychic world. As Jung puts it, "Man is not a machine in the sense that he can constantly maintain the same output of work. He can only meet the demands of outer necessity in an ideal way if he is also adapted to his own inner world, that is to say, if he is in harmony with himself." [4] When the over-development of one of the psychological functions has resulted in an unbalance in the psyche, a part of the psychic energies flows backward and downward away from experience. In doing this, they take the emphasis off the over-developed function and, by activating contents in the unconscious, they bring to the surface materials which may eventually establish a new

[4] *Contributions to Analytical Psychology*, p. 43.

equilibrium in the psyche. The regression of libido is therefore a necessary phase of psychic life; without it, the individual cannot gain access to the unconscious as he needs to do in order to find the elements necessary to build an inner balance. The inference is plain. The movement of libido involved in neurosis is an essential precondition for the full integration of the personality. The individual will not find himself unless he is forced to make the search.

LIBIDO REGRESSION AND THE OPENING OF THE UNCONSCIOUS

The correct way to think of neurosis in Jung's terms is not that it is a necessary condition for creativity—as is sometimes said—but rather that it, or its psychological equivalent in terms of energy movement, is a necessary stage in the process of gaining access to the deeper levels of the psyche. It is the psychic process—the regression of libido—that makes possible a new integration or creativity for the personality.

There is, however, another aspect of this process, in which the individual derives his neurosis directly from the nature of the society in which he lives—and from its time in history. Jung points out that the ubiquitous psychic process of libido regression varies according to the historical context in which it develops. In particular, he notes that there are times of transition in history, in which old values are breaking up and new values, though on their way in, are not yet fully accepted. In these situations, it is inevitable that some individuals will have difficulty in finding their values and will be torn by conflicting loyalties. Such personalities are subject to the strain of unresolved tensions within the psyche and to the pressures of autonomous complexes struggling within them to take control of the personality. They manifest in their lives the individual case of neurosis when it occurs as a phenomenon of historical change. They experience the situation of confusion which results when the psyche is sundered into separate parts by autonomous partial systems, each of which uses its energies to take the person in a different direction.

THE HISTORICAL NATURE OF PSYCHOLOGICAL SPLITS

This is the psychological condition characteristic of every period of historical transition; but, according to Jung, it is particularly characteristic of modern man. The Western European is beset by uncertainty because the established values no longer seem true to him, and he has to search alone as an individual for new meanings for his life. On the one hand, he is drawn to the conventional beliefs to which his traditional sentiments cling even while he sees them collapsing; on the other hand, new, even strange beliefs come upon him from within and from without, and he is drawn to them too. Each has the energic force of an autonomous complex within his psyche, each working independently to drive him along its particular path. The mind of modern man is full of "demons," as Jung calls them, for the complexes which express the conflicting values of our time act within the psyche as though they had a will of their own. There are many persons in the modern psyche, and they are conflicting persons. It is the split within personality that prevents the harmonious expression of the psychic energies and leaves the modern individual in the confusion which means neurosis. Because the symbols of the dominant religions and systems of value no longer carry the absolute conviction they must have if they are to answer the individual's need, the modern man is cut loose to find the meaning of life for himself, even while he is beset from within by the conflicting demons of his psyche. This is why, in our day, as Jung says, "neurosis is the hall-mark of civilized man." [5]

To the extent that an individual in any society is able to identify his psychic energies with an established system of meaning and belief—and is able to experience as "psychologically true" the corresponding religious symbols—he is safe from neurosis. He gives up his individuality and receives the psychic security of social values. In this regard, the difference between modern civilization and other civilizations is merely that it is more difficult for an individual to find a satisfying belief with which to identify himself. But in any society, when an individual sets out to gather truth for himself—when he seeks to transcend the beliefs which are socially "true" and to integrate his personality in universal terms—the precondition is necessarily a regression of libido, and therefore a neurosis. The literature of the world, and especially of religion, is filled with symbols of the psychic process involved in this search. It is expressed in the story of how Buddha foreswore his secure position in society and withdrew in solitude to receive his message; and again in the episode of Christ being "tempted" by the devil. The regression of libido into the unconscious involves an inherent psychic process, and its symbolism expresses a universal aspect of the psyche.

SYMBOLISM OF THE LIBIDO REGRESSION: INCEST

When a religious doctrine speaks of the "Nurse Mother" of the world, we may be sure that it is not merely a figure of

[5] *Two Essays*, p. 15.

speech. The fact that it is taken up and made a doctrine of belief, personified by the image of a woman and worshipped by the devotees of the religion, indicates that it expresses something that has a strong inner meaning for those who experience it. It has been pointed out that the objective elements of the unconscious, the underlying psychic processes, are expressed by archetypes, each of which are symbolic expressions of a specific process. The movement of the libido is portrayed by a wide variety of symbols. What the symbol represents always depends on the context of the myth or fable or whatever unconscious product is being studied. But, "from different directions the analysis of the libido symbolism always leads back again to the mother incest," [6] and the various aspects of incest symbolism are the most important representations of the regression phase of the libido.

The word "incest" has a curious history in the study of the unconscious. Freud based his system on the analysis of the Oedipus Legend, which, he said, expressed a psychological process consistently recurring in the human race. He referred to the desire of the son to murder his father and possess his mother. The inference that Freud drew is that the desire to commit incest with the mother is a suppressed element in the unconscious of everyone, and he buttressed this view with analyses of many other myths and religious stories in addition to personal dreams and fantasies, all looked at from the same angle. This particular doctrine, while it is among the most fundamental, is also the most objectionable and questionable in Freud's thought. In a sense, the symbols are there, and when one is disposed to read them in Freud's way because of one's theoretical orientation, the

[6] *The Psychology of the Unconscious*, p. 230.

incest analysis may easily seem "self-evident." This, however, is one of the great problems in the correct interpretation of unconscious symbolism. The unconscious speaks only in symbols, and symbols leave the individual the greatest leeway for "reading in" whatever his own unconscious is disposed to see there. When one proceeds with the assumption that the unconscious harbors an instinctual desire to rape the mother, it is quite natural to interpret a phrase like "entering" the mother—or its symbolic equivalent—to mean the act of coitus. One can readily see, however, that it can also be interpreted in other ways, and especially in terms of the desire to be "born again."

The conception of "rebirth" is an especially strong symbol, for example, in the Christian religion. Its meaning is that one can have "new life," can be "born again," if one believes in Christ. This means, interpreted further, that the individual identifies himself with the figure of Christ who was born of a virgin mother in a womb which bore no other child. The new life or rebirth is thus acquired *through* the symbol and it means, in psychological terms, a psychic rebirth. The "testimonials" at the conversion meetings of the various evangelical sects indicate that a new life actually has been acquired in the here and now. The individual's libido had been in regression—for the testifiers, each a modern St. Augustine, always begin with a tale of their "sin" and "failure." The result of "believing," that is, of identifying with the symbol, is that the libido is born again, is set free through being identified with the son of a virgin mother who has "eternal life." Such symbols are, of course, found in many varieties throughout the East and Near East, as well as in primitive mythologies. The symbol indicates that the libido having regressed, seeks a new source from which its potency can be renewed. Its original source was the "mother," who is also conceived of as "Nature," the most inclusive conception of the source. Thus we reach the phrase "Mother Nature" and find that in many unconscious expressions the symbols of mother and nature are interchangeable. Once back in the source, in the "womb of nature," the libido can renew itself as life energy. It can thus be born again, and this "second birth" means that the inner conflict has been resolved, that the obstacle to progressive libido movement has been removed. It means that the energies of life have been set free.

The ease with which this can be misinterpreted as physical incest is increased by the fact that one of the main symbols of libido is the phallus or, by derivation, some symbol for the phallus. Consequently, when Freud analyzed the contents of religions from the point of view of the unconscious, in one way or another the interpretation came to be that the phallus was inserted into the mother. In this light, he can hardly be blamed for drawing the conclusion that mother-incest was involved. The all-important point that did not occur to him is the fact that the mother and the phallus are themselves symbols in this case—as we would expect them to be in the unconscious—symbols of psychic processes. In making such a criticism of Freud and Freudian-type analysis, the possibility must equally be allowed that Jung's own interpretations may be colored by his theoretical orientation. The nature of the symbolic material that is being handled makes this unavoidable and recalls Jung's remark that every psychological theory is the "subjective confession" of the man who constructs it. In the case of Jung's treatment of the incest question, however, we must recognize the fact that his work represents an effort to interpret the phenomenology of incest symbolism in the largest possible context.

In his most recent treatment of the subject in his *Psychologie der Uebertragung,* Jung considers some of the possible ways in which incest can be interpreted. Is there really an instinctual drive toward incest as Freud supposed? Or is it, as Adler thought, that incestuous fantasies are one of the "arrangements" worked out by the "will to power" in its protesting effort at compensation. Or should incest be understood as a representation of the regression of psychic energy —a drawing back of energy from the "present moments" of adult life to the ways of childhood because of the fear of being unable to meet some new life-problem? This was a concept which Jung himself developed in the days when he was just beginning his redefinition of psychoanalytic concepts. In his *Psychology of the Unconscious* he remarked that he felt he was giving "the word 'incest' more significance than properly belongs to the term. Just as libido is the onward driving force, so incest is in some manner the backward urge into childhood. For the child, it cannot be spoken of as incest. Only for the adult who possesses a completely formed sexuality does the backward urge become incest, because he is no longer a child but possesses a sexuality which cannot be permitted a regressive application." [7]

---

[7] Ibid., p. 530. A good statement of Jung's position on this point is to be found in a paper entitled "The Psycho-Analytical Background of the Parent-Child Relation" delivered by H. G. Baynes before the Medical Society of Individual Psychology in London on October 8, 1936. It has been republished in Baynes' *Analytical Psychology and the English Mind,* Methuen, London, 1950. Rediscussing the symbolism of Hamlet, Dr. Baynes remarked, "Since no one actually wants to

At the present stage of his thinking Jung rejects all three of these views of incest symbolism: the instinct theory of Freud, the "arrangement" of the "will to power," and the regression to childhood. His conclusion now is that the material brought out in incest fantasies is to be understood in a purely symbolical sense. It does not refer to actual physical incest, but it is rather an expression of a fundamental and essential psychic process involving the downward movement of libido. The appearance of the symbolism of incest symbolizes to Jung now a "reactivation of the incest-archetype." It expresses the withdrawal of libido from consciousness and the reciprocal attachment of energy to contents in the unconscious. The life-energies of the individual are withdrawn from the surface of life into the 'womb of the Mother (Nature, the unconscious); thence they re-emerge with new qualities and a new vitality. This is a recurrent motif in the history of mythology and religion, and it involves the essential psychic process in neurosis, as Jung understands it.

THE UPWARD REVERSAL OF ENERGY MOVEMENT

The downward movement of libido is the psychological aspect of a conflict which the individual experiences in terms of his external relationships. A difficulty in outer life has sent the energies back and down into the depths of the unconscious, where, it turns out, they may be replenished. The inward-turning of the libido is a painful time for the individual, a time of crisis, and often of illness. "If the libido

---

sleep with his mother or fears to be castrated by his father, is it not better to regard incest and castration as idiomatic expressions of the archaic backward-drawn states of the libido." (p. 13.)

See also, C. G. Jung, *Die Psychologie der Uebertragung*, Rascher, Zurich, 1946, especially pp. 22-28.

remains arrested in the wonder kingdom of the inner world, then the man has become for the world above a phantom, then he is practically dead, or desperately ill." [8] The energies that are needed for the adaptation to reality are then not available to consciousness. The individual becomes increasingly withdrawn into himself and goes further and further out of contact with his surroundings. "But if the libido succeeds in tearing itself loose and pushing itself up into the world above, a miracle appears. The journey to the underworld has become a fountain of youth, a new fertility springs from his apparent death." [9]

We thus come upon the basic psychological principle, that "spiritual transformation always means the holding back of a sum of libido." [10] Without the regression of psychic energy the contents of the unconscious could not be reactivated. The archetypes of the psychic processes—in which the great universal truths about the nature of man are contained—rest in the deepest recesses of the objective unconscious. While libido moves up toward life, latent symbolisms of knowledge remain unactivated within the individual. Only when a failure or obstacle of some sort sends the libido downward are the deeper resources of the psyche opened. The fact that suffering is a most important and constantly recurring symbol in the religions of the world expresses a fundamental psychological experience. The suffering of the God-Man in Christianity has been a most powerful symbol just because the suffering on the Cross—"He died for me" as the saying is

[8] *The Psychology of the Unconscious*, p. 330.
[9] Ibid., pp. 330, 331.
[10] *Psychological Types*, p. 291.

—epitomizes a universal psychic process. The suffering of the god symbolizes the suffering and regression of the libido in each individual psyche. It may be expressed in many ways, depending on historical circumstances; but whatever the symbol, the psychic process is the same. The neurosis of modern man, growing though it does out of a critical period of transition, reflects "essentially a universal problem." [11]

The effect of the regression of psychic energy is to reactivate the contents of the unconscious. It carries the danger of psychosis because of the possibility that the autonomous forces in the unconscious may not be kept under control; but it also holds the potentiality that the descent into the depths of the psyche will bring forth a new insight and feeling for life. Neurosis is, then, to be understood as the downward movement of psychic energy resulting from a splitting off of autonomous factors in the psyche; it has the special function of arousing the larger areas of the unconscious so that they may be integrated with consciousness to form a "reborn" unified personality. In terms of the structure of Jung's thought, the most important aspect of neurosis is its function, which is, that it is the expression in personality of a basic psychic process. In the pathology of our times it takes many forms, and these have become the subject matter for the specialized studies of individual psychology. But the underlying significance of neurosis is that, at the critical moment when a weakness appears at the surface of consciousness, it brings the Ego into renewed contact with its unconscious resources. The psychic process involved in neurosis is one of the steps preceding the integration of the personal-

[11] *Two Essays*, p. 19.

ity. Consequently, as we come now to discuss the resolution of disharmonies and the balancing of the psyche, we have to ask some further questions about the nature of the phenomena of the unconscious, and particularly of dreams.

V I

DREAMS AND THE INTEGRATION
OF THE PSYCHE

THE DIFFICULTY OF DREAM INTERPRETATION

In its regression movement the libido loosens the unconscious and activates the contents of the lower levels of the psyche. The very fact of libido regression indicates a weakness in the conscious attitudes; consequently, it is at such a time that non-assimilated, unconscious products tend to come to the surface. The formation of unconscious materials may take place either in the psyche of the individual or in the group as a whole. In the first case, the unconscious may express itself in the arts, dreams of all sorts, and in individual religious experience. In the latter case, unconscious products emerge in the form of myths, sagas, fairy tales, customs, rituals, enthusiasms, and mass possessions of various kinds.

The difficulty then arises—and it is really the imponderable at the heart of all depth psychology—that we need a way of finding out what the symbolism of the unconscious actually means. The problem is particularly delicate because the unconscious "thinks" in an undifferentiated way—that is, not with specific ideas as consciousness does—and we can never overcome a basic uncertainty which must remain when we attempt to convert the unconscious to the terms of conscious reason. The forms in which the unconscious expresses itself cannot be taken literally or at their face value as can the

135

thoughts offered by consciousness. We have, rather, always to look for something hidden, and the interpretation necessarily involves a process of conversion or "reduction" of unconscious manifestations to the terms of consciousness. In the process of working out these interpretations, a great variety of theorists have come forward, each with his favorite "principle" for the conversion of unconscious symbolism. Each works under the same difficulty, however, that even unintentionally he cannot avoid forcing the material to fit the pattern of his own theories. Because the symbols of the unconscious are so ambiguous when looked at from the point of view of consciousness, each of these theorists must at some time be guilty of reading his own "principles" into the dreams he is interpreting.

Jung's own principle for the interpretation of dreams is simply that there is "no general theory of dreams." [1] Some critics have made the observation that he carries his approach of caution to such an extent that he requires a different principle of analysis for each individual. Actually, in so far as this is true, it only points to the extreme flexibility that Jung tries to maintain in refusing to categorize the psychic products of any individual according to a predetermined psychological theory—even if the theory is his own. We have to give Jung credit for trying conscientiously to avoid dogma in his dream interpretations, and at the same time we have to point out the coincidence that the dreams which he reconstructs tend to fit the pattern of his general approach to psychic phenomena. In other words, he does have a theory of dreams and it has a definite place in his total conception of the psyche.

[1] *The Integration of the Personality*, p. 98.

JUNG'S CONCEPTION OF DREAMS

The key to Jung's dream interpretations is his underlying principle that the manifestations of the unconscious are to be studied in their relation to the psychic processes. This means that dream materials are necessarily set in terms of what they are tending *toward*. Jung applies here his teleological point of view based on the principle that the continuing development of the psyche is the one constant factor on which an analysis can be based. In so far as dreams express the latent or potential development of the psyche, or as they express obstacles that may be encountered, it is correct to say that dreams have a "message," and it is valid to ask of a dream what it is trying to say. The answer must then be in terms of the processes which are active in the psyche, and the dream products are to be understood as symptoms, or at least as characteristic expressions of these processes.

In a sense, it is correct to say that Jung is eclectic in his way of reading dreams. He is apt to apply the point of view of any school of thought in his dream interpretations. For some types of individuals—mainly extraverts at certain points in their lives—he holds that a Freudian approach is warranted; for other individuals, mainly introverts, he prefers an Adlerian approach. But his point in using whichever approach is applicable to the individual is only that all the sides of a dream-meaning must be grasped and set into the perspective of the development of the personality. "Dreams," Jung says, "have many aspects," and because of this, "they can be studied from many sides." [2] All their sides, however, are part of the continuity of the individual's personal-

[2] *Psychology and Religion*, p. 118.

ity, and Jung claims that the reason dreams can occasionally be taken as a basis of prediction is that they express tendencies that are still only latent in the unconscious in advance of the time that they can be brought overtly into consciousness. The policy of looking at the dream from every point of view and of using every theoretical approach that can fit the individual is in this sense not really eclecticism, but rather an effort to maintain flexibility in the face of an extremely obscure subject matter.

SYMBOLISM AND THE DREAM SERIES

In the same vein, Jung takes the position that there are no fixed meanings for the symbols of the unconscious. It depends always on the dream, and particularly on the dreamer. In the case of myths, the meaning of the symbols also depends on the background of the peoples among whom the myth has developed. It is incorrect to say that any given object or figure necessarily has the same significance when it appears in the dream of one individual as when it appears in the dream of another; or that any given element of a myth has the same significance for one nation as for another. It is always a matter of the context supplied by the continuing development of the psychic processes.

In order to get at this context for the analysis of dreams, it is necessary to study not one but a series of dreams. Jung warns that a single dream taken in isolation may be highly misleading because one cannot tell at what point in the total development of the individual it is taking place. One cannot tell from it either the nature of the processes at work within the individual's psyche or the significance of particular symbols in terms of his unconscious. In Jung's phrase, "the series is the context, and the dreamer himself supplies it."[3] In one of his most illuminating dream interpretations he used more than a thousand dreams, fantasies, and visual impressions produced by a single individual over a period of many months.[4] The special value of such a study is that it makes it possible to understand the symbolism with which the particular individual's unconscious expresses itself, and to observe the development of the various psychic processes leading toward the integration of the psyche.

In particular, given a long series of dreams to study, one can observe a change in the nature of the dream material at given stages in the dream series. In the first dreams Jung found a large proportion of purely personal material, much of which referred to everyday life situations. Gradually symbols that were less familiar began to appear, and they became increasingly strange as the series progressed. Their relation to the individual's life was not at once clear because they did not in themselves come out of personal life experiences. The reason for the changes in the nature of the dream contents is that, at the beginning, the dream material was coming from levels of the unconscious close to the surface, since the psychic energy, just beginning to regress into the psyche, was activating material from the Personal Unconscious. As the libido continued in regression it went to the layer below these personal experiences, activating ever deeper contents of the psyche. At this point, the figures brought to the surface were no longer personal in nature, but had a mythologic quality and represented, with archetypal symbols, more basic processes of the psyche.

[3] *The Integration of the Personality*, p. 101.
[4] See Ibid.

When these lower levels are reached, the dreaming process does more than merely reveal what is in the unconscious. Dreams that contain archetypal images tend to be experienced in a deeply moving way by the individual. Jung reports that many of his patients have described to him their emotional condition accompanying these dreams as being either of great intensity or of deep peace, similar to that of a religious or artistic experience. Because of this, dreams have a double function. As they uncover the material in the Personal Unconscious, they reveal the specific content of neurosis, they provide the basic facts for diagnosis. But, when they have progressed to the deeper levels of the psyche, they have the much more important function of acting as an avenue by which the individual experiences the generic potentialities of his Objective Unconscious. This involves an inner reintegration and carries with it a change in the individual's total feeling for life.

THE ASSOCIATION TEST

As an auxiliary method for finding a clue to the psychology of an individual, Jung developed the technique of the Association Test. This test is based on the principle that the unconscious represses or inhibits those mental contents that are related to its conflicts and complexes. The subject is given a series of words with instructions to give an instant response while the tester observes his reactions. Words that have no emotional involvements generally receive a ready answer; but words that stir up something in the unconscious make the subject confused, uncertain, and sometimes able to answer only with great difficulty. By observing these differences, by correlating the "reaction time" on individual words, and by other techniques, it is possible to find some of the things that the individual is hiding from himself, and in this way to find a clue to some of the sources of a neurosis.

In any judgment of the Association Test, however, it has to be kept in mind that it is very largely limited to the level of the Personal Unconscious, because the association method can touch only those psychic contents that are relatively close to consciousness. In this sense, it is the equivalent of the first or more superficial dreams in a dream series which have a purely personal content. Its limitation is that it is not able, by itself, to reach the deeper layers of the psyche, and also, more importantly, that the association test cannot be experienced as intensely and intimately as a dream that is presenting archetypal symbols. Certain types of dreams—when they express something deep enough in the psyche—have an energic force that is equivalent to their having actually been lived, and these dreams through the force of the experience, may play an important role in the reintegration of the personality.

BIG AND LITTLE DREAMS

In a dream series Jung has observed that the question of whether the dream symbols have a personal or an archetypal character depends on the level of the psyche from which the dream material comes. On his trip to Africa, he found a primitive tribe that is accustomed to make the same distinction. "The Elgonyi, natives of the jungles of Elgon," says Jung, "explained to me that there are two kinds of dreams, the ordinary dream of the small man, and the 'big vision' that comes only to the great man, the medicine-man, or the headman. The little dreams are of no account, but if a man has a 'big dream' he calls the tribe together and tells the dream to all.

"How is a man to know," Jung continues, "whether his dream is a 'big' or a 'little' one? He knows by an instinctive feeling of significance. He feels himself so overwhelmed by it that he would never think of keeping the dream to himself. He is forced to tell it on the assumption—which is correct psychologically—that it is significant for everybody." [5]

Jung was very much impressed by finding this evidence among the primitives, and he refers to it often in the course of his writings. It appears to him as clear verification of his basic distinction between personal and racial unconscious materials, and, by corollary, it appears to endorse his more fundamental doctrine on the structure of the psyche. Actually, practically every system of mythology carries such a distinction implicit in its attitude toward dreams and vision. It distinguishes the subjective dreams which grow out of the individual's personal life and the illusionary visions of false prophets from those prophecies which are felt to come "of the Lord." The latter speak to the people as a whole and have a meaning that goes beyond the individual person by whom they came. They are the "big" dreams, the "legitimate" prophecies, and their authority in every culture is based on the fact that they are felt to be more than personal in origin, expressing the inspired revelation of a cosmic reality. Jung does not pass judgment on the metaphysical basis of such views, but he points out that they have a psychological aspect which we actually perceive phenomenologically in the fact that these profound cosmic visions come from deeper levels of the psyche. Their meaningfulness over long periods

* *Two Essays*, pp. 189, 190.

of history is possible because they are the manifestation of archetypal figures that have a generic meaning to man. When the Elgonyi shares his "big" dream with everyone in the tribe, he can feel assured that the dream will be meaningful to others because it refers not to his own limited, personal experience, but to something that is present in all of them.

In understanding dreams, it is always important to place them in their proper psychological context. Dreams are not entities in themselves, and neither are the symbols of the dream. They are expressions of the unconscious and, like the material brought forth in the association tests, they are important just in so far as they reveal information about the operation of the psyche. The analysis of dream contents may make it possible to trace the flow of the psychic energies, and it may give a clue to what is taking place at the various depths of the unconscious. In this sense, the dream is a tool for the interpretation of personality. But more important is the fact that the dream life is actually a very vital part of the lived experience of the individual. Certain kinds of dreams are not only indications of psychic processes at work, but they themselves constitute an important part of these processes. Such dreams may play a central role in the most fundamental of all psychic processes: the unification of the personality.

THE PROCESS OF INDIVIDUATION

Jung's conception of the integration of the personality constitutes the core and culmination of his theories regarding the psychology of the individual. As he uses the term "integration," it is not at all to be understood merely as an aim of personal development—as one speaks, for example, of the "mature" personality. Integration is rather a process inherent in the nature of the psyche, transcending and including all others, and it is therefore the most basic of all the processes in the psyche. Jung's name for it is "Individuation."

Individuation has two aspects. On the one hand, it is the basic psychotherapy for the individual; on the other hand, as a universal psychic process, it is interpreted as a key to the underlying symbols of the great world religions and philosophies. In its first aspect—that is, in the treatment of his patients—Jung focuses on correcting what he calls the "over-valuation of consciousness." In this sense, Individuation involves a balancing and a harmonization of the psyche. In its second aspect, used as a key to the interpretation of myth and symbols, Individuation refers to the quest of self-realization as an archetypal psychic process on the principle that it is the essential sub-structure underlying the multitude of forms by which mankind experiences its spiritual life. The symbolism of mythology can then be read as variations on a single theme, so that Jung feels he is on sound theoretical ground when he turns to prehistoric myths to learn from man's primordial psychological insights into the nature of personality integration.

It would be beyond the scope of our present study to go into the details of the method by which Jung attempts to achieve Individuation through psychotherapeutic techniques. That has now become a separate and specialized field, and we are more concerned here with the social and historical significance of his conception of personality. Nevertheless, it is important to note for our historical context that Jung's therapy has one pervading characteristic—and limitation—that restricts its application to a particular sociological area.

He himself has acknowledged that the nature of his technique is such that it is principally applicable to individuals in whom there is an over-development of consciousness. He has to point this out in order to indicate that since his therapy is designed to loosen the contents of the unconscious, it may be extremely dangerous for a person who does not begin by having a strong conscious standpoint. If the individual is already over-balanced on the side of the unconscious, such a therapy may only intensify the disharmony.[6] The consequence is that his approach to therapy has value mainly for those individuals in whom a disequilibrium has developed out of an overstress on the conscious segment of the psyche.

SOCIO-HISTORICAL CONTENT OF JUNG'S THERAPY

It would not be correct, however, to say that Jung's therapy is restricted to any particular psychological type. The over-development of the conscious functions is not a characteristic just of, for example, the thinking type, but it is rather an aspect of the modern period of Western civilization as a whole. Because of this, just because his method is

* Jung's approach can operate successfully for the opposite type, but it must be manipulated very delicately and skillfully by the therapist. In the case of schizophrenics in whom the unconscious is stronger than consciousness, Jung's method is to try to catch hold of the thread of reality in the segment that is split off and is taking over the psyche from the unconscious. That is to say, the principle he works with is to find a way of relating some element of the vision or the "voice" of the schizophrenic to a corresponding element in consciousness and then, once this connection has been established, to proceed by means of it to strengthen the conscious position. Only when consciousness has been strengthened sufficiently so that it balances the unconscious can the therapist proceed in his efforts to integrate the opposites in the psyche.

directed at the over-balance of consciousness in the psyche, Jung considers that his therapy is designed for the particular problem which psychology must face in this historical situation. He sees the psychological problems of individuals as arising out of the broad historical movements, the inordinate faith in science, the stress on rationality in individual life, which are the trade-marks of modern culture. Here Jung finds the sociological root of the discordance between consciousness and the unconscious, which underlies modern psychological problems. In focusing on those individual cases, therefore, where the difficulty arises from the disproportionate development of consciousness—even though it limits the type of person whom he can treat successfully—Jung feels that he is engaging the most fundamental issue of our time.

In proportion as the conscious segment of the psyche is over-developed, there exists a condition of unbalance with relation to the rest of the psyche. The aim of individuation is to achieve a balance, a harmony, in which consciousness and the unconscious complement each other in a relation of "reciprocal relativity." It involves the integration of the psyche as a unity.

Fundamentally, the test of personality is whether the dominant attitudes within it are functioning effectively. Like a good shoe, as an old saying goes, when it fits, the person is not even aware that he is wearing it; but when it does not fit, it makes the whole body uncomfortable. When the dominant conscious attitudes are functioning well, the person is not even aware that he has them; but when they come into conflict with daily experience, he becomes all too acutely aware of his conscious position, and his entire psyche is thrown into disorder.

THE COLLAPSE OF THE PERSONA

In terms of Jung's analysis, the conscious attitudes are contained within the Persona, the mask of personality, and when a "collapse of the conscious attitude" takes place, it involves a breakdown of the Persona.[7] It means, functionally, that the energies can no longer flow smoothly out toward life, but now regress into the psyche. As this is a painful personal experience, the individual may try to stem the inward tide of his energies by trying to form new conscious attitudes, a new Persona, at a lower level. When the individual decides that his Persona broke apart because he was "shooting too high," and when he then sets out to build a new conscious attitude that will not require so much of him, Jung speaks of the "regressive restoration of the Persona." It is the means by which the individual finds peace through building a compromise version of what he had previously thought himself to be.

If the individual, however, does not make this compromise, the downward and inward flow of the libido continues and involves increasingly deep areas of the psyche. In time, the unconscious brings up to the surface psychic contents that are more than personal, archetypes that focus the individual's energies toward questions that are cosmic or religious. At this phase of the development, the individual is being led to find the materials for a more complete resolution of the problem of opposites out of which the break-up of the Persona was precipitated. While more fundamental symbols of psychic processes are coming into consciousness, the individual is still seeking a basis for building a new Persona, and he will very often find the necessary materials by relat-

[7] *Two Essays*, p. 173.

ing these newly activated unconscious contents to some movement that is current in his particular culture. In this way, the break-up of the Persona in the individual frequently leads, if it progresses far enough, to a reintegration of personality based on a newly found religious belief or a newly developed philosophy of life.

The important point is that the regression of psychic energies brought about by the collapse of the Persona leads ultimately to the activation of archetypal material in the unconscious. The possibility therefore opens for the individual that a break-up in his conscious attitude can be superseded in time by a new integration at a more basic level of the psyche. If this is accomplished, it means that consciousness has been brought into a closer relationship with the unconscious and that the new conscious attitude is on a more solid base.

Apart from this, however, the opening of the deep levels of the unconscious by the regressing libido has a special consequence for the process of individuation. We have to refer again to the "autonomous partial systems," which have been described as operating under their own force within the psyche. Of these, the Persona represents the conscious side, while the Anima represents the unconscious in general, including everything "spiritual," the "soul" side of man. The most important aspect of the partial systems is that they have the power of "possession," that is, they may take over the total personality of the individual in "moods" or "tempers" or "inspirations" and intrude themselves into the individual's life without the control or guidance of consciousness. While the autonomous complexes are active, the individual is subject to their whims, and he cannot have the freedom to integrate his total personality until he has brought them under control. Therefore, Jung says, "fundamentally the aim of individuation is to free the self from the false wrappings of the Persona on the one hand, and from the suggestive power of the unconscious images (i.e., the Anima) on the other." [8]

THE CONTROL OF THE AUTONOMOUS COMPLEXES

To achieve this is far from a simple matter. To become conscious of them is merely the very first step. Jung follows with another suggestion which he uses as a main technique in his therapy. He advises that the Persona and the Anima should be treated as they themselves behave in dreams; since they personify themselves as separate individuals and act as separate personalities, we should regard them as such. Because they act with a power of their own in the psyche, we need to learn, he says, to think of them— and to deal with them—as separate individualities. Jung quotes one of his patients as an example of how strongly an autonomous Anima may be described when a person is making an effort to come to grips with it:

"I recognize that a psychic factor is active in me that can free itself from my conscious will in the most incredible way. It can put extraordinary ideas in my head, and can provoke unwished for, unwelcome moods and affects, can lead me into astonishing behavior for which I can take no responsibility, and can disturb my relations with other people in an irritating way. I feel myself to be helpless in the face of this fact, and what is worse, I am in love with this thing so that I can only wonder at it."

[8] Ibid., p. 185.

Jung adds, "Poets often call this the artistic temperament; unpoetical people excuse themselves in other ways." [9]

We may understand, even looking at it from the outside, that what is being described here is a difficult and painful process. In making such an effort to come to grips with his very nature, the individual is forcing himself to take an objective attitude toward his most innerly subjective psychological forces. He is speaking of his own psychic contents, beliefs, values, and so on—all of which he is accustomed to think of as "himself"—and yet he talks of them as though they were not "him," as though they were strangers. Indeed, the aim is to be able to speak not *of* them, but to them, to be able to *address* them as separate individuals.

A main step in achieving this is to separate what is conscious in the individual from what is unconscious. As the process proceeds, it appears that very little belongs to consciousness and that by far the greater part of the psychic life belongs not to the conscious "I" but to the unconscious archetypes; we have merely given them specific forms, and given the forms our names. Now, in being objective toward the unconscious complexes, the individual can realize that what he thought was his own personality was not his own personality at all. It was only his Persona, the mask he wears in society. At this point he can understand that, though the purpose of the Persona was to impress others, it has accomplished something else. He himself is the one who has been deluded, because he has not only acted a part but believed it. When he thought he was making his own choices, it was not he who was choosing. It was the Anima working with the Persona, creating a conscious attitude so deftly out of the unconscious that he mistook it for consciousness. And now the process is to be reversed. Now the Anima is to be addressed not as part of himself, but as a separate individual. A major point in Jung's concept of individuation is that the individual must be able to speak to the Anima, to enumerate its qualities, and declare to it that its power in the psyche is over. Certainly this is difficult, and it requires a special psychological situation to be possible at all. Jung, citing the Hindu saying, refers to this process as being as difficult as walking on a "knife-edge"; but he regards it as a necessary step in the accomplishment of the process of full individuation.

THE EMERGENCE OF THE SELF

If we now assume that the individual has had the stamina with which to bring the Anima to consciousness, what are the consequences? The Anima will no longer be free to act autonomously in the psyche. It will have lost its force; in Jung's words, it "can no longer exercise the power of possession." The individual will now be free from the control of the unconscious complexes. It has already been pointed out that the Anima, as the symbol of the unconscious and of all the archetypes, has an extremely large concentration of libido energy. In fact, Jung considers the libido intensity of the Anima to be so great that he refers to it as "mana," as having a miraculous—that is, extraordinarily powerful—quality.[10] When the Anima is raised from the unconscious and "depotentated," this great force of energy is let loose in the psyche. Consequently, the crucial question in Jung's development of the process of individuation becomes: what happens

[10] Ibid., p. 252.

to the psychic energy of the Anima when it is raised to consciousness?

As he describes it, the unconscious has clearly lost this large sum of libido. On the other hand, the conscious ego has not gained it. There is, then, this great quantity of psychic energy, powerful and with very unusual qualities attached to it, situated between consciousness and the unconscious, and belonging to neither one. Where does it go? Jung's answer is that it stays where it is. The psychic energy which formerly belonged to the Anima comes to rest in a twilight zone where it performs a unique function: it acts as a bridge between the conscious and unconscious divisions of the psyche. It becomes the point of meeting, where the opposites of the psyche may be integrated into a unified personality. It becomes the point on which the psyche balances itself and through which a constant equilibrium may henceforth be maintained. The libido sum which formerly belonged to the Anima now becomes the "central point of the personality." [11]

It is even more than that, Jung says. This newly created focusing point emerges as a new component of the psyche. It is the result of the constant battling of the opposites in man. It is the "Self."

The Self is created, Jung says, "as a kind of compensation for the conflict between the inner and the outer worlds." It is "something that has come into being only very gradually and has become a part of our experience at the cost of great effort. Thus the Self is also the goal of life, because it is the most complete expression of that fateful combination we call

* Ibid., p. 245.

"individuality." [12] The harmony that is established when the conflict of opposites is resolved is expressed in the creation of the Self. The principle of opposites still remains; there are still consciousness and the unconscious. But now the opposites balance each other, and the Self, as the midpoint, maintains an even tenor in the psyche.

What is most significant for the psychology of consciousness is that at this point the ego has an altogether new position. It is no longer the center of the psyche as a whole. Though it remains the center of consciousness, consciousness itself is now in a dependent relationship. The Ego now finds itself revolving around the Self "very much as the earth rotates around the sun." [13] The Self is now the center of the psyche and the source of all its energy. In conceiving of it in this way, Jung virtually reverses the usual view of psychology, according to which the Ego is the center of the personality. It is almost a literal description to say that, with his conception of the "Self," Jung has undertaken a "Copernican Revolution" in psychology. [14]

MANDALA SYMBOLISM AND INDIVIDUATION

A large proportion of Jung's interest in seemingly strange symbolism may be understood as his effort to find the terms in which the Self is expressed and described in the religions and psychologies of other peoples and other times in history. His interpretation of Alchemy, which has struck

[12] Ibid., p. 268.
[13] Ibid., p. 268.
[14] The description of individuation presented in this chapter is intended merely as an introduction to the subject. The reader who is interested in a more advanced discussion is referred to Jung's *Aion* and his *Psychologie und Alchemie*.

many critics as an unduly obscure subject matter, hinges on his psychological reading of what the Alchemists mean when they speak of the transmutation of the base metals into gold. It signifies to Jung "the transformation of the personality through the merging and binding together of the noble and base elements, the conscious and the unconscious." In psychological terms this is the Unifying Function of the psyche, by which the conflict of opposites is transcended and the Self emerges as the centerpoint of a new harmony.[15]

In a similar vein, Jung finds in the "Mandala" a symbol which expresses the integration of the personality and the emergence of the Self. The Mandala is a figure or design found in the art of virtually all peoples. It is based on a perfectly balanced square or circle, in which the mid-point is given a particularly great importance. Jung has found many instances of Mandalas in the religious art of the Orient, as well as in the art and dances of primitive peoples. The main evidence of Mandalas that comes to him from the modern world, however, is in the dreams of his patients. The central content of such dreams—taken from the psychological point of view—is a symbolic portrayal of the conflicting opposites and of the harmony that is established when the Self emerges as the centerpoint of the psyche. The following is an example of a Mandala dream told in the words of one of Jung's patients; the reader may perhaps be able to visualize from the description something of the form and type of content that characterizes Mandala dreams.

"I climbed the mountain and came to a place where I saw seven red stones in front of me, seven on either side, and

---

[15] *Two Essays*, p. 243. The phrase "unifying function" is sometimes translated as the "transcendent function."

seven behind me. I stood in the middle of this quadrangle.
The stones were flat like steps. I tried to lift the four stones
that were nearest to me. In doing so I discovered that these
stones were the pedestals of four statues of gods which were
buried upside down in the earth. I dug them up and so ar-
ranged them that I stood in the middle of them. Suddenly
they leaned towards one another so that their heads touched,
forming something like a tent over me. I myself fell to the
earth, and said, 'Fall upon me if you must for I am tired.'
Then I saw that beyond, encircling the four gods, a ring of
flame had formed. After a time I arose from the ground and
overthrew the statues of the gods. Where they fell to the
earth four trees began to grow. And now from the circle of
fire, blue flames shot up which began to burn the foliage of
the trees. Seeing this I said, 'This must stop. I must go into
the fire myself so that the leaves may not be burned.' Then I
stepped into the fire. The trees disappeared and the ring of
fire contracted to one immense blue flame that carried me
up from the earth." [16]

We may assume that such a dream has many layers of
meaning. Yet we can see the conflict of opposites expressed
in the patterns involving the number four, and the emergence
of the Self in the "one immense blue flame." A dream such as
this is important to the individual because the psychological
forces that are involved in it are deeply experienced; they
have more than an intellectual effect because they actually
take place much below the surface level of consciousness.
When they occur, such dreams signify that some phase of the
process of individuation is taking place within the personality. Nevertheless, we must remember that, while the dream

[16] *Two Essays*, pp. 246, 247.

holds an important place in the psychological development of the individual, the dream is not itself the reality but
is to be understood as the manifestation of the psychic
process that is taking place in the psyche.

THE SIGNIFICANCE OF THE INDIVIDUATION THEORY

The large point that is important in Jung's concept of individuation is that, with the emergence of the Self, an altogether new force comes to birth in the psyche. The meta-
phoric reference to "rebirth" then has a quite substantial
meaning. When the conflicting opposites have been integrated and brought into a peaceful relationship, it is actually as though a new individual has been born.

In considering the value of this conception, we are bound
to observe that the Self as Jung describes it has not been
proved by scientific standards. The entire formulation has
to be taken as a hypothesis, or better, as a schematic way of
approaching a very difficult and elusive psychological experience. To evaluate Jung's position on this point, we may put
the following question: is Jung correct in stating that the
something new which emerges as the Self is *qualitatively*
more than the mere integration—or balancing—of the contending forces in the psyche? If he is wrong in this, his psychological system must be restricted to the analysis of the
movements of energy in the layers of the psyche. If he is
right, he has found a starting point for a creative study of religious experience capable of going beyond psychology. We
may say, therefore, that, on the one hand, Jung's concept of
Individuation is the culmination of his psychological studies,
and, on the other hand, it opens the possibility of new and
enlarged conceptions of the psychological nature of man.

Part II

JUNG'S SOCIAL CONCEPTS
AND THEIR SIGNIFICANCE

V I I

THE PSYCHE IN SOCIETY
AND HISTORY

SOCIETY AND INDIVIDUALITY

In the preceding chapters we have discussed the essential concepts that Jung uses to analyze the processes underlying psychic phenomena. The context for all these processes is the psyche as Jung conceives it, but up till now we have spoken of the psyche only in terms of the factors involved in the development of the individual personality. The principles developed within this range of problems constitute, of course, the basic core of Jung's theoretical work, since, as a psychiatrist, he is interested primarily in clarifying the situations of his individual patients. But now we turn the focus of study in a different direction. We turn from the individual to the group and ask how Jung's description of the processes of the psyche contributes to an understanding of culture and historical change.

Before we go ahead to work out Jung's specific social concepts, it is important that we be clear about just what is involved in this shift of perspective from the individual to the group. In a certain sense, we are changing not only our focus but also our subject matter, since the phenomena of society are qualitatively different from those of the individual personality. There are questions of the structuring of societies, the organization of economic and political systems, problems of

population and group mixture, and these move on a level
that is, at least externally, largely independent of psychological factors. Since he does not take a sociological point of
view, Jung is not concerned with such questions at all. His
interest is, rather, in the various kinds of belief, the different
ways of thinking, the driving power of some symbols as compared to others, the formation and disintegration of life-
attitudes. His interest, in short, is not in the external forms
of social groups, nor in the history of economic or political
movements, but in what can be called the inner content of
history. In treating this special side of social phenomena, he
deals with the factors that are most directly expressed in the
character formation of individuals, and, in this sense, his
studies of society are a necessary consequence of his main research into the problems of personality. He needs to know
not only the historical background of personality, but, because of the nature of his conception of the unconscious, he
must study the historical contents of the psyche. Jung's treatment of social issues is carried out altogether with the purpose of answering psychological questions, but it has an additional result. Dealing with the inner contents of history,
and then analyzing the psychic processes which underlie
them, he reaches, almost inadvertently, the inner dynamics of
social change. He does not develop any integrated approach
to history, but his way of applying his psychological theories
to the varieties of culture and of cultural change leads to concepts which in time may very well crystallize into a theory of
history. These are the concepts that we shall develop and
discuss in this chapter.

Jung's approach to society differs from that of other psychologists in one outstanding and fundamental way. The

usual practise is to begin with the notion of the individual, conceived either as a biological organism or as a hypothetical primal man, and then to generalize a theory based on a multiplication of the individual case. Freud's *Group Psychology* follows such a pattern. Jung avoids the common tendency of psychologists to regard society as merely the plural of the individual, since he realizes that the social quality of man is something inherent in human nature. He works with the opposite of the view handed down by the liberal tradition, namely, that society has been formed by individuals who came together, either by force or for their own convenience, to form some kind of social compact. In other words, first the individual, then society. Jung reverses this. Man is by his very nature social, he says. The human psyche cannot function without a culture, and no individual is possible without society. By making this his basic assumption, Jung frees himself from the main pitfalls of studying society from a psychological point of view. That is to say, he does not carry over to the study of society interpretations based on the analysis of the human being as an individual. Instead, he makes it his principle that all analysis must start from the primary fact of the social nature of man.

The fact that Jung starts with an inherently social definition of man—rather than a biological or epistemological one —has two main roots in his thought. One is the nature of his conception of the psyche. He derives the deeper levels of the unconscious not from individual experience, but from the great communal experiences of mankind, and he thus places social factors at the origin of the psyche. The second root lies in his intellectual sources. On this question of the social nature of man Jung has not at all been influenced by psychological writers, but has rather worked out his basic conceptions in the spirit of Durkheimian sociology. That is to say, he begins with the view that society is the primary reality, and therefore the primary datum in the study of man. Because he starts this way, the logical order for thinking of the problem is: first society, and then the individual. If he took the other point of view, that is, if he took the individual as his starting point, the problem would be reversed, and he would have to turn his analysis to the question of how it is that society emerges from the concourse of individuals. But Jung assumes society, and he assumes that the nature of man is inherently social. Society, therefore, is not his problem for study, but it only serves to provide a foundation for the interpretation of individual human beings. He is thus accepting a sociological point of view and adding to it the extra dimension of his analysis of the unconscious. Further than this, Jung assumes history; he begins with the assumption that man is not only social by nature, but *social in the continuity of time*. He goes further than Durkheim in this regard and works with the underlying view of Jacob Burckhardt that society and history are inextricably bound to each other. Since he thinks in these terms, it is logically necessary that his conception of the individual must have both a social and a time aspect inherent in it, and Jung's view of society is basically designed to make such a conception possible. His approach to society grew out of his effort to solve the problems of individuality, and it is formulated in such a way that the two main factors, the social and the time aspects of the human being, can be worked out, at least provisionally, in some detail.

The key to understanding Jung's work in this field is to keep firmly in mind the way in which he thinks of society and the individual and of their relation to each other. It is a side of Jung's work that can be quite misleading, and it has, in fact, resulted in much misunderstanding in the past. The twofold situation is this. From the practical point of view of a psychiatrist, Jung is interested primarily in the individual; but from the larger perspective of the study of man, he regards society as the prior fact. Society and the social experiences of history are ultimately the main suppliers of the contents of the individual psyche. It comes about, then, that while his primary focus is on the individual personality, the conception of individuality is not a given fact for him but only a derivative from the more fundamental category of society.

It should be clear that in putting it this way we are not presenting any doctrine that Jung has stated explicitly, but are rather trying to show the inner relation of the ideas within his formulations. He does not postulate a category of society, nor does he even speak of it in such terms. But the idea is present in his work; it is constantly being applied, and has far-reaching consequences throughout his studies, even though he does not state it in so many words. It is one of the basic views of the Durkheimian sociology and is implied in all the questions that Jung has dealt with coming from that quarter. There is the difference, however, that while the concept of society is present as an active idea in Jung's thought, it does not have the same form as in the French sociology. It comes out couched in his own characteristic terminology. To Jung the social is essentially the unconscious, and more particularly, the deeper layers of the Collective Unconscious. In understanding the individual as a derivative of society, he is following his more fundamental idea that "consciousness comes from the unconscious." In other words, just as the process of bringing psychic contents to consciousness involves a sharpening and clarifying of the ambiguities of the unconscious, so the individual emerges out of society by a process of differentiation and individualization. To Jung this is not an analogy, but parallel processes, essentially two sides of the same development. It means that his conception of consciousness and his analysis of the nature of individuality are very closely related to each other.)

The framework for Jung's understanding of consciousness is the psyche as a whole, which means the totality of the psychological aspect of the person. It is his all-inclusive concept for the cognitive side of the human being, formulated with the purpose of defining in a more specific way what Descartes called *res cogitans*. When he uses the term "consciousness," Jung means just a very small part of this. He limits his idea of consciousness to a carefully circumscribed area at the surface of the psyche, a relatively tiny segment of the total cognitive process. It is the part of the psyche that is altogether related to individuality. That is why Jung says in the definition section of his *Psychological Types*, "By consciousness I understand the relatedness of psychic contents to the ego in so far as they are sensed as such by the ego." [1]

The problem of the nature of consciousness is then carried one step further and depends on the meaning of the term "ego." "By ego," Jung says, "I understand a complex of representations which constitutes the centrum of my field of consciousness and appears to possess a very high degree of continuity and identity." [2] Many people have felt that this is.

[1] *Psychological Types*, p. 535.
[2] Ibid., p. 540.

a definition which goes in a circle. On the one hand, consciousness is defined in terms of its relation to the ego. On the
other hand, the ego is defined as the "autonomous complex"
which acts as the center or, so to speak, the axis of consciousness. It recalls the situation of the man who inquired
as to the identity of two children whom he met. He was told
that the boy was the brother of the girl, and that the girl was
the sister of the boy; but he was not told whose children they
were. Actually these definitions are misleading because, in
giving such brief formulations, Jung does not do justice to
his full ideas. In his fuller descriptions and applications of
his conception of consciousness, he indicates much more than
merely its relation to the ego. He explains it in terms of its
position in the psyche as a whole, and of its relation to the
contents of the various layers of the unconscious. The cir-
cular nature of the two definitions has larger implications.
What is most significant is that from the very fact that Jung's
formulation of consciousness and the ego goes in a circle,
we can see the inherent inter-relation of consciousness and
the ego to each other—the ego as the focus of personal identity, and consciousness as the manifestation of the individual's
awareness of himself and of the outer world. It emphasizes
the closeness of the relation between consciousness and individuality in Jung's thought.

To stress further the relation between Jung's conception
of the individual and the entire context of his analysis of consciousness, we should underline the distinction between individuality and individuation. Individuality is centered
around the ego and involves the small surface part of the
psyche which is consciousness. Individuation, on the other
hand, is the integrative process affecting the entire psyche.

One of the most important aspects of individuation is that it sets individuality in context. Jung's basic conception is that consciousness rests on the unconscious in a constant tension, out of which individuality emerges. Individuation involves a release of tension by means of the balancing of opposites and the setting up of a relation of harmonious dependence between consciousness and the unconscious. The ego remains the center of consciousness, but the Self emerges as the center of the psyche as a whole. It is a process that takes place within the individual, but its essential meaning is that it gives personality a larger aspect, opening beyond the particularities of the individual. Individuation eliminates the illusion of individuality and yet retains the centrum of specific personality. It therefore brings to the fore of Jung's psychological theories the problems not only of what the individual is and how it happens that the individual comes into existence as a psychological entity, but what is the relation of the social and historical sources of individuality to the enlargement of personality in the process of individuation. From several directions, the need constantly re-emerges in Jung's work for an ever-more refined definition of individuality. Fundamentally, Jung's thought on these issues follows parallel lines, from the unconscious to consciousness, from society to the individual. The problem of the emergence of personality is at the heart of his theories of society.

PARTICIPATION MYSTIQUE AND THE EMERGENCE OF
CONSCIOUSNESS

Jung comes to the question of individuality from two main intellectual traditions: German philosophy and French sociology. His basic idea that personality develops as an unfolding out of a depth layer of the unconscious has its roots in Schopenhauer and Hartmann. He carries over their conception that the individual depends on a substructure of reality expressed in unconscious principles and forces prior to individual existence. This, however, is the philosophical side of the question, and Jung shies away from it even though he is well aware that his own work makes use of such concepts. Because of what he considers his "phenomenological" (i.e., pragmatic) point of view, he feels the need for a conceptual scheme in which the emergence of the individual can be traced in a more factual way. In this regard Jung has been much influenced by Jacob Burckhardt's idea that the sources of the individual go far back in history and that images present in primordial man still are active in the modern personality. Nietzsche, also, was important to Jung on this question, since his work is permeated by the idea that the individual expresses something in addition to his conscious individuality in his life experiences. With Nietzsche, the awareness of splits within personality became a consciousness of unconscious factors at work as though they were, in a sense, a multiple individuality in one person. This was, as we indicated earlier, very important to Jung in his understanding of the autonomous factors in personality.

For the specific concepts with which he analyzes the emergence of the individual in the social process, however, Jung is most indebted to the sociological concepts of Emile Durkheim and Lucien Lévy-Bruhl. Like Durkheim, Jung postulates society as a primary human datum, and he agrees that the individual must be understood in terms of the social situation in which he lives. He also takes over Durkheim's basic conception of the "collective representations." By this is meant the basic beliefs and assumptions about the nature of things, the world, and the conduct of life held in common by the members of the group, imposed on them by the pressures of the group, and transmitted from generation to generation. Individuals share in the collective representations not as individuals but as members of the group and, in this, sense, their individuality is submerged within their culture. The individual partakes of the collective representations by a fusion of himself with the group; it involves the loss—or absence—of individuality for him. Jung realized that something of this is present in every social relationship, and he therefore followed the question further to ask what is the psychic process involved in the participation of the individual in the collective representations.

In treating this problem, the anthropologist, Lucien Lévy-Bruhl, postulated what he called the "law of participation." We should note that the word "participation" as Lévy-Bruhl uses it does not mean merely to share or to take part in; it means actually to fuse, to identify oneself with an object in such a way that all distinctions are obliterated. Participation means that no conscious discrimination exists between the subject and the object, or between two objects. Lévy-Bruhl developed this idea in his effort to analyze the nature of the thinking processes in primitive tribes. He came to the conclusion that primitive tribes have a different manner of thinking, what he called a different "mentality," from civilized men. The collective representations of primitive tribes, he said, differ from those of modern civilization in that they are based on the "law of participation," specifically "participation mystique." Lévy-Bruhl meant to convey the idea that primitives see real relationships between things where these relationships are imperceptible to us. A primitive may believe, for example, that he is not only himself, but also a bird; or he may feel that the failure of a hunting expedition was caused by his chance meeting with a neighbor. The "mystique" consists not in the beliefs themselves, and not in the correctness or error of the primitive's interpretation of the relationships. The "mystique" is simply the primitive's immediate sense of a power or force binding the two events together. Lévy-Bruhl referred to this as "pre-logical mentality." He was careful to point out even in his first book on the subject that he did not mean to imply by the term that "pre-logical mentality" constitutes an earlier stage in the evolution of thought; and also that he did not mean either that primitives are a-logical or anti-logical. He meant merely that primitive societies do not feel bound to follow the principle of contradiction as we do for the simple reason that, since their collective representations permit the "law of participation," they see no incongruity in one thing being two things at the same time. His careful disclaimers and modifications, however, did not prevent Lévy-Bruhl from being criticized constantly for things he did not say, mainly on the basis of the unfortunate connotations of the term "pre-logical." The issue has been beclouded by argument, and Lévy-Bruhl's contribution has tended to be lost sight of in the haze. Jung, however, has been convinced from the first that the principle of "participation" represents a very definite psychological fact and that it is important to understand the psychic principles involved in Lévy-Bruhl's formulation.

In the first place, the term "pre-logical" is not only misleading because it confuses Lévy-Bruhl's true meaning, but it is really beside the point. It is not a question of logic.

Jung points out that primitives are no less logical than we are—*when we understand their assumptions*. It is all a matter of context, and when we see the ideas of the primitive within their own frame of reference, they look much more logical than when we see them from the outside. In the second place, the discussion of the principle of "participation" in terms of primitives alone gives an altogether wrong impression. Examples of what Lévy-Bruhl has called "pre-logical" mentality can be found in many groups in the modern world. Not only that, but the collective representations which go to make up the modern world-view—from the faith in science to the belief in a standard of living based on material goods or commercial success and the conflicts in world ideologies—are full of "participation mystique." In attributing pre-logical thought exclusively to the primitives, we are ascribing to them something that is also present in ourselves. "Participation" appears to be a universal psychic element, and Jung discusses it in a general psychological context.

The main characteristic of "participation" is that it involves a fusion between subject and object, a failure to differentiate. The individual identifies himself with another person, with an animal, a bird, or an inanimate object. He projects something of himself into the object and then draws the two together. "Participation" is clearly an unconscious process expressing the way in which the unconscious thinks. That is to say, the unconscious expresses itself in dreams or by other symbolic means in which one object is transposed into the form of another and the principle of contradiction has no application at all. Also, when a psychological function such as thinking, feeling, etc., is in the unconscious, it is undifferentiated and it tends to fuse objects together in an un-

clear way. It operates by "participation." When an individual
lives completely within the spell of the collective representations, fusing himself with the group and identifying himself
with the collectivity, the images of the group dominate his
unconscious. Such an individual lives constantly in a relation
of "participation mystique" with the collective representations. He does not distinguish the ideas of his own thinking
processes from the collective images—or if so, only barely—
and in this condition he can hardly be said to be individualized.

It appears, then, that "participation" is a condition that
prevails where the psychological process of differentiation
has not yet taken place. "Participation" is the characteristic
of unconsciousness; differentiation is the characteristic of
consciousness. "Participation" is also characteristic of the fusion of the individual with the group via the collective representations; differentiation, which involves the breaking-up
of the "participation," means also the emergence of individuality. These psychological interpretations, which Jung has
added to Lévy-Bruhl's conception of the "participation mystique," are an essential part of his analysis of the relation of
society to personality.

Despite his disclaimers, it is a fact that, with his roots in
the sociology of Auguste Comte, Lévy-Bruhl did carry over
in his mind some of the assumptions of evolutionism, particularly the assumption that there are gradations in consciousness from the pre-logical up to the scientific. In Jung's context it is not a question of gradations at all. The principle of
"participation" is significant to him not as part of a general
theory of culture, but as a description of a development
within the psyche, in which contents move out of the uncon-

scious by the process of differentiation and are freed from the condition of "participation mystique." Sometimes Jung uses the phrase "pre-conscious" in a way that is roughly analogous to Lévy-Bruhl's use of the term "pre-logical." When he does so, however, he applies it in a very specific way so that it cannot possibly carry any overtones of referring to an inferior or early stage in cultural evolution. The phrase "pre-conscious" has for Jung the purely heuristic purpose of describing the means and steps by which thinking proceeds from the unconscious to consciousness, from the lower levels to the surface of the psyche.

Jung's analysis of the emergence of consciousness runs parallel to his interpretation of the principles underlying the emergence of individuality from the group. In discussing the mentality of the primitives, he is not mainly interested in the characteristics of their thought as a cultural type. He finds examples of primitive thought—that is, thought based upon participations—throughout modern culture, and the significance of primitive mentality is that it indicates most clearly and graphically what happens in the first dim appearance of consciousness as it emerges in the individual, whether the individual is considered as having been submerged by "participation mystique" in the collective representations of a particular group, or whether the individual is considered abstractly as emerging to personality in any historical situation in general.

In this analysis Jung's key concept is that "our individual conscious psychology develops out of an original state of unconsciousness or, in other words, a non-differentiated condition."[3] What is important to him is to have a conceptual

[3] *Two Essays*, pp. 225, 226.

structure with which to handle the relation of the unconscious to consciousness. Even while, for example, in the following quotation, Jung refers explicitly to "primitive mentality," its meaning for him is to explain how the psyche functions *whenever* its symbols are active in the depth levels of the unconscious. "Primitive mentality," he says, "differs from the civilized chiefly in that the conscious mind is far less developed in extent and intensity. Functions such as thinking, willing, etc., are not yet differentiated; they are pre-conscious, a fact which in the case of thinking, for instance, shows itself in the circumstance that the primitive does not think *consciously* but that thoughts appear. The primitive cannot assert that he thinks; it is rather that 'something thinks in him.' " [4]

This introduces an idea other than "participation," namely, "possessions" coming from the unconscious, or what Jung calls "partial systems," capable of acting autonomously in the psyche—that is, without direction by the ego and frequently even prior to the emergence of an ego. It is obvious that much more than primitive psychology is involved in such concepts. William James, for example, in a similar vein but from another direction, pointed out that we should not say "I think" but "it thinks," meaning "our thoughts think" in us and for us. The whole question of consciousness is put in another light when treated in such a context, and the reality of the individual becomes a quite nebulous question. [5] It would seem that, in so far as consciousness is identified with individuality, it involves the degree of "directed thinking" that can be carried out. This

[4] *Essays on a Science of Mythology*, p. 100.

[5] William James, *Principles of Psychology*, Dover Publications, New York, 1950, Vol. 1, pp. 224-230. James uses the term "Self" to cover the general question of the continuity of individual identity in his reasonings on the existence and the nature of the person.

involves a change in the area of "autonomous" functioning in the psyche. Whereas "partial systems" operating as "autonomous complexes" carry out the thinking of the individual's thoughts in the "pre-conscious" state, the step up to consciousness means that the individual ego takes control of the thinking process. But the ego itself is defined as an "autonomous complex," and its own position is in the nature of a "possession" of the psyche as a whole. The ego comes out of the unconscious and becomes the center of unconscious contents which are described as conscious on the basis that they "sense" themselves as being conscious. This expresses once again the difficulty of giving an absolute definition of consciousness, but it takes the problem one step further because it indicates that while consciousness and individuality may be associated, both of them draw their main characteristics from their relation to the rest of the psyche.

From one point of view, the nature of the ego and the extent of its autonomous power depend on the degree to which it has been able to differentiate itself and to emerge from the "collective representations." This is the sense in which consciousness, coming forth from the unconscious, runs parallel to the development of the individual out of society. When a condition of "participation mystique" binds the individual within the collective images, it means that individuals are still undifferentiated from each other; that is to say, they have not yet been self-consciously broken up into individual personalities. On this "pre-conscious" level, the individual is covered over by his participation in the "collective representations"; he does not experience his own individuality as separate from the life of the group, or at least he experiences his individuality with such slight intensity that it is readily resubmerged into the collectivity, which is to say, also, into the unconscious. Thinking, feeling, and all the other psychological functions are still undifferentiated at this stage of cognition, and they retain the characteristics of unconscious materials in the sense that they are, in Jung's phrase, in the nature of "things that happen to one." They are not under the control of the ego and consequently, since they are not particularized to meet the needs of individuality, they remain in an undifferentiated state.

ARCHETYPES AND INDIVIDUALITY

The archetypes exist in the unconscious as undifferentiated symbols appearing to the individual as a kind of dream-reality, and to society in historical forms as "collective representations." In the process of being applied to life, the archetypes take on specific forms. Since they cannot be expressed abstractly, but only in particular manifestations, the archetypes of the Objective Unconscious reach the level of daily living only *via* the individual human being. The nature of the archetype is to individualize itself—more or less in proportion to the degree that it is expressed in consciousness. "It must individualize itself," Jung says, "as soon as it manifests itself, for there is no way in which it can express itself except through the single individual." [6] In this sense, the individual in society is altogether dependent on the archetypes, since his personal psyche can come into existence as an entity only by being differentiated out of the collective representations of his period of history. Consciousness emerges as a result of this process of individualization. Self-consciousness consists in the intuition of the process by which the individual is differen-

* *The Integration of the Personality*, p. 296.

tiated from the symbol and experiences himself as directing his own thought processes.)

In the over-all pattern of Jung's thought, differentiation, the individual, and consciousness are all aspects of a single underlying psychological process. All three originate in the unconscious and in historical symbols. His conception of society as a whole corresponds to the objective psyche in the sense that it represents a generalized formulation that transcends the individual and precedes the differentiation that leads to consciousness. The crux of the matter is that the archetypes of the collective experience, which are the symbols of the society, must be expressed through individuals; on the other hand, individuals must rely on collective material for the basic content of their personalities. This inter-weaving relationship, coming together from opposite directions, is at the heart of the interpretation of the individual in society. Jung is particularly aware that the question must be approached from two points of view at the same time, and he also realizes that the opposites must be linked by a unifying concept which can draw them together. His formulation and analysis of "psychic energy" in society is designed to serve such an intermediary function.

PSYCHIC ENERGY IN PERSONALITY AND CULTURE

The assumption that society is the natural and necessary condition of human life leads to the inference that it must correspond to some psychic process deeply imbedded in the nature of the human being. Jung's analysis takes a starting-point that is not dissimilar to Freud's to the extent that it points to the crucial impact which society has on the raw, instinctual energies of the human creature. Unlike Freud, however, Jung does not conclude that the fact of social life leads directly to the neurotic situation. He interprets it from a functional point of view, and asks what happens to instinctual energy in the course of its contact with society. The first, most obvious point is that this raw libido is immediately curbed in its free impulsiveness, since it is restricted as to the means by which it can express itself. This is the negative side, however, and the positive side is that the raw libido is thereby harnessed and focused in specific directions. The fact of group life "channelizes" the energies of the individual, converting them from one form to another in terms of a variety of psychic values and psychic intensities. It is a process that Jung considers to be inherent in both society and the individual, and which he describes under the term, "the transformation of the libido." [7]

The development of this concept proceeds by drawing an analogy between the process of energy transformation as it occurs in the physical world and in psychological phenomena. Jung takes this merely as a pragmatic assumption for its value in formulating the issues, and he is not concerned *a priori* with a metaphysical "parallelism" or any other doctrine of correspondence between the physical and mental worlds. On this level, too, Jung follows the methodology of Freud very closely in treating the question of "energy" in the manner of the physical sciences. He speaks of "energy values" and "intensities," as Freud does, in a purely functional, non-moral, non-evaluative sense, in an effort to get at least an approximately quantitative basis for comparing and relating psychic contents. He uses also, as Freud does, the general hypothesis of "equivalence" of energy borrowed from physics, and

[7] *Contributions to Analytical Psychology*, pp. 45, 46.

adapted to mean that a given quantity of psychic energy may be transformed from one psychic content to another while maintaining the same energic intensity.

In applying this theory to society, Jung points to the example of the steam engine, in which we see the "conversion of heat into the pressure of steam, and then into the energy of motion." "Similarly," he says, "the energy of certain psychological phenomena is transformed by suitable means into other dynamisms." [8] He goes on to say that the entire life process as we observe it in nature is a "transformer of energy, life participating in some still unknown fashion in the transformation process. Life takes place through the fact that it makes use of natural physical and chemical conditions as a means to its existence. The living body is a machine that converts the amount of energy taken up into its equivalents in other dynamic manifestations. One cannot say that physical energy is converted into life, but only that the transformation is the expression of life." [9]

Jung draws his analogy along in three steps, following the process of energy conversion in modern machinery, in the human body, and in society. "The adaptations to physical and chemical conditions . . . have the value of machines that make other forms of transformation possible. Thus, for example, all the means employed by an animal for the safeguarding and furthering of his existence, not to speak of the direct nourishment of his body, can be regarded as machines that make use of natural potential in order to produce work. When the beaver fells trees and dams up the flow of water, this is an effort of work conditioned through his differentiation; and

[8] Ibid., p. 45.
[9] Ibid., p. 46.

this latter is a natural culture, which, like a machine, functions as a converter of energy. Similarly, human energy, as a natural product of differentiation, is a machine; first of all a technical one that uses natural conditions for the transformation of physical and chemical energy, but also a mental machine using mental conditions for the transformation of libido." [10]

The transformation of energy in society occurs on two levels: the physical or animal level, involving physical energy; and the psychic level, involving the "transposition of the libido." The latter process is the special function of human culture. It is a distinctive feature of the human race, and it sets off human culture as being basically different from all other means of energy transformation. Jung marvels at the subtlety of the culture mechanism, and he concludes that the very fact "that man should have discovered this machine" indicates that it must be "something rooted deep in his nature, in the very nature, indeed, of the living creature as such." [11]

In working out this analysis he postulates that the raw materials of society are basically the human energies, that is, physical energy and psychic energy. Ultimately both are derived from the instinctual urges of the human being, but the peculiar nature of psychic energy is that it involves something more than the biological. Jung derives it as a manifestation of the principle of opposites, holding that psychic energy could not develop beyond a very rudimentary stage were it not for a constant tension which arises within the psyche out of conditions inherent in social life. On the one hand, the impulsive drives of the animal nature of man press forward, seeking to be expressed without restraint; on the other hand, the preser-

[10] Ibid., p. 46.
[11] Ibid., p. 46.

vation of the group requires that these forces be held back, or at least that they be allowed to come forth only according to a socially acceptable pattern. The result is conflicting pressures in the psyche: biological pressures driving upwards, social rules pressing them down; and it is within this conflict that psychic energy is generated. Jung takes a basically Freudian position and adapts it for his own context when he says, "The collision between infantile instinctiveness and the ethical order can never be avoided. It is . . . the *sine qua non* of psychic energy." [12]

A highly significant corollary may be drawn from this. Since it is the pressure of society that converts physical to psychic energy, it follows that if the conditions of man's life were not social, psychic energy would not be brought forth. The fact of living in groups is a necessary prerequisite for the emergence of psychic energy, and it is just this type of energy that characterizes the human being. The line of thought goes further to point out that, since man is by nature a social being, the development of psychic energy is inherent in the human species. Psychic energy and society go together as complementary aspects of a single thing. Jung interprets them as two sides of the basic psychic process which involves the functioning of the individual in society. It leads him to his theory of social symbols as the link between the personality and the group, which we shall discuss in detail presently. Jung's underlying postulates on this question are that the individual psyche is an essentially social phenomenon; and also the converse that the symbol structures of society are expressed *via* individuals.

[12] Ibid., p. 64.

SYMBOLS IN SOCIETY

In relating energy to society, Jung points out that while the tension which arises in the psyche creates psychic energy, it has, at first, no direction in which to express itself. It is energy with no place to go. *It is energy, too, that is not immediately drawn into life because it is in excess of what is physically necessary for survival.* The development of culture, Jung says, has been possible only because "man possesses a relative superfluity of energy which is capable of application over and above the merely natural flow." [13] The question is then how this excess energy is channelized into society, and how it is focused into particular fields of activity. It is once again the question of the "transformation of the libido," meaning in this case, the transformation of psychic energy into cultural phenomena.

Jung's thinking on this issue begins in a deceptively simple way. "The psychological machine which transforms energy," he says, "is the symbol," [14] and as he uses it here, the term "symbol" has a relatively uncomplicated meaning. It is defined functionally in terms of the role that it plays in drawing the individual into the social process. It has also, however, a more specifically psychological meaning at other points in Jung's thought, where it relates to the psychic processes. In his discussion of social change, it takes on an historical meaning; and, in still other areas, where it is a question of man's experiencing his relation to the cosmos, the term "symbol" carries with it unmistakable philosophic overtones. To a large degree,

[13] Ibid., p. 53.
[14] Ibid., p. 50.

the various aspects under which Jung discusses the meaning of "symbol" correspond to the several levels on which he analyzes the psyche as a socio-historical phenomenon. For this reason, in working out the different sides of his definition of "symbol," we can gradually piece together Jung's conception of the total cognitive process as it takes place in society.

The point from which the analysis begins is the observation that, while symbol formation is a process inherent in the nature of the psyche, it emerges as a psychological phenomenon only after the primary life needs have been satisfied. Jung's view is that the human organism takes care of the rudimentary requirements of existence on a level that is prior to psychology, and that it is natively equipped with more energy than it needs for physiological purposes alone. It is this remainder of the over-supply of energy that is available to bring the individual into contact with society, and finally results in the emergence of "psychic energy." "Symbols," Jung says, "are the manifestation and expression of the excess libido. At the same time they are transitions to new activities, which must be specifically characterized as cultural activities in contrast to the instinctive functions that run their course according to natural law." [15]

This is the point which we referred to previously in stating Jung's basic formulation that the emergence of psychic energy and the social nature of human life are complementary phases of the same phenomenon. They are, so to say, opposite sides of the same coin. Both are possible only on a basis of biological energy, but they function one step above the physiological level. On the one hand, psychic energy develops through the tension between instinctual energy and society; on the other

[15] Ibid., p. 53.

hand, society functions in terms of, and by means of, psychic energy. The two belong together, and the link between them is the symbol.

SYMBOLS AS ANALOGUES

On this level, the symbol is to be understood in terms of its function as the vehicle by which psychic energy moves from its origin in instinctual energy to some cultural activity. In the tension that is set up within the psyche by the conflict between biological energy and society, the symbol is the means by which it becomes possible for quantities of libido to pass through and find expression in life. What can then be expressed is not actually psychic energy, however, but specific sums of energy carried in the form of some image or figure that is experienced strongly. Jung refers to this phase of the symbol as the "libido analogue," by which, he says, "I define a representation that is suited to express the libido equivalent, by virtue of which the libido is led over into a form different from the original one." [16] The "analogue" is then the symbol in its specifically functional aspect, in which it serves as a transformer of energy.

THE SOCIAL EXPRESSIONS OF ARCHETYPES

What are the qualities of the analogue? Of what kind of psychic materials does it consist, and what is the source of its contents? In raising these questions, we are led from the functional side of the symbol to its psychological aspect, and specifically to the types of symbols that are able to function as "analogues."

[16] Ibid., p. 54.

JUNG'S DEFINITION OF SYMBOL

To answer this, we have first to understand why, in his definition of "symbol," Jung goes to such pains to exclude the function of communication. What he means by "symbol" covers something altogether different from the function performed by language in any of its forms. A particular five-letter word, for example, "chair," may be taken as a symbol of a particular wooden object; or a given Greek letter may be used as a symbol for an abstract mathematical formula; or a certain flag may stand for a particular country. Regardless of the strength or extent of the connotations that may be attached to such "symbols," they all denote something definite. Each of them refers to something that is ascertained in advance, and the purpose of the symbol is to *convey* a meaning that is already known. Jung holds that what is involved in such a situation is not a "symbol"—according to his definition—but only a "sign." It serves only a "semiotic" function when a word or figure is used as an "analogous or abbreviated expression of a known thing." [17] That is to say, when a definite *known* object is taken as a point of reference, the "symbol" for it is really only a "sign" by which it is designated and therefore specifically limited in its meaning. When, however, a figure or object is used to refer to a "relatively unknown thing," its function is not semiotic but *"symbolic."* [18] Very often a single object serves as both a sign and a symbol, under different circumstances. Jung describes an instance of this in the case of the Cross in Christianity. "The *explanation* of the Cross as a symbol of Divine Love," he says, "is *semiotic,* since

[17] *Psychological Types,* p. 601.
[18] Ibid., pp. 601, 602.

Divine Love describes the fact to be expressed better and more aptly than a cross, which can have many other meanings. Whereas the interpretation of the Cross is symbolic, which puts it above all imaginable explanations, regarding it as an expression of an unknown and yet incomprehensible fact of a mystical or transcendent, i.e., psychological character, which simply finds its most striking and appropriate character in the Cross." [19]

In Jung's first example above, the conception of "Divine Love" is understood as the symbol, whereas the Cross serves merely as a sign for it, that is to say, as a means of communicating the symbol. In his second example, the Cross is the symbol because it is experienced as the point of contact with an illimitable reality. The characteristic of the symbol is that it opens up beyond itself, touching in the form of a representation something that the understanding does not fully encompass, but into which it wishes to reach. The symbol, taken in this sense, therefore, cannot be a means of communication, since it does not refer to any specifically known thing. It is a direct, continuing experience of something real, which is yet indefinable for Man, and in itself is in need of signs in order that its presence may be communicated.

The symbol, as Jung defines it, does not come from the world of outer experience. It is expressed in society, but it does not develop out of social intercourse. In taking this view, Jung has a position that is directly contrary to the mainstream of Sociology as it has developed in the traditions of Neo-Kantianism, Positivism, and American Pragmatism. Actually, the very nature of Jung's conception eliminates the possibility that symbols can come through the senses or

[19] Ibid., p. 602.

through intellectual thought. They emerge through the autonomous processes of symbol formation in the psyche, and they are therefore prior to sensory experience. Developing out of the dynamics of the depth of the unconscious, they are intuitive representations, autonomous glimpses into phases of reality that are not otherwise known. According to Jung's view, the symbol that emerges from the unconscious and is truly effective for the individual is "a living thing" for him. It provides a way for the individual to see and to understand the outer world in a way that would not be possible for him without his particular symbol. It is "pregnant with meaning," illuminating the world for the individual with a light that he cannot find in other symbols. Having this special quality, the symbol is "alive"; but should it cease to be the source of new meanings and new inspirations, it becomes a "dead" symbol. Then, as Jung remarks, "it possesses only an historical significance." [20]

The interesting point is that it is not within the individual's power—nor the society's for that matter—to make a "dead" symbol come "alive" again. A symbol derives its living quality from its emergence out of the psyche. It must "come" to the individual. It cannot be deliberately and consciously developed, nor can it be intellectualy worked out and rationally believed in. If one attempts to work out a symbol in an intellectual way, the reasoning must be in terms of specific and *known* pieces of experience, and therefore "semiotic." Efforts to construct a symbol are impossible by definition because they have to work with materials on the external level of experience, and not with the inner, autonomous forces of the psyche. The gap cannot be bridged, Jung says, because "an expression that stands for a *known* thing always remains merely a sign, and is never a symbol." That is to say, it can never become a symbol. "It is quite impossible to make a living symbol, i.e., one that is pregnant with meaning from known associations, for what is thus manufactured never contains more than was put into it." [21]

The heart of Jung's conception of the symbol is that it is a *spontaneous formation* out of the unconscious and that it comes forth "pregnant with meaning" as long as it is a "living reality" for the psyche. In this sense, the symbol is a general frame of reference for consciousness, and individual aspects of the symbol supply the contents for the basic attitudes. From the functional point of view, the symbol is primarily a "transformer of energy," and this means that libido coming up from the unconscious is expressed in social events *via* conscious attitudes. The channelizing effect of the symbol is therefore accomplished by means of consciousness. The "attitude of consciousness" taken toward the symbol has an important effect on the "libido analogue." If the symbol is joined with the ego so that it becomes the center of consciousness, and if it is experienced inwardly with an intimate sense of personal identification, it becomes the focus for the major energies of the individual. On the other hand, if the individual does not take up the symbol from within, if it does not come to him "naturally," but if he comes to it merely through the external signs and figures by which it is communicated in society, it does not really function as a symbol for him. "Signs" that are taken from the outside and made the center of conscious attitudes can have a lasting effect only if they make contact with some element in the individual's unconscious

[21] Ibid., pp. 602, 603.

and thereby put a foundation underneath their position in consciousness.

All this is another way of saying that the libido analogue can function well in consciousness only if it rests upon a psychic content with a strong position in the unconscious. The reason Jung can make the absolute statement, that "symbols are never thought out consciously," is that *by definition* symbols come from the unconscious. What is created by consciousness must be drawn from outer experience, and therefore cannot be a real symbol in the sense of being deeply placed in the psyche, or of being able to act as a transformer of energy in more than a tentative way. The nature of a real symbol is that it is a product of the unconscious and that it comes into consciousness not by reason, but by the direct force of a "revelation or intuition." Jung remarks that "judging from the close relation of the mythological symbol to the dream symbol. . . . it is more than probable that the greater part of the historical symbols arise directly from dreams, or at least are inspired by them." [22] We have to understand that when Jung speaks in these terms he is not necessarily referring to dreams as such, but rather to the general fact of a pre-conscious psychic content arising out of the very lowest levels of the psyche. He thinks of mythology as the dream of the race, and correspondingly of dreams as expressions of mythological material. In this sense, while the libido analogue may carry the kind of symbol that occurs in dreams, it is also necessary that it be a symbol that comes out of the depth levels of the psyche. This means that it can come only from the kind of dream that has a more than personal content. We recall the distinction made by the members of the

[22] *Contributions to Analytical Psychology*, pp. 54, 55.

Elgonyi tribe between "big dreams" and "little dreams." The "little" dreams had purely personal connotations, and the tribesmen felt that they were of interest only to themselves; but the "big" dreams left them with a sense that something more than their personal experiences was involved, something of either social or cosmic significance (and often both), and so they told the dream in the company of the whole tribe, where all could share it. The libido analogue has to come from the same level as that at which the mythological symbols are formed. It is particularly necessary that it come from the collective level because the analogue has to be able to function for large groups of people. If it came from the Personal Unconscious, it would have meaning for some and not for others. Only by the fact that it comes from the collective, supra-personal, layer of the unconscious is it able to function as a transformer of the psychic energies of large historical groups consistently and over long periods of time. The libido analogue operates best when it is composed of objective psychic material and consequently, analogues tend to be manifestations of archetypal symbols in historical forms.

LIBIDO ANALOGUES IN HISTORY

In one sense the analogue is the history-making function of the psyche. It takes up the symbol that is "alive" in the depths of the psyche and adapts it to the cultural time and place in which the human being lives. From another point of view, however, it is the universalizing function because, while it provides a means of energy transformation in a given historical situation, it does so in terms of psychological contents that are generic to the race. In his later writing, Jung referred to these universal elements as "motifs," meaning the archetypal core of the varying symbols that recur throughout history. The "motifs" express basic phases of the process of individuation; therefore, their significance is closely related to the integration of the personality and to the emergence of the Self. At this point, since we have already discussed the archetype within the general structure of Jung's psychological system, we can take the issue a step or two further and inquire into the historical and ontological aspects of the motif.

What is it that gives a motif its universal quality? We can say that it is simply because the nature of the human being is everywhere the same, and the motif is an expression of human nature; but we should have a more specific answer. Approaching from another direction, we can say that the biological structure of man is always the same, and that the motif expresses something biological in man. Jung would answer that this points toward the truth, but that it is not yet the whole truth. The motif is, after all, a psychological phenomenon, and it cannot be comprehended merely in terms of its biological roots. Nevertheless, the motif is an expression of a psychic process, and every psychic process is somehow related to the fact that the human being has a body. Psychic factors emerge out of a physiological context. Jung begins with this point, but as we follow his thought through, we realize that he is not thinking in terms of an interrelationship between the physical and the psychological, and not of a parallelism either. When we go one step back beyond psychology, and when we go one step back beyond biology, we reach a point at which they are not differentiated from each other and at which neither biologic nor psychologic characteristics can be specifically discriminated. We come to a third category which is neither biological nor psychological, but in which the rudiments of each are contained.

THE SOURCE OF THE MOTIF

To define this third category is extremely difficult because it is somewhere out of reach of intellectual formulations. It does, however, correspond to a specific phase of reality. If we think of Jung's conception of the psyche as a kind of infinite area within man, a spaceless space, and if we follow it down to the lower layers where it is less and less differentiated, it gradually fuses into something that cannot really be defined as psychological. Down at this "depth," as Jung remarks, "the uniqueness of the psyche is a magnitude that can never be made wholly real; it can be realized only approximately," though it is always "the absolute basis of all consciousness." [28] Here, where it is very far from consciousness, the psyche has a quality that consciousness cannot readily comprehend. The "autonomous functional systems" operate at this level without any restriction or guidance at all. At the opposite of consciousness, they just happen of themselves. They function "naturally," as cosmic forces function in the world of nature, and they are lost, as Jung says, "in the body of materiality." Now the point is that the concept of "materiality" does not really express this most underlying category that Jung has in mind. What is "material" or "physiological" is only a part of it, just as what is "psychological" is only a part of it. It is deeper, more autonomous, more spontaneous, more brutish even than "brute matter." It is more primal, more archaic, more primordial still than materiality. As far back as matter

[28] *Essays on a Science of Mythology*, p. 127.

goes, it is one step further. It is of the cosmos itself, deeper down, hidden at the center of the very nature of Nature herself. When, therefore, at this level, the primal, cosmic element in man begins to differentiate itself, it breaks into biological and psychological aspects. Despite this, no matter how finely it is differentiated, the specific manifestations retain some degree of the primal quality. In its most fundamental essence, "the psyche is simply 'world.'" It carries the cosmos implicit in it. "In this sense," Jung says, "I hold Kerényi to be absolutely right when he says that in the symbol the *world itself* is speaking." [24]

We can now see how the several aspects of Jung's interpretation of the symbol express his underlying conception of the largeness and essential unity of the cognitive process. First, in its *psychological* aspect, symbols appear as natural products of psychic processes and emerge from the unconscious into conscious attitudes. Secondly, in its *social* aspect, which is also the functional side of the symbol, it channelizes the energies of the individual out into the activities of the group. Thirdly, in its *historical* aspect, the symbol comes forth in various and changing forms according to factors of time and culture. And fourthly, Jung comes to what must be called the ontological aspect of the symbol in the sense that here the symbol is understood as the means by which Man articulates, unbeknown to himself, the mode of primal being which it is his nature to manifest.

It must be understood, of course, that all four aspects belong together as parts of a single, unitary conception. As the symbol is the expression of the primordial quality of man, it

*Ibid., p. 127.

constitutes at the same time an intuition of itself. That is to say, at the most archaic levels of the cosmos, where the psyche is not yet differentiated, the symbol begins dimly to emerge as a concomitant of the "autonomous functioning systems." As these systems become more clearly differentiated into psychic processes, the symbol is also more individualized and tends to become a clearer expression of the autonomous psychic process to which it corresponds. As it moves upward into consciousness, it carries these vestiges of the archaic, and it dresses them with cultural overlays taken from the immediate environment. Now the symbol becomes social, and it takes on the cohering function of holding large groups together in the midst of historical change. Through all its variations, however, and through all the elaborations added upon it, the symbol retains the qualities of the psychic process which it expresses, and as it comes to consciousness, it retains the dim intuition that some ancient meaning is imbedded in itself. This is why the symbols that come out of the depth of the unconscious can be experienced with such great intensity. It is not only that by expressing the archetypal psychic processes they touch the intimate parts of the individual's inner life; but also that, by such symbols, the individual participates in something that is borne in upon him as a primal contact with reality. To say that this is more than psychological means that the individual has touched something that is cosmic, touched it within himself, and that there it has come "alive." The reason that such mythological motifs may be experienced with the greatest psychological intensity is that they are a link between the individual and the universe.

THE CHILD MOTIF

The figure of the "Child" is one of the most interesting examples of an archetypal motif. On several occasions Jung has felt impelled to work out detailed analyses of the "phenomenology of the child-archetype," as he calls it, because myths based on the "child-hero" tend to include all the main aspects of the process of individuation. It is an archetype that is expressed in many symbolic representations. Often the child is born among many hardships and dangers. The mother who has borne him dies at his birth, or else she has to leave him or give him away. In several cases the "child-hero" is left to be fished out of the waters and there to be taken care of by animals or by strangers. If the birth goes well and the parents remain with the infant, his well-being is sure to be threatened by some unfriendly influences, as the Christ-Child had to be taken into hiding by Joseph and Mary.

The child coming forth as new life out of the darkness is a particularly apt representation both for the regression of libido energy, and for the emergence of the Self in the process of individuation. The first phase, the regression phase, in which the life energies descend into the unconscious, is expressed by entry into the womb, the womb of the mother, or the womb of Mother Nature. None of these symbols, however, should be interpreted as referring specifically to physical organs. If they were, they would lose their character as symbols, since they would be functioning only as "signs" for particular known objects. Jung refers at one point to a ceremonial performed by the Watschandies tribe in which the primitives dig a hole in the earth, "surround it with bushes so that it suggests the female genitals," and in the course of an erotic dance, during which they are forbidden to look at a woman, they plunge their hunting spears into the opening. Jung's point is that to interpret the hole in the earth simply as referring to the female organs would be "to interpret the symbol semiotically" and would deprive it of its meaning. On one level, the semiotic interpretation is likely to be correct, however; that is, up to the point where it indicates what the hole and the spear correspond to. Only when the semiotic interpretation is taken as the whole meaning does it obscure the issue, because then it is impossible to see the ceremonial as an effort to fructify the earth by simulating a cosmic process. Similarly, in religious mythology, the portrayal of the birth of the child-hero refers to the biological process on the *semiotic level;* but representations like the Divine-Mother, the womb of a virgin, and so on, have a symbolical significance that opens into a much wider area of meaning.

The second phase of the child symbol which brings out the special meaning of the emergence of the Self is indicated by the fact that the symbol of the child tends to have a "numinous" character. That is to say, the child-archetype carries with it a sense of divinity, a special saving quality, which shows that it is a motif very deeply imbedded in the psyche. "The symbol of the child," Jung says, "fascinates and grips the conscious mind," [25] and thereby is enabled to set loose an intensity of psychic energy strong enough to dissolve a psychological conflict. The "redemptive" quality of the child-archetype consists in the fact that it is able to move up from the unconscious with a force that breaks through the conflict-

[25] Ibid., p. 121.

ing opposites and can even establish a new situation in the psyche. This new condition, a new state of consciousness, is symbolized by a rebirth of the person and may be experienced in terms of a new-born divine child emerging from the darkness of the womb and from other dangers in order to begin a life of extraordinary power. Jung points out "the paradox that in all child-myths is that the 'child' is, on the one hand, delivered helpless into the power of terrible enemies and in continual danger of extinction," while, on the other hand, he is altogether invincible.[26] The processes of libido regression and rebirth are vividly portrayed in such symbols. "The 'child' is born out of the womb of the unconscious," Jung says, "begotten out of the depths of human nature, or rather out of Living Nature herself. It is a personification of vital forces quite outside the limited range of our conscious mind; of possible ways and means of which our one-sided conscious mind knows nothing; a wholeness which embraces the very depth of Nature. It represents the strongest, most ineluctable urge in every human being, namely, the urge to realize itself."[27]

Jung's underlying point is that the reason the child-hero is found universally as a motif in mythology and religion is that it represents an archetypal psychic process. This means that, one way or another, it is psychologically necessary for every individual to go through the experience indicated in the saying, "Except ye become as little children. . . ." because the experience of rebirth is an inherent part of the individuation process. If the personality can make that a reality in its own life, it does not need the symbol; but since

[26] Ibid., p. 123.
[27] Ibid., pp. 123, 124.

most people cannot actually live it within themselves, they turn to a "mythological projection." The child-archetype and the psychic process which it represents are then experienced indirectly—not in lived life, so to say, but in a lived symbol; and because it comes only through a representation, it "requires religious repetition and renewal by ritual." [28] Ceremonials and rituals are the means provided by society for periodically drawing up the sums of energy attached to symbols, lest the symbols sink back into the unconscious. In this way, psychic contents that would tend to become weak and ineffectual if left to themselves are reactivated, and their libido is channelized into social purposes.

THE FUNCTIONING OF SYMBOLS IN HISTORY

We have the further question of how libido analogues change in history. On the surface, it would seem to involve mainly a change in the symbols that serve as "transformers" of psychic energy. The nature of the symbol, however, is that it comes from within the psyche. New symbols cannot be brought in from the outside, but can come into consciousness only by being drawn out of the deeper levels of the unconscious. The significance, then, of the individual's contacts with society and of the pressures society exerts on him is not that they create, but rather that they activate symbols already present, though latent, in the psyche. What is present in the psyche is not the particular historical form of the symbol, however, but rather its archetypal motif; that is to say, it is present in potentiality in the psyche just through the fact that it is the expression of a psychic process. When an archetypal motif is activated by experience in the social

---

[28] Ibid., p. 121.

world, it is filled in with the contents present in the society. The form that the libido analogue takes in any given culture, then, is the bridge between the universal and the historical; it is the point at which the archetype becomes particularized into its social manifestations. In terms of his general theory of levels, Jung maintains that the symbol active as an analogue is on the level closest to consciousness. It is the one that serves as the basis for the conscious attitudes out of which the Persona is formed. The analogues that previously were in consciousness but have dropped from use go down below, at first only as far as the upper layers of the unconscious. The longer they remain in disuse, the further down they drop into the deeper historical recesses of the psyche. Jung maintains the general point that those symbols that have been strongly in the consciousness of a people are not altogether lost when they cease to maintain their position in consciousness. He holds that they remain in the unconscious as latent memories and also as potentialities more specific in form than the mere archetypal motif. Over the ages, as each people expresses its basic psychic processes in terms of the symbols that emerge out of its particular historical experience, it tends to accumulate a characteristic set of symbols in its unconscious. These may not be apparent immediately on the surface of consciousness, but they are present in the lower reaches of the psyche and they assert themselves when an appropriate psychological stimulation appears.

The basic conception of historical layers of symbols contained and accumulated within the psyche of a people has many applications in the interpretation of cultural history. How does it happen, for example, that we find essentially similar cultural beliefs in widely separated nations, where culture contact seems highly unlikely? Jung does not give much importance to the old "borrowing" theory of cultural exchange, and he rejects the equally dated idea that culture has been diffused from a single original "cradle of civilization." He takes the position, rather, that the basic symbols arise spontaneously out of the nature of the psyche itself, and that the underlying sameness of mythological symbols expresses the fact that they are derived from archetypal motifs. Such a view, however, does not come specifically to the question of how some cultural materials are extended from one people to another at particular times in their histories. Actually, the crucial question is not only why a particular symbol was accepted, but why it was rejected at a particular time, or why it was accepted at one point and later discarded or radically altered.

Jung has a rather general, but fertile concept with which to approach this question. He says that when a new symbol is brought into the life history of a people, it may be adopted as a result of momentary contingencies, but the question of whether it will last depends on whether there exists in the unconscious of that people some historical experiences which dispose it to accept such symbols and to find them meaningful within the preconscious areas of the psyche. In other words, the acceptance or rejection of new libido analogues depends on whether there is a *"psychic readiness"* for them. If there is not this "readiness," they will not be able to function, the psychic energies will not be able to flow freely through them, and in time they will either disappear through disuse, or they will be modified in order to admit psychic elements which are more in conformity with the historical layers of the psyche. A main point is that this "psy-

chic readiness" does not depend on the surface of consciousness, and it cannot be maintained by the deliberate exercise
of intellectuality. It cannot be made to last if it does not fit
the historical archetypes which are held as dormant potentialities in the lower levels of the unconscious. An individual
or a group may be able for a limited period of time to build
and maintain a conscious attitude that has no relation to
the underlying historical symbols; but Jung's judgment is
that such a situation is always precarious and that as soon as
the conscious attitude breaks down under any external stress,
the images that are more deeply rooted in the unconscious
will upset the power of the ego and will take control of consciousness.

The history of Christianity in Northern Europe offers an
interesting and suggestive instance of such a situation. Here,
a religious myth whose source was in a Semitic nation
was subsequently developed by a Mediterranean people, and
finally superimposed on the quite alien mythologies of the
North Europeans at a barbarian point in their history. From
the point of view of an historical conception of the psyche, it
would seem self-evident that the resulting psychological conditions would have to be unstable—as they certainly have
been. Jung carries the point even further and holds that the
constant unsteadiness of Christianity in Europe, its wars and
schisms, the frequent adaptation of Christian ritual to pagan
symbolism, and the overpowering upsurge of the "anti-
Christian" ideologies of modern times, are the psycho-
historical consequences of imposing on a people a set of symbols which did not conform with the historical tendencies of
its unconscious. It is not only recently, but for several centuries that the European man has been "divided against him-

self." When Jung approaches the psychological problem of the Western man, therefore, he sets it in the context of historically discordant symbols—the pre-Christian paganism, the Graeco-Hebrew religiosity, the militant Protestant intensity —and finds in the resulting tension a source of the inner turbulence that has come to the surface in recent years.

THE STABILITY OF CONSCIOUS ATTITUDES

In general, Jung's view is that as long as the conscious attitude is strongly held, it will be able to keep the autonomous forces of the unconscious in control. Only when there is a weakness in consciousness can the contents of the unconscious move up to the surface. On this basis, Jung seems to have been correct in his prediction that, "as the Christian idea begins to pale, we may anticipate a corresponding renewal of individual symbol formation." [29] His point is that, inasmuch as Christianity has been providing Western civilization with its main social symbols, when these cease to function as transformers of energy, there must be a corresponding weakening in the dominant conscious attitudes. As the symbols which Christianity has provided serve less and less effectively to channelize the individual's energies into life, these energies must regress within the individual and in their downward movement activate the deeper layers of the unconscious. New figures must then be brought to the surface of the psyche, since fantasy formation, including dreams, becomes increasingly active and frequent. On one level, this means that when the social symbols lose their power, the individual is turned back into himself; and, on another level, when the dominant attitudes break up for any reason, unas-

[29] *Contributions to Analytical Psychology*, p. 55.

similated material is brought to the surface from the unconscious. A weakening, then, in the social bases of consciousness
has the effect of turning the libido back into the psyche,
where it reactivates dormant historical symbols.

At the close of World War I, Jung came upon a very significant instance of this condition. "As early as 1918," he writes,
"I noted peculiar disturbances in the unconscious of my German patients which could not be ascribed to their personal
psychology." [30] He found that symbol formations were being
brought to the surface from a level deeper than the Personal
Unconscious. In terms of his theoretical framework, Jung
then concluded that the psychic energies of these Germans
were in marked regression as a result of a strain on their conscious attitudes. From the nature of the symbols which were
brought to the surface, he judged further that the libido
movement in these individuals had gone below the level of
Christian symbols to earlier historical layers of Germanic
mythological figures. Consequently, the old German god,
Wotan, was brought to the surface out of the pre-Christian
past, and he came surrounded by "mythological symbols
which expressed primitivity, violence, cruelty, in short, all
the powers of darkness." [31] The collapse of conscious attitudes, then, resulted in an increase in individual fantasy formation drawn from the lower historical levels of the psyche,
and finally reached a point where these figures were drawn
together into a mass movement embodying the pagan fury
which the figures had expressed.

On the one hand, a break-up in the dominant conscious at-

---

[30] C. G. Jung, *Essays on Contemporary Events*, Kegan Paul, London,
1947, p. X.
[31] Ibid, p. XI.

titude can result in an upsurge from the unconscious. On the other hand, a situation in which certain attitudes are too specifically fixed in consciousness may result in an equally dangerous situation, but from an opposite point of view. Jung holds that when a culture becomes too highly rational-ized, or when it becomes too thoroughly devoted to its con-ventional forms, its individuals are not able to experience the natural flow of unconscious materials. By following the precepts of ritual or propriety too closely, they focus their psyches toward the surface of consciousness so that the un-conscious is not able to be expressed. What results is a condi-tion in the psyche in which the upper and lower layers have no point of contact. The individual loses touch with the ac-tive forces in the unconscious and has to place his faith in the "conventions," which, in Jung's phrase, "are soulless mechanisms that can never do more than grasp the routine of life." The psychological situation becomes over-balanced in this condition, leaning too far over toward consciousness. Psychic energy then accumulates in the unconscious, since it cannot come to the surface, and it finally bursts loose in un-controllable upsurges without reference to consciousness. As the principle of opposites thus asserts itself, "it comes about that, when the mere routine of life in the form of traditional conventions predominates, a destructive outbreak of the cre-ative forces (i.e., the archetypes) must follow." [32]

The over-stress on conventions may act as a decoy. It gives the individual an easy means of making his decisions so that he does not have to rely on himself. "The mechanisms of convention," Jung says, "keep people unconscious, and then, like some wild game, they can follow their customary run-

[32] *The Integration of the Personality*, p. 195.

ways"—and not need to bother making up their minds. They are freed from the necessity of making conscious decisions, and this very convenience, this ease with which routine can be substituted for deliberated action, is the greatest psychological danger of all. "When new conditions not provided for by the old conventions arise, panic seizes the human being who was held unconscious by routine, much as it seizes an animal, and with equally upredictable results." [33]

In the case of a break-up in the conscious attitude, contents come to the surface from the unconscious simply because consciousness can no longer hold up its part of the tension maintaining it in a "reciprocal relativity" with the unconscious. Unconscious materials then come up through the fissure in consciousness. In the other type of situation, however, where consciousness is excessively strong and in which the unconscious cannot really express itself at all, psychic energies pile up in the lower areas of the psyche until they accumulate to a point where they can no longer be contained. They then become an uncontrollable element in the psyche, activating deeply buried symbols and surging into consciousness with them. Consciousness is taken over by an unassimilated content which, having constellated other contents with tremendous energy around it, has gone wild in the psyche. When this occurs in a single individual, it is manifested as a psychosis because it disorients his conscious attitude and takes him out of the context of his social world. When it occurs in many individuals, however, it may become a "movement" with a tremendous driving force. The lunatic is an individual who has been more or less overcome by the unconscious; but "the same condition may exist to a less degree

[33] Ibid., p. 195.

in the case of a person whom we cannot characterize as lunatic. We have then to deal with a man who is only partially
overcome by the unconscious. . . . On such occasions strange
ideas may seize otherwise sound individuals. Groups and societies, even whole peoples, may have seizures of a similar
kind; they are mental epidemics. In such a case only malevo-
lent critics speak of a psychosis, while others speak of an
'ism.' The ordinary lunatic is generally a harmless, isolated
case, and since everyone sees that something is wrong with
him, he is quickly taken care of. But the unconscious infec-
tions of groups of so-called normal people are more subtle
and far more dangerous." [84]

POSSESSIONS IN HISTORY

The important point in this type of analysis is not to put a
psychiatric label on a social movement—which would be a
purpose alien to Jung's basic approach—but rather to stress
that large groups as well as individuals are subject to "possessions" which "derive from the autonomy of unconscious
processes." The symbols which serve as the centrum for these
"autonomous partial systems" come out of the historical layers of the psyche, and this is why newly arising social movements tend to be based on seemingly forgotten historical
symbols. In the reactivation of the Wotan symbols which
Jung discovered in his analysis of his German patients after
World War I, there was an indication of the kind of symbols
which were moving into German consciousness. While they
came from the depths of the historical unconscious, taking
over the psyches of individuals, they did the same on a mass
scale in the Nazi movement. "When such symbols occur in a

[84] Ibid., pp. 8, 9.

large number of individuals," Jung says, "and are not understood, they begin to draw these individuals together as if by
magnetic force, and thus a mob is formed; and its leader will
soon be found in the individual who has the least resistance,
the least sense of responsibility, and because of his inferior-
ity, the greatest will to power. He will thus let loose everything which is ready to break forth, and the mob will follow
with the irresistible force of an avalanche." [35]

The term "demonic" is particularly apt for describing the
irrational force with which these autonomous complexes take
over the psyche. They shoot up into consciousness without
regard for previous conscious attitudes, and Jung's contention is that the modern man is particularly susceptible to
such "possessions" just because his psyche is over-developed
on the side of consciousness. The classic example of "demons"
arising in the modern psychological situation is German Nazism, where a country in the forefront of the rationalistic attitude toward life was taken over from behind by archaic
images which sprang up, like demons, to overwhelm consciousness. In general, Jung says—and this is partly to belie
the charge of his sympathy for Nazism—"It is—and always
was—my opinion that the political mass movements of our
time are psychic epidemics, i.e., mass psychoses." [36] On the
one hand, the demons come into consciousness as the bearers
of a mental sickness; on the other hand, they are expressions
of the underlying continuity in psychological life. They always involve the reactivation of archaic images latently present in the unconscious in the form which they took in past
historical eras, as were the Wotan symbols of the pre-

[35] *Essays on Contemporary Events*, p. XI.
[36] Ibid., p. 79.

Christian Germanic mythology. On this basis, when an attitude is breaking up within the consciousness of some historical period, or when, for any reason, independent contents from the unconscious are moving up to the surface, we can know that the arbitrariness with which they impinge on consciousness will be determined by the nature of the historical symbols out of which they emerge. The demons, then, are manifestations of the psychic forces which bind history together since they come out of the historical side of the psyche. While the attitudes in consciousness may vary according to the environmental situation, the historical symbols in the psyche constitute an inner continuity for a people's history, since they hold as a source of supply the mythological figures which will ultimately move into consciousness either as demons or as settled psychological conditions.

In one sense, the demons are arbitrary usurpations of consciousness by unconscious segments; but, in a more basic sense, they are in a very close relation to religious phenomena. Actually, while a demon may come into consciousness as an autonomous complex unrelated to other areas of consciousness, it may in time become the centrum of a large enough constellation of psychic contents so that it will be established as a dominant condition in the psyche. This total process involving the transition from demon to stabilized psychic situation is really the basis on which Jung interprets religion as a psychological phenomenon in society. "Every religion," he says, "is a spontaneous expression of a certain predominant psychological condition." [*] That is to say, a religion begins in the form of an autonomous complex, a "partial system" which splits off from the unconscious and

[*] *Psychology and Religion,* p. 108.

first appears in consciousness in the unassimilated, independent form of a demon. These are the visions, the revelations, the direct religious experiences on which religions are founded. As they activate the corresponding archetypal symbols in other individuals, a movement arises which, over a period of time, becomes firmly established in consciousness both for the individual and for the society as a whole. At this point, religion serves the double function of binding together the psyche of the individual and also of drawing together the psychological life of the culture as a whole. Religion, then, is the stabilizing factor in historical change, and whatever may be the "predominant psychological condition" on which it is based, it can be a symbol only of archetypal quality, one that is deeply placed in the psyche, so that it is capable of transforming and channelizing, as an analogue, large quantities of libido.

ASPECTS OF RELIGION

The nature of religion, Jung says, is "essentially symbolic." If we keep in mind the particular definition of symbol which he uses and the way he applies it as a spontaneous formation out of the psyche, we realize that the whole interpretation of the nature of the symbol which we described above constitutes essentially a phenomenology of the religious process.[88] Religion expresses itself on all the levels on which Jung described the various aspects of the symbol. It is psychological in the sense that it expresses the inner processes of the psyche; it is social in the sense that it maintains the interrelation of individuals and the group in terms of shared values and beliefs; it is historical in the sense of maintaining

[88] See p. 150.

the continuity of a people in terms of a mythologic origin which gives a frame of reference to its present history. And, above all, and including all, religion is ontological in the sense that it provides a means by which individuals can experience some intuition of the ultimate meanings of life. In the discussion of the symbol on these levels, the point was made that a symbol must be "alive"; it must be "lived" if it is to function with its full force for the psyche. This means that it must be experienced at the lower levels of the psyche, and in terms that are more fundamental than rationality. Religious experience, since it contains the most basic elements of personal and social life, must take place prior to consciousness, and then, depending on the strength and authenticity with which the religious experience occurs, it can be established in particular conscious attitudes.

The relation of religion to consciousness is one of the foci for Jung's diagnosis of the modern psychological situation. He finds the historical roots of the problem in the attack which was made during the Enlightenment on the traditional views of Medieval Christianity. The question during that period was whether a religious belief can be conformable to "reason." To those who maintained the Catholic tradition, the articles of faith seemed self-evident; to those who adopted the methodology of "reason," faith seemed an altogether arbitrary concept. In Jung's view it was a situation that clearly exemplified his basic formulation that, since religious beliefs are expressions of historical archetypes, they are not understandable on the surface of the psyche unless they are first deeply experienced in the unconscious. To say that an individual has "faith" is to say, psychologically, that he can *live* his symbols, that they are *alive* within him; and to say that an individual is "sceptical" means that the symbols are no longer spontaneously active or alive within him. In these terms, individuals who can no longer "live" their archetypal symbols are bound to find them meaningless, and the fact that they hold their symbols up to the criteria of consciousness indicates that the symbols in themselves are no longer "pregnant with meaning" for them.

The most important area in which this change has taken place in the modern mind is in the expression of the archetype of God. From the point of view of the psyche, God is a symbol like other symbols, a phenomenological manifestation of an archetypal motif. It is different only to the extent that, of all motifs, it has the greatest energic force attached to it, and that the individual comes *via it* to his most direct encounters with the ultimate realities of life. It was, in Jung's words, "only through accepting the reality of the symbol that humanity came to its gods." [39] Every symbol, however, in so far as it is a "natural symbol" rooted in the very nature of the psyche, corresponds to some basic psychic process. The process on which the motif underlying the God-symbol is based is the movement of psychic energies. The symbol of God, in other words, corresponds to the life-process itself. It is an expression and an intuition of the presence of life in the individual and particularly of its manifestation in libidinal energy. Jung follows this hypothesis into detailed analyses of the meaning of the God-archetype in relation to mystical and cosmic experiences. However, these are not necessary for the present discussion, although they are exceedingly interesting. His basic point is that the symbol of God is the expression of life-energy in the psyche and therefore has

* *Psychological Types*, p. 157.

the greatest degree of energy attached to it. From an ontological point of view, it is through this symbol that the individual may experience his relation to the total life process;
and from the psychological point of view it is the symbol that
carries the largest sums of concentrated energy in the psyche.

Like other symbols, the God-archetype originates in the
unconscious and becomes the centrum of a constellation of
psychic contents. An "autonomous partial system" then develops and moves upward into consciousness, where it establishes its power by effecting a "possession" of consciousness.
It carries with it a dynamic of psychic energy which the individual is not always able to control; just the opposite happens in fact. Far from being able to dominate the complex,
the ego, expressing the conscious attitudes of the individual,
becomes dependent on it, and the individual is able to experience himself only through the constellation formed by
the attracting power of the symbol. The particular quality
of the God-archetype is that, because of its superior force, it
achieves the greatest momentum in the psyche and the largest measure of autonomy. It is therefore the symbol which,
more than any other, places the ego in a dependent relationship.

There arises, then, a most paradoxical situation in the
psyche. As the God-complex comes to consciousness, it carries
the greatest psychic force, and the individual interprets its
contents as though they were beliefs which he himself has
chosen consciously and freely. He willingly and wholeheart-
edly associates himself with them and enshrines them in his
conscious attitudes. "The ego is sucked into this focus of energy to such a degree that it becomes identified with it and
thinks that it wishes and needs nothing further. But in this

way there develops a craze, a monomania or possession, a most exaggerated one-sidedness which endangers the psychic equilibrium most seriously." [40] In the process of choosing what he thought was a conscious attitude, the individual becomes the slave of a complex of unconscious contents which have the power to act autonomously in his psyche. The "highest operative value"—whether it be a god in the heavens, a god of flesh and blood, or a god of dollar bills—then becomes a passion which the personality is no longer free to disobey. "A man believes he wills and chooses and does not notice that he is already possessed, that his greatest interest has become a master that has arrogated to himself the power." [41]

This contains the irony inherent in religious psychology— and in the psychology of every social situation in which a symbol is really "lived." While the symbol of God embodies the greatest power in the psyche, it is a power which the individual must also serve. Religious systems recognize the psychological necessity of this situation by saying, in various forms, that the individual must "give himself up to God," and they mean that he must give himself up to the autonomous complex of God. The most vigorous activities may then result because the individual's conscious life becomes a channel for the vast energy potential contained in the God-archetype. Great energy forces are then set free, but they may go in either of opposite directions; strong devotion to the God-complex may, in itself, result as easily in the conquering furies of a "holy war" as in the visions of the Prophets. It depends on the nature of the "god" that is being

[40] *Two Essays*, p. 74.
[41] Ibid., p. 75.

served. The same psychological phenomenon is expressed whenever God in any form is conceived as a supreme ruler whose "commands" the believer must obey. It is the autonomous complex constellated around the God-symbol that is the giver of these commands. It speaks not from the burning bush or from the mountain top, but—and no less legitimately —from the depths of the unconscious.

It is inherent in the nature of the autonomous complex that the individual is not aware of its separate existence, but identifies it with himself. Because he does this, he cannot realize that he is projecting the complex into the world and is imputing objective reality to phenomena that come from the archetypes of his own soul. In describing the vision of God as the manifestation of an autonomous complex, Jung does not intend, by any means, to impugn or to limit the truth which such "revelations" may bring. On the contrary, the whole spirit of his studies is committed to the view that the deepest insights into life come through the symbols of the unconscious, and he holds that this is particularly true of religious experiences which make contact with the archetypal layers of the psyche. The point to stress merely is that, when we speak of "god" in Jung's terms, we mean a symbol that emerges from the unconscious as an expression of the archetype of life-energy in the psyche, and that this symbol, constellating the greatest intensities of libido around it, takes "possession" of consciousness as an autonomous complex.

THE LIFE AND DEATH OF GODS

The "possession" may come in either of two forms. It may suddenly appear in consciousness as a demon unrelated to other conscious contents, in which case it will have an upsetting effect on the psyche; or, in its other form, it may be securely established as a psychological condition integrated into consciousness to the point where the ego identifies itself with it. In the latter situation, the God-complex is the focus around which other symbols gather, and from it comes the energic force with which they may be vitalized into a "lived religion." From Jung's point of view, everything depends on the position of the God-archetype, since it is the main supplier of energy, and no constellation of symbols can function as a religion in the psyche unless its particular symbol for God is "alive."

When such a condition does prevail in the psyche, and when it is experienced generally throughout a community, the "archetypal images," in the form provided by the particular symbol structure of the culture, seem "so significant that people never think of asking what they mean." They are simply assumed and lived in as the unquestioned and unquestionable realities of life. Then the God-archetype, expressed as an autonomous complex, maintains the pattern of beliefs which constitute the basis for the conscious attitudes of the individuals in the society. The God-archetype, expressing the most essential function of the symbol, holds the society together by cohering its values, and it integrates the psychological life of individuals by channelizing their highest energic force into a social system.

From an historical point of view, everything depends on how well the constellation of symbols continues to channelize the energies through its conscious attitudes. The stability of consciousness varies directly with the strength of the God-complex in the unconscious. If the constellation based on the God-image weakens, the position of consciousness also becomes uncertain. Jung points out that the gods can maintain their position only so long as they are experienced as having a "divine" background, which is to say, as long as their "commands" are felt to have a validity that is greater than merely human institutions. When this sense of divinity is lost, it means that the God-symbol can no longer be experienced in the unconscious with the same strength. The gods are still looked for in the outer world, but the symbol is no longer "alive" and the god can no longer be found. The miracle is prayed for, but it does not come to pass. Since the symbol is no longer effective in the unconscious, the god is no longer as "godlike" as he was, and he cannot perform his special favors in the daily world, as he was previously wont to do. A people that loses its god, or more properly, its ability to believe in and experience its god, has to live a disillusioned and precarious life without divine protection. "That the gods die from time to time," Jung says, "is due to man's discovery that. . . . they are good-for-nothings made by human hands."⁴² When a god dies, a void is left in the psyche of the people for whom the symbol was once alive, and there results then a painfully critical interval until a new god-symbol is awakened in the psyche.

Jung offers a very interesting hypothesis to explain what happens when the God-symbol ceases to function. The sum of energy that had previously been channelized through it is now set free in the psyche. Because the intensity of libido attached to the God-symbol is so great, Jung says, it is bearable only as long as it is harnessed to some particular social activity. When it is not under direct control, the momentum of its own power causes it to split off as an autonomous com-

⁴² *The Integration of the Personality*, p. 80.

plex, and it may ultimately result even in a dissociation of personality. Specifically, the energy is turned within, and the complex takes on the qualities that had previously been found in the god, so that the individual is subject to the delusion that a superhuman power belongs to his own person.

As an historical example of this condition, Jung points to the psychological situation of the Germans as it led to the "mass psychosis" of Nazism. "Did not Nietzsche prophesy that God was dead, and that the Superman would be heir to the divine inheritance; that fatal rope dancer and fool? It is an immutable psychological law that a projection which has to come to an end always returns to its origin. So when somebody hits upon the singular idea that God is dead, or does not exist at all, the psychic image of God, which represents a definite dynamic structure, finds its way back to the subject and produces a condition in which the thinker believes himself to be "like unto God"; in other words, it brings out all the qualities which are only characteristics of fools and madmen and therefore leads to a catastrophe." [43]

In this sense Nietzsche was a prophet in reverse. He did not come, as other prophets come, to announce the birth of a new god; but he came to proclaim the death of an old god, the Christian God, who had lived so precariously in the German psyche. The Nazism which finally ensued was not an intellectual derivation of Nietzsche's thought, but rather a consequence of the same situation; it grew from the fact that the Christian God had died in the German psyche, as Nietzsche said, and that vast sums of psychic energy were set free to craze certain individuals with delusions of power.

To speak of the death of God, then, refers to a psychologi-

[43] *Essays on Contemporary Events*, pp. 69, 70.

cal occurrence which has actually taken place in modern times. It involves not only the weakening of the theological beliefs in God, but also the loss of feeling and fervor for the whole pattern of social values. The death of a god is always an historically important phenomenon because the God-symbol is the core in every society of the system of symbols by which the society functions. When a god dies, the structure of values loses its support; its vital quality is gone; it loses its meaningfulness, its authority, and its ability to inspire. Energies which would ordinarily be directed through these symbols out to life no longer move outward but turn back into the psyche, where they activate dormant elements of the historical unconscious. The whole equilibrium of personality is then upset, and it remains unstable until a new god, a new "predominant psychological condition," is established in the psyche to provide the link between the conscious attitudes and the unconscious symbols. Even if a new god is not "born" at once, the tendency of the psyche is to draw to the surface those psychic contents that carry a sense of authentic meaningfulness for life. They are brought to the surface, systematized and conventionalized, for only in this way can the individual avoid the psychological problems which arise when there is no institutional base for his conscious attitudes.

"Whenever there is an external form," Jung says, "be it ritual or spiritual, by which all the yearnings and hopes of the soul are adequately expressed—as for instance in some living religion—then we may say that the psyche is outside and no spiritual problem strictly speaking exists." [44] The individual is then able to move out toward the world in terms of beliefs that he does not need to question, and so he is not

[44] *Modern Man in Search of a Soul*, p. 232.

caused to develop an introspective frame of mind. When the conscious attitudes are securely fixed in institutions, the attention is focused away from the psyche toward outer objects; but when the symbols fail to function, the individual becomes acutely aware of the fact that there *are* forces that are active within him. "As long as all goes well, and psychic energy finds its application in adequate and well-regulated ways, we are disturbed by nothing from within. No uncertainty or doubt besets us and we cannot be divided against ourselves. But no sooner are one or two of the channels of psychic activity blocked, than we are reminded of a stream that is dammed up. The current flows backward to its source; the inner man wants something that the visible man does not want, and we are at war with ourselves." [45]

THE SITUATION IN OUR TIME

In these terms, the development of psychology as a specialized field of study expresses in itself the disharmonies which permeate the psyche of our age. There would not have been the stimulation to apply systematic analysis to psychological phenomena if it were not that, by its disorders, the psyche calls attention to itself. In the ordinary, harmonious course of living one is hardly aware that the psyche exists; certainly in no system of lived symbols is it spoken of as an objective entity. Only when the psychic energies turn back on themselves and disturb consciousness is the individual's attention drawn to the fact that the psyche is a reality; and only when symbols have ceased to be "alive," can the psyche be looked upon objectively. It is very significant, as Jung observes, that "it was men of the medical profession who were the first to

[45] Ibid., p. 233.

observe" the psyche. Psychology emerged directly from the sickness, the spiritual uneasiness of modern man. In this sense we can agree with Jung's statement that the entire tradition of psychoanalysis, with its tendency to interpret modern man by means of psychiatric tools of analysis, has been possible only because Western civilization has been passing through a crisis in its deepest beliefs.

Jung's final conclusion concerning the present situation of consciousness is that it is a vacuum. The enigmatic phrase that has shocked his empirically-minded critics is the key to his ultimate evaluation of the present psychological condition. Modern man *is* in "search of a soul." Old gods have died. New gods have not yet been born, although psychological labor pains are apparent in many areas. New gods will in time be brought to birth; Jung is sure of that. The human race can do nothing else, unless it exterminates itself. The psyche, by its very nature, must continue spontaneously and autonomously to produce out of itself new symbols, and from these symbols it will fashion new gods, and ultimately find a new soul to dedicate to these gods. To say, therefore, that modern man is searching for a soul is to say that he is searching for a meaning for his life, a meaning that he can experience from within himself, prior to consciousness, and on a base more fundamental than intellect. The psychological problem of our time, then, as Jung sees it, goes deeper than psychology. It is a religious problem, but here even the word religion is inadequate and misleading. The psychological problem is a problem of religious need, but not a need for religious rituals. It is a need for symbols that may be lived spontaneously, intensely and naturally, and that can be "alive" in the psyche; for only in the emergence of a new way

of life which may be deeply experienced and lived can the
modern man find his new soul. In the meanwhile, the characteristic of modern man is his searching. His religious
problem is actually the absence of religion. His psychological problem is the problem of the person overcome by the
meaninglessness of his individual life, even while he lives in
the midst of one of the most meaningful periods of history.
Between the death of old gods and the birth of new gods,
between rejected beliefs and awaited prophecies, lies the
vacuum which is the modern psyche. The merit of Jung's
conception of the psyche and its contents is that it draws psychology and history together to provide a large and unifying
perspective for understanding what may fill this vacuum.
It is the kind of view that somehow eludes academic social
theory, and yet one feels that these are concepts which must
soon be put to use. In the search for the meaning of life in the
modern world, very little can be accomplished until we understand at least the first axiom—that it is only out of the historical depths of his being that man may find what the future
holds in store.

V I I I

HISTORICAL IMPLICATIONS
OF JUNG'S THOUGHT

Now that we have a more or less comprehensive picture of Jung's system of thought, we can come to the crucial questions: what does Jung's psychology actually accomplish? And where do his social concepts lead?

Fundamentally Jung's work must stand or fall with the validity of his conception of the psyche and his analysis of its contents. This must be clear to us when we consider that in the final analysis what he has developed is a conception of the cognitive nature of man. The specific doctrines within Jung's scheme of analysis have to be understood merely as hypotheses on given subjects, subject to change with further investigation. It is only in the larger aspects of his analysis that we find the spirit and import of his work.

When we speak of Jung's conception of consciousness, we must keep in mind the different levels of his discussion. In Jung's terminology, consciousness refers only to the small segment of awareness that centers around the ego; the rest of the psyche is classified as "the unconscious." It is altogether misleading, then, to compare what Jung calls "consciousness" with what other writers speak of when they treat the larger aspects of consciousness, or what we can call cognition in general. In Jung's work, that is understood not as

221

consciousness, but as the totality of the psyche. In getting a perspective for evaluating Jung's contribution on this point, we should see that while it is true that Jung's way of formulating the unconscious is the most important concept in his work, it can be understood properly only in terms of the psyche as a whole. Its significance in his schema depends on the role that it plays in relation to the other parts of the psyche. *The important thing is to understand Jung affirmatively as having developed not a psychology of the unconscious, but a perspective for all the contents of the psyche.* In an earlier chapter we discussed some of the misunderstandings that have arisen around the theory of the unconscious, particularly the fact that it was viewed as a negative concept. In Freud's work the unconscious is understood as containing materials that are "repressed" from consciousness, and Freud carried his implied contrast so far that he identified consciousness with health, and the unconscious with illness. As a carry-over from his earlier studies, Jung displays a similar tendency at certain points in his writings, and a phrase like his "unconscious processes" carries these negative implications. But it also has a more positive meaning, and when Jung speaks of psychological processes as "unconscious," he means that they have an existence prior to individual rationality and that their force is derived from a more fundamental level of the psyche.

Throughout his works, Jung speaks of a relation of "reciprocal relativity" between consciousness and the unconscious, one balancing the other in a constant, dynamic tension. When we say, however, that Jung's ideas must be understood in terms of cognition as a whole, we mean that the basic concept is neither consciousness nor the unconscious, but rather the psyche which includes both of them. In this inclusive sense, the term "total cognition" seems to be preferable, when it is understood to mean all the faculties of human awareness: those that turn outward to the external world and those that deal with internal phenomena. The point to stress is that the key to Jung is that, after he posits the reality of psychological phenomena, he maintains that there is an essential unity of structure in the area in which they take place. Then, within this unity of the total processes of cognition, he speaks of layers within the psyche, which means, simply, stages in the total process of cognition. Taken in this sense, consciousness and the unconscious are not opposites, but rather degrees of depth within the psyche, unified by the fact that they participate as particular aspects of the full cognitive process.

The unconscious is, then, not a negative element in the psyche. It plays an affirmative role because the entire conception of the psyche has an affirmative meaning. When Jung diverged from Freud in his conception of the unconscious, he stated that what Freud had referred to as the unconscious was really just one aspect of the psyche, namely, the part that is related to individual experience but is not fixed in consciousness. At that level of his studies, Jung's contribution was simply to show that there are layers in the psyche deeper than those to which Freud had called attention. To articulate his point he then developed his distinction between the Personal Unconscious and the Collective Unconscious, mainly to give Freud's original conception a large and historical dimension. There is little question that these concepts involved a step forward in the analysis of the unconscious; and yet they seem awkward and unsatisfactory, perhaps because Jung was still too deeply entangled in psychoanalytic terminology when he constructed them. The Personal Unconscious remained for Jung an essentially negative concept, as the unconscious in general had been for Freud. On the other hand, the deeper layer of the psyche, the Collective Unconscious, emerged as the positive element, the creative force in the psyche. It could not be negative, as Jung understood it, for the simple reason that its existence is prior to all the other levels of consciousness. It is, so to speak, the source of supply, both for the Personal Unconscious and for consciousness. It contains the potentialities which the individual possesses generically both as a member of the human race in general and as a particular organism. It is the primal level of consciousness, and though the phrase "unconscious" is used to refer to it, it has the sense of pre-conscious or potentially conscious. Far from being a negative element, the Collective Unconscious is the most creative component of the psyche, since all the layers of consciousness are dependent on it for their psychic contents. Here we have the essence of Jung's view of consciousness, that the psyche is a dynamic unity and that its deepest level, misnamed the Collective Unconscious, is the creative source of the materials which finally emerge as the contents of individual consciousness.

From an operational point of view, then, it turns out that the distinction between consciousness and the unconscious is not of primary importance. Even though Jung constantly places them in juxtaposition to each other, it is very clear that the two terms must be understood mainly as analytical tools used pragmatically for their value in studying the still uncharted depths of the psyche. We can definitely see the

tendency in Jung to move away from the idea of the unconscious toward a unified view of the psyche based upon a virtual infinity of depth layers. Such a development is logically
implied in his affirmative conception of the unconscious. It
would indicate to us that Jung himself is not satisfied with
the terms "consciousness" and the "unconscious" and that,
really, they are a handicap to him in his thinking. There is
always the feeling in reading Jung that his work suffers because of his terminology, and that if it could be reformulated in terms free from even reminiscence of psychoanalytical theory, the result would be clearer and more fertile. It is
particularly so on the question of the relation of the unconscious to consciousness, where the important idea to convey
is the creative and affirmative aspects of the psyche as a
whole.

The problem here stems from Jung's basic relation to
Freud. It grows from the fact that while he gained so much
stimulation from Freud's concepts, he remolded them to the
point where they took on altogether different connotations.
Nevertheless, the fact remains—and it is important to keep
in mind for the history of Depth Psychology—that Jung is
the only one of Freud's original disciples who has maintained the conception of a dynamic unconscious and carried it
further than Freud himself took it. In a theorist like Alfred
Adler, for example, the demiurgic aspect of the unconscious
is virtually eliminated, and there has been a similar tendency
for psychoanalysis in general as part of its blending with
academic psychology. On the specific question of the active,
pulsating nature of the unconscious, Jung has remained the
closest to Freud, and the confusion in terminology comes

largely from the fact that while his conceptions are so very close to Freud's in their origin, they have been developed in an altogether independent way.

RECAPITULATION OF THE SOCIAL THEORY OF PERSONALITY

Within the psyche Jung's main tool of analysis is his conception of psychic energy. As he first developed it, it was intended also as an improvement on Freud's doctrine of libido energy, to expand it beyond the limitations of Freud's mainly sexual connotations. When Jung treats psychic energy on this psychological level, it is conceived as the quantitative force attached to psychic contents, varying in intensity according to the situation in the psyche. The various psychic processes are expressions of the movement of energy, and in this sense Jung speaks of the progressive and regressive movements of libido; that is to say, energy may move forward into life or it may move backward and downward into the psyche, activating the contents in the lower levels of the unconscious. At this point, and to this extent, Jung's conception of energy does not differ markedly in its general aspect from the view of the Freudian psychoanalytical school. What is different, however, is the spirit in which it is applied to the study of society and in which it is made a link between personality and history.

Whereas Freud takes a romantic point of view and regards the individual as being in conflict with society as such, Jung posits that psychic energy is derived from the fact that the human being is inherently social by nature. His idea is that individual life basically involves a flow of energy out into the world and that the flow can take place only by means of symbols. He understands "symbols" as having a dual form, being psychological in their universal aspect, and social in their particular historical manifestation in the individual. In other words, the media through which the energies of the individual are poured out into life depend on the social form which the archetypal symbols take, and the development of the individual personality depends on how these symbols function. Jung refers to these social symbols as "libido analogues," since they transform psychic energy from its raw state to one in which it serves some social purpose. Further than that, the specific nature of the conscious attitudes which the individual develops comes from the fact that the individual emphasizes some particular aspect of the social symbol according to his talents or his situation, and develops an "autonomous complex," which is then integrated into his personality. This outer side of personality which the individual displays in society, Jung calls the Persona, and he holds that it is generally derived from the social symbols. The Persona, he says, is "an excerpt of the collective psyche." The excerpt is made in terms of the specific characteristics of each individual, his psychological type, his introverted or extraverted nature, his relation to his parents; but always the Persona must be formed out of social symbols which are meaningful to the group as a whole.

The above terms constitute the basis on which Jung analyzes the structure of the personality in society. When the social symbols provide an effective channel for the individual in terms of his particular psychological traits, the psychic energies flow out smoothly toward life. The individual's conscious attitudes are then secure, and he easily establishes a Persona that is satisfactory to himself and to society. He maintains his Persona by adapting the dominant functions of his psychological type to the active libido analogues of the culture. If, however, the qualities of his psychological type are out of harmony with the prevailing libido analogues, the individual finds it difficult to maintain a place for himself in his society. He cannot find adequate channels through which to express his energies in life, and he is then not able to hold up an adequate Persona before society. In such a situation, the psychic energies which would flow out into society dam up within the psyche, and instead of continuing a progressive movement into action, they follow a regressive movement down into the lower levels of the unconscious.

The turning away of libido from the social problems of life is the condition which Jung terms neurosis. Actually, from a functional point of view, all the aspects of the withdrawal of the attention to life are merely symptoms, and the neurosis itself is expressed in the regressive movement of libido. In terms of the individual's adaptation to life, the break-up of the Persona may involve merely a discordance between the particular "excerpt of the collective psyche" which the individual was trying to take for himself and the attitudes of his psychological type; he may, in other words, have been in the wrong field. In this case, after a period of energy regression, the libido can return to life and build a new Persona. If it was a situation in which the Persona fell apart because it was on too high a level to be maintained for long, a period of libido regression is followed by what Jung calls the "regressive restoration of the Persona"; that is to say, the individual must readjust his sights in order to find a channel through which to focus his energies into life.

The rebuilding of the Persona involves the readjustment

to life on the outer level of consciousness in terms of the individual's role in society. It therefore always requires a progressive movement of libido, at least in some degree. If, however, the energy movement continues to regress into the
psyche, it goes further and further away from consciousness
until it comes into contact with the contents of the deeper
levels of the psyche. When this takes place, the adaptation
that the individual has to make is not mainly to the outer
world; it becomes more important for him to work out a harmony within his own psyche. At this point, the difficulties
which take place in the outer world, in the building and
maintaining of an adequate Persona in society, result in a
transfer of the psychological problem from the outer to the
inner world. The key problem of individuality then no
longer involves an adaptation to life on its external side, but
requires finding the meaning of life itself.

From a social point of view, the question of whether the
individual feels that he knows the meaning of life depends
on whether any major libido analogues are functioning for
him. Jung holds that the meanings of life are carried by
those symbols that are integrated in the structure of each society and that they manifest themselves in the individual
through the conscious attitudes of his Persona, where they express the individualized form of the social meanings of life.
When the symbols are not strongly experienced by the individual, the meanings of life are in doubt, and ultimately a
break-up in the Persona is sure to come. When it does come,
it results in a deep regression of libido, since the individual
must find a new set of symbols to give meaning to his life.
The libido is forced to move down to the deeper layers of the
pysche because only there can it contact symbols with suf-

ficient strength and wide enough significance to make possible a new point of view. In its essence, Jung holds, the problem of neurosis involves the absence of the meaning of life for an individual. It means that the individual does not experience the meaningfulness of his existence within the context of his society. It means that the society has not given him a meaningful social role on which to build a strong Persona. Failing to have strong analogues through which to move out into society, the life energies must regress in an effort to find new symbols within the psyche.

THE PSYCHE AND HISTORICAL CHANGE

From the historical point of view, such a situation is a sign of weakening in the social values of a culture. If its symbols cannot provide the meanings of life for its members in a satisfactory way, the culture is subject to increasing disaffection from within, and in time the social structure itself cannot hold together. Without taking the point further than a psychological formulation, Jung maintains the basic thesis that a society can continue to function effectively only by providing its individuals with meanings in which they can have a living faith. Only then can the psychic energies be directed out into the world and into the socially productive enterprises which a community requires. If a culture fails to maintain psychologically effective symbols, its individuals withdraw from the social areas of life and turn into themselves in search of new meanings. The basic psychic process underlying such a social development may be referred to as "neurosis," but not in the sense of a diagnosis; it is merely a description of its kind of libido movement, that is, of regression away from outer life and into the depths of the psyche.

On a cultural and religious level, it means that new doctrines of all kinds will be sought after, and that nothing
will be too strange or too unconventional to try out. Sociologically, it indicates that as large numbers of individuals
are unable to function in terms of the customary symbols,
changes must soon follow in the basic beliefs and in the
whole pattern of "mutual expectations" of the society. The
psychic process which Jung describes is, then, a symptom of
transition in the fundamental social values of any period of
history, whether the declining days of Rome or modern
Western civilization. With regard to the contemporary situation, he finds many signs of the regression of energies, the
relentless introspection of modern literature and psychoanalysis, the searching for new religions and exotic doctrines in
distant corners of the world, the total questioning of intellectual and moral values and the search, throughout Western
civilization, for the meaning of life. Jung interprets all of
these as signs that the traditional symbols of Western civilization are ceasing to be operative, that they are becoming
less and less able to hold together the personality of the Western individual, and that therefore new symbols must soon
come to the fore.

The methodology that Jung provides for obtaining historical perspective on this point takes us to the heart of his
contribution to social thought. When the libido is seeking
symbols strong enough to give new meaning to life, it must
regress very deeply into the psyche because that is where the
archetypes are. In one sense, the archetypes are the univer-
sals in man, the psychic potentialities latent in mankind as a
whole. But that is only their abstract form. The main quality of archetypes is that they are experienced not abstractly,

but only as they are manifested in some particular symbol. In Jung's analyses of the unconscious, the forms in which the archetypes come to the surface correspond to the social symbols in which they were experienced in past times. The figures of pre-Christian symbolism, for example, are very commonly found in European dreams. And not only in dreams, but in the actually lived symbols of the present time, ancient Druid and Etruscan beliefs are found, hidden more or less deeply in the Irish and Italian mind, even while they are quite overtly expressed in the forms of the Catholic religion. The past lives on in the psyche and comes to the fore again long ages after it was thought to have died. To have perspective on human history we have to deal with the time-contents within the psyche.

Certainly at this point, a new simile is necessary to describe the unconscious. The old analogy in which the mind was described as an apartment house in which the unconscious is the basement no longer holds. The psyche has depth downward, but it also extends backward, across, through time so that somehow history is latently contained and unconsciously expressed in each individual. This is Jung's great hypothesis for the study of history in terms of the psyche. It makes possible a dimension of time-study in which time is a unitary category for personality and social history. As Prof. Eaton pointed out some years ago,[1] this aspect of Jung's

[1] See remarks by Ralph M. Eaton in Preface to W. M. Kranefeldt, *Secret Ways of the Mind*, Holt, New York, 1932.

Jung's most recent thought centers around the development of his conception of the essential wholeness of the psyche and of the implications which may be derived from such a viewpoint. For an advanced discussion of the concepts with which he is currently working, see his very important article, "Der Geist der Psychologie" in the *Eranos Jahrbuch*, 1946, Band XIV, pp. 385-490, espec. p. 441 ff.

theory of the psyche must one day be very profitably integrated with the philosophies of time of Bergson, Husserl, Whitehead, and G. H. Mead.

With regard to Jung's accomplishments in the field of social thought, we must realize that his contribution is still in the realm of hypothesis. Jung himself has nowhere worked out a detailed study of society, but he has rather formulated principles of the psychic-depth and time-depth of man which now need to be tested in specific application. For this reason we believe that the test of the value of Jung's work does not lie ultimately in Jung himself, but in the use that will be made of his ideas by thinkers who will come after him. The true measure of the fertility of his concepts will come when we can see how well they contribute to still larger, more specific, and more dynamic formulations of the nature of man and history than Jung himself has yet worked out. We do not mean, of course, that Jung is to be judged by the work of those of his "followers" who keep their studies altogether within the terms of his definitions and terminology; such "schools" tend to become doctrinal and rigid (as certainly happened with the "orthodox" Freudians), and it is very unlikely that such groups can develop the potentialities latent in Jung's essentially flexible ideas. We mean rather that the creative adaptation of Jung's concepts must finally be done by independent thinkers, who will take their primary stimu-

---

In his long essay, "Synchronizitat als ein Prinzip akausaler Zusammenhange" published in *Naturerklarung und Psyche*, Rascher, Zurich, 1952, Jung undertakes to apply his conception of the psyche to Time and Causality. He develops there a line of thought that may ultimately have the most far-reaching consequences. It is, however, still in an early stage of development and it is much too soon to attempt to evaluate it.

lation from Jung and then apply his ideas in terms of a fresh starting-point. By the strength and originality of the conclusions which these non-Jungians reach and by the still new areas of study which they open, we shall be able to judge the value of Jung's contribution in a large and lasting context.

THE WORK OF HEINRICH ZIMMER

For the unitary study of man, that is, for the point of view that seeks an integrated study of personality, society and history, the most significant doctrine in Jung's work is his concept of the "archetypes." It has a pivotal importance because, on the one hand, it involves the universal, the unchanging side of man; and, on the other hand, it deals with the materials out of which the varieties of historical symbols are formed. Up to the present time, the most creative studies carried out in terms of Jung's hypotheses have centered on the archetypes, and it is from these studies that we can draw our first conclusions as to the path that research, drawing inspiration from him, is likely to follow in the future. The works of two main scholars stand out in this regard, those of Heinrich Zimmer and Carl Kerenyi, and it is valuable for us to see how each of them has developed the concept of the archetype as the link between the nature of man and the study of history.

Zimmer focused his main attention on the study of Indian mythology and its symbolism, but his interests later expanded to include the field of mythology as a whole—particularly the mythos of pre-Christian Western Europe. Up to the time of his premature death in 1943, while still at the height of his creative work, Zimmer had accumulated a vast amount of mythologic data which he had not been able to put into systematic form. It is quite possible that he might have altered his perspective and developed additional concepts had he lived long enough to work out an integrated interpretation of this material; but unfortunately that is something we can never know. In the writings which have been published, his theoretical concepts are expressed more or less incidentally within the framework of rather literary elaborations of the various myths and legends. We therefore find his point of view indicated only piecemeal, with his theoretical constructs brought in only to fit the subject matter of each particular myth. Nevertheless, Zimmer's approach to the problem of the archetypes is especially valuable for its flexibility. Certainly, his studies of Hinduism constituted an excellent preliminary discipline. He was occupied for many years with the questions of the One and the Many, the universal and the particular, the timeless and the transitory; and these are essentially the issues that are involved in the interpretation of archetypes.

STUDIES ON THE ARCHETYPES

One of the main aspects of research on the archetypes has been a large-scale process of fact-gathering designed to identify and analyze the various archetypes as they are found in the symbols of world mythology. Once the archetype concept was formulated, this was a necessary step in order to test the hypotheses. Many persons have therefore been engaged in research seeking out the motifs underlying the figures and symbolism of the myths and religions of primitive and advanced cultures. The papers published in the *Eranos Jahrbuch*, in particular, have been contributions in this direction. A large part of Zimmer's work is devoted to studies of this nature, which point out the archetypes expressed in the form of figures in a Hindu or a Buddhist or a Celtic myth. For example, he finds in the Arthurian figure of Merlin "the archetype of the Wise Old Man, the personification of the intuitive wisdom of the unconscious. By his inspiration and secret advice," Zimmer says, "he guides the conscious personality, which is represented by the knights and the king. The figure of Merlin is descended, through the Celtic Druids, from the ancient tribal priest and medicine man, supernaturally endowed with cosmic wisdom and the power of witchcraft, the poet and divine who can conjure invisible presences with the magic of his songs. Like Orpheus, the singer and master of the mysteries and initiations of Ancient Greece, whose harmonies tamed the wild animals and moved the mute stones to arrange themselves into walls and buildings, Merlin can command the stones." [2] He adds other examples of the form in which the archetype appears—as the Chinese aged sage, "The Old One," Lao Tse of Taoism; and also the Guru of Hinduism. The basis of this archetype, it should be noted, is that the figure of the Wise Old Man corresponds to the psychic process whereby the contents of the unconscious move into consciousness in terms of and guided by the principles inherent in the archaic layers of the psyche. The Wise Old Man is understood as the personification of the voice of the age-old past in man as expressed in the deep unconscious. Zimmer holds that all myths have many levels of interpretation—a virtual infinity of levels de-

[2] Heinrich Zimmer, *The King and the Corpse*, Bollingen Series XI, Pantheon, New York, 1948, p. 134, fn.

pending on the interpreter—but the general pattern in his elucidation of myths is to point out the archetypal figures contained in the myths and then to indicate the psychic processes which they represent.

He points, for example, to the great number of Anima symbols in the Celtic mythology, the many "beautiful princesses," which represent the soul-side of the male. Correspondingly, he notes that the figure of Sir Lancelot is an Animus image, representing the soul-side of the female. Zimmer remarks that "in contrast to the paucity of animus-figures in the Arthurian romances, representations of the opposite, the anima-archetype, abound." [3]

A most interesting illustration that Zimmer uses for another psychological concept, the archetype of the Persona, is the figure of Abu Kasem and his slippers.[4] This is an old Arabian tale about a wealthy merchant who persisted in wearing a pair of very old and tattered slippers. When they began to get him into difficulties that were very costly, he tried to get rid of them, but each time they would return to him and bring with them a greater calamity than before. In the tale, the slippers take the role of the Persona, expressing an archetypal psychic process. Zimmer says, "The life accomplishment of a man, his social personality, the contoured mask shielding his inner character: that is the shoes of Abu Kasem. They are the fabric of their owner's conscious personality. More, they are the tangible impulses of his unconscious: the sum total of those desires and achievements in which he parades before himself and the world, and by

[3] Ibid., pp. 133, 179.
[4] Ibid., p. 9 ff.

virtue of which he has become a real personage. They are
the life sum for which he has struggled."[5] Zimmer points
out the psychological insight contained in the tale as it
shows how the slippers, (representing Abu Kasem's social
personality, especially his business ability, which he prizes
most) hold a sway over him from which he cannot free
himself. To Abu Kasem the slippers "mean unconsciously
. . . his greatest, most consciously cultivated virtue, his merchant's avarice. And all of this has brought the man a long
way, but holds more power over him than he supposes. It
is not so much that Abu Kasem possesses the virtue (or vice),
as that the vice (or virtue) possesses him. It has become a
sovereign motive of his being, holding him under its spell."[6]
(In other words, as a Persona, the slippers also have the pos-
sessing power of an autonomous complex.)

PSYCHOLOGICAL CONCEPTS IN MYTH

Jung's psychological conception of the autonomous complex, the "autonomous partial system," is interpreted by Zimmer as having especially great significance when applied to
the world view of Hinduism. In discussing the myths centering around the god and goddess, Shiva and Shakti, Zimmer points out that "Shakti is the materialization of the
vital power of her spouse;"[7] that is to say, Shakti as the
feminine principle represents the embodiment of Maya,
the life-force, and the life-illusion. In order to interpret a

[5] Ibid., p. 17.
[6] Ibid., p. 17.
[7] Heinrich Zimmer, *Myths and Symbols in Indian Art and Civilization*, Bollingen Series VI, Pantheon, New York, 1946, p. 193.

seventh century Hindu relief which depicts the "Goddess slaying the Buffalo-Demon," Zimmer describes the psychological significance of the background myth of the goddess conquering the monsters, who are the illusionary forms of life. "The lesson," he says, "may be read psychologically, as applying to ourselves, who are not gods but limited beings. The constant projection and externalization of our specific shakti (vital energy) is our 'little universe,' our restricted sphere and immediate environment, whatever concerns and affects us. We people and color the indifferent, neutral screen with the movie-figures and dramas of the inward dream of our souls, and fall prey then to its dramatic events, delights and calamities. The world, not as it is in itself but as we perceive it and react upon it, is the product of our own Maya or delusion. It can be described as our own more or less blind life-energy, producing and projecting demonic and beneficent shapes and appearances. Thus we are the captives of our own Maya-Shakti and of the motion picture that it incessantly produces. Whenever we are entangled and enmeshed in vital, passionate issues, we are dealing with the projection of our own substance. That is the spell of Maya. That is the spell of creative, life-engendering, life-maintaining energy." [8]

In this sense the demonic forces in man may be understood as coming out of man's own inner nature. As they have a great force, it is derived from man's own energy within the psyche, and yet man himself is not able to control it. The autonomous power of the complexes created in the psyche is expressed in the figures of the demonic animals who, having

[8] Ibid., p. 194.

a power of their own, are nevertheless understood by the myth to be projections of man's own inner world of Maya, or illusion.

Zimmer is inclined to carry the interpretation even further than psychology. As "the shapes and figures projected by the angered and embattled Hindu gods represent a very revealing psychological insight," they involve also "a philosophy and a metaphysic." In the Hindu way of thinking there is a correspondence between the psychological and the cosmic. "The Highest Being is the lord and master of Maya. All the rest of us—the lower gods, the demons, human beings—are the victims of our own individual Maya." That is to say, the delusions of life on the cosmic plane spring from the delusions that are given reality within the psyche. Human energies brought forth by the individual take on a power of their own as though they were demonic monsters; the individual, like the goddess represented in the myth, has to struggle with beings which he himself has brought forth. Zimmer thus states the meaning of the Hindu myth in terms that correspond directly to Jung's concepts. "We fall prey," he says, "to the spell of our own vitality as it infects us with its blindness, passion, and obsessions. Its processes in our psyche are autonomous, beyond our control; our reactions to them are compelled. Our state is, thus, one of serfdom and bondage to the life-supporting, life-rushing spell of Maya-Shakti. Were this not the case, we should not be *individuals* at all, we should have no history, no biography. The very essence of our personal life is our life-illusion."⁹

Zimmer here shows his strong identification with Hindu ways of thinking, and especially with the paradoxical Hindu

⁹ Ibid., pp. 194, 195.

concept that man's illusions in life actually constitute the realities of his life. His interest, however, is in bringing out the archetypal quality of the Hindu symbols and in showing the subtlety with which they penetrate the nature of the psyche. The Hindu myth is profound and metaphysical in the way it expresses its psychological insights, but the Celtic myth, while much simpler, conveys the same archetypal conception of the psyche. The typical Celtic tale portrays the struggle of the psyche for individuation, using mainly the adventures of a princely hero as its symbol.[10]

CELTIC "LORE OF THE SOUL"

Zimmer gives an excellent example of such an adventure, the images of which, he says, "still carry the force of the primitive pre-Christian lore of the soul." [11] The tale of Conn-Eda, set in the context of the Druidic mythology, possesses the main symbols characteristic of its type. The hero, born of noble parents, is tricked at the most promising point in his life into playing an enchanted game with his stepmother, the wicked queen. He loses, and the penalty which

[10] For an analysis of myth in terms of the pattern of hero stories, see, Joseph Campbell, *The Hero with a Thousand Faces*, Bollingen Series XVII, Pantheon, New York, 1949. Campbell has developed the concept of the "monomyth" to represent the basic structure of the cycle of action which underlies hero stories. It is a very interesting theory, but it has one fundamental weakness, which is that Campbell intends it as a theory of myth in general, whereas it actually describes only one particular type of myth. Campbell interprets the figure of the hero and its adventures as *the* archetype of the soul, and therefore he feels that his theory of the monomyth can have a universal application. It must be understood, however, as just one aspect of the archetype of the soul, and the fact that Campbell concentrates on the hero and hero symbolism weights his theory in the direction of Celtic and Celtic-type mythologies.

[11] *The King and the Corpse*, p. 33.

the queen imposes on him is a hazardous journey to a fairy kingdom which is surrounded by fire and from which he must bring back three golden apples. The prince realizes that he is in great danger, and he goes to a Druid priest for advice. The priest tells him to "take yonder shaggy little horse" and go to find a certain bird with the power to give him further directions. The prince mounts the magical horse and is soon taken to the wise bird, from whom he receives the instructions to "remove the stone just under your right foot and take the ball of iron and the cup you will find under it; then mount your horse, cast the ball before you, and having so done, your horse will tell you all the other things you will need to know." [12]

Conn-Eda obeys the bird and throws the iron ball ahead of him. The ball rolls along of its own accord and the shaggy horse understands that he is to follow it. By and by they come to a river with three terrible serpents. The prince does not know what to do, but the shaggy horse tells him that if he can throw three pieces of meat, one into the mouth of each of the serpents, they will get across unharmed. Conn-Eda makes the throws successfully, and the horse gets him across with a single leap. They then continue to follow the ball until they come to a "great mountain flaming with fire." Once again the horse gets Conn-Eda over the obstacle in safety, but the prince complains that he has been "greatly scorched." The horse then says that he has in his ear an elixir called "All-Heal," which Conn-Eda should use. The prince applies the "All-Heal," and his burns are cured. They set out again following the iron ball and finally come to the fairy city, which they find to be guarded by two towers of

[12] Ibid., pp. 28, 29.

flame. The shaggy horse makes a surprising request. "Take a small knife from my other ear," he says, "and with this knife you shall kill me and flay me. When you have done this, envelop yourself in my hide and you can pass the gate unscathed and unmolested. When you get inside, you can come out at pleasure, because, when once you enter, there is no danger, and you can pass and repass whenever you wish; and let me tell you that all I have to ask of you in return is that, once inside the gate, you will immediately come back and drive away the birds of prey that may be fluttering round to feed on my carcass—and more, that you will pour any drop of that powerful "All-Heal," if such still remains in the bottle, upon my flesh to preserve it from corruption." [13]

The prince is shocked and refuses to kill the faithful horse, but the animal insists and finally Conn-Eda agrees. He raises the knife hesitantly when suddenly, "as if impelled by some magic power," the blade plunges itself into the horse and kills him. Conn-Eda covers himself in the hide of the horse, enters the fairy city, and returns to the carcass to fulfill the horse's last request. He applies the All-Heal, and the body of the dead horse is transformed into a handsome young man, the brother of the king of the fairy city, who explains that he was kept in bondage as a shaggy little horse by the magic of a Druid priest. He says that in order for him to be set free it was necessary that Conn-Eda do all the things that he has done. Now all is well. The new youth tells the secret behind the whole episode. It was his own sister who set everything in motion by deliberately influencing the wicked queen to require the

[13] Ibid., p. 30.

golden apples of her stepson. She did it only with good
motives, he tells Conn-Eda. "She only wanted to free you
from all future danger and disaster, and recover me from
my relentless enemies through your aid." Conn-Eda gets
the three golden apples and returns to his native land.
When the queen sees him returning, she commits suicide
in despair; Conn-Eda plants the golden apples, and they
come forth as trees and crops which make his country pros-
perous for ever.

Such a tale is full of archetypal images, as Zimmer points
out. The old Druid priest whom Conn-Eda consults at the
outset represents the "Wise Old Man." The mysterious bird
who gives advice symbolizes the higher spheres, as birds are
often the symbols of angels. The wicked stepmother and
the beneficent sister of the transformed youth are the dark
and light sides of the Anima. The "All-Heal" elixir is an
archetypal symbol of the liquor of life and eternity which
appears in countless forms—the "Ambrosia" of the Greeks,
the "Amrita" of the Indians, as Zimmer mentions. The journey itself is an archetypal representation of the course of
struggle over which the soul must pass in reaching self-
realization. The obstacles on the way, the passing through
fire, the jumping over water, the feeding of the serpents,
are part of the pattern of initiation by which the soul is
tested before it is allowed to see through to the realities of
life. Conn-Eda is like Buddha, pure and naïve, unsoiled by
life before he is brought face to face with its cruel realities.
The figure of the hero, then, represents the life of the
psyche, even to the point of distinguishing its separate parts.
Conn-Eda is the conscious ego carried along and guided by
the trustworthy intuitive base of personality. Finally, how-

ever, the unconscious must itself be transformed by an act of consciousness, and then consciousness and the unconscious, the ego and the instincts, are brought into a new integrated relation to each other. The unconscious is transformed from a dark, lower area of the personality to a beautiful, higher spiritual level. (It is transformed by being loved in its ugliness and imperfection—the "Beauty and the Beast" theme.) At the same time, consciousness is enabled to return to the field of its native proclivities, now fortified with a new potency and with a strength that protects it from future calamities. The pagan tale of the hero is, then, a story of the individuation of personality, told with archetypal symbols which express the underlying psychic processes.

Zimmer finds the same fundamental message in the Celtic as in the Hindu mythos. Both are based on archetypal images expressing the nature of the psyche; and both base their approach to life on the psychic nature of man. The differences lie mainly in the fact that each contains the archetypes within its own characteristic modes of expression —each with the symbolism that has become peculiar to it for historical and cultural reasons, and in terms of its own indigenous feeling for life. The Celtic mythos, with its extraverted cast and with its disarmingly child-like qualities, visualizes the struggles of the inner life in terms of the adventures of the young and handsome hero-prince, who hunts in the forest and perhaps wins the prize of a lady-fair. The Hindu mythos, on the other hand, more introverted and introspective, has the dark, disenchanted view of an older civilization. It is not susceptible to the easy enthusiasms, the fairy land of naïve joy that entrances the Celtic spirit with its happy endings. The Indian psyche sees its symbols through the prism of eternity, looking through the axle of the wheel of rebirth in its endless turnings. The Hindu hero cannot look forward to living "happily ever after" as the Celtic hero can; he knows his joys must disappear in the cycles of time, since both sadness and joy are parts of the illusion of Maya. But these are the outer differences of form, and they express the historical differences of time and place which constitute the source of the variations in symbols. They are underlain by a fundamental sameness in the archetypal intuition of the psyche that is at the root of both the Hindu and the Celtic mythology.

ZIMMER ON MYTH AND ARCHETYPE

Zimmer's studies of myth, then, come squarely into the two-sided issue that is at the heart of the study of archetypes. On the one hand, we have the kind of investigation that looks for the archetypal element as it underlies the variety of historical forms in which symbols appear. On the other hand, we have the more integrative and evolutionary study, which seeks to interpret the nature of the historical differences, the basis for the variations, and their significance for the development of individual personality within their context.

The first type of study, the search for the archetypes, constitutes a large, informal research project carried on individually by ethnologists, mythologists, philologists, anthropologists and analytical psychologists, searching for examples of the universal motifs which underlie the symbolism of psychic processes. It is a necessary fact-finding operation, especially within Jung's theoretical context, but it also has a negative side. It has a tendency to fall into a pattern of

categorizing, and to allow its studies to become merely a process of classifying symbols so that they can then be filed in
the pigeon-hole of the proper archetype. On this level, the
study of archetypes follows an analytical methodology that
reduces the myth to terms that can be fitted into intellectual groupings; thus, one symbol is reduced to "nothing
but" an Anima archetype, another to "nothing but" the
Persona archetype, and so on. (Unfortunately, it is a tendency within Jungian research that is to be expected to increase as Jung's following crystallizes into a "school.") It is
a type of study that is all too similar to the Freudian psychoanalytical method of reducing a myth or any other content
of the unconscious to the terms of some neuro-psychiatric
mechanism. It corresponds within the Jungian framework
to the Freudian approach to anthropology, with the main
difference that it devotes itself to isolating and classifying the archetypes instead of the "mechanisms of neurosis" as the Freudians do. Both are subject to the same basic
criticism that, since they follow a reductive method, they
do not develop the dynamic, historical aspects of their material.

We have to admit that Zimmer's work is not always above
this criticism. Now and then he lapses into a style of thinking that expresses the intellectual classifications of the static
side of Jungian thought, namely, the explanation of myths
by reducing their symbols to archetypes; but these are only
lapses, and they are not characteristic of the main tenor of
Zimmer's work. When he defines his own approach to
myth, it is, in fact, just the opposite. He does not believe in
fixed meanings for symbols, or even in a fixed style of interpretation. "There is always the risk," he says, "that the

opening of one vista may be the closing of another." [14]
Therefore, he would set out with no predetermined theory;
and even when he takes up a theory, he would hold it as a
hypothesis, or better, as a tentative methodology. Zimmer's
fundamental attitude is that there is a "virtual infinity" in
the meanings and interpretations of each myth and, in this
sense, "our primary task is to learn, not so much what they
are said to have said, as how to approach them, evoke
fresh speech from them, and understand that speech." [15]

This very approach, with its stress on openness and ten-
tativeness, involves a particular conception of the nature and
function of myth. Zimmer's view is that myth serves as a
medium for the thought of the underlying strata of a population. It may also contain the esoteric wisdom of deep
traditions, and, on occasion, it can combine both by carrying esoteric teachings in a form that common people can
understand and experience. Myth is capable of doing this
because it comes from the deep layers of the psyche and because it expresses in its non-literal forms the symbolic figures
and actions of the unconscious. "There is no explicit com-
mentary on the meaning of the mythological action. The tale
goes straight to the listener through an appeal to his intuition, to his creative imagination. It stirs and feeds the unconscious. By an eloquence rather of incident than of word,
the mythology serves its function as the popular vehicle of
the esoteric wisdom of yoga experience and of orthodox religion." [16]

The reason they can be experienced immediately and

[14] *Myths and Symbols*, p. 41.
[15] *The King and the Corpse*, pp. 4, 5.
[16] *Myths and Symbols*, p. 40.

deeply by great numbers of people is that "the tales are not the products of individual experiences and reactions. They are produced, treasured, and controlled by the collective working and thinking of the religious community. They thrive on the ever-renewed assent of successive generations. They are refashioned, reshaped, laden with new meaning, through an anonymous creative process and a collective, intuitive acceptance. (They are effective primarily on a subconscious level, touching intuition, feeling, and imagination) Their details impress themselves on the memory, soak down, and shape the deeper stratifications of the psyche. When brooded upon, their significant episodes are capable of revealing various shades of meaning, according to the experiences and life-needs of the individual." That is why Zimmer believes that "the myths and symbols of India resist intellectualization and reduction to fixed signification"; and that is why the underlying spirit of his work is opposed to the intellectual reduction of myths to archetypal motifs.[17]

HISTORICAL CONCEPTIONS OF THE PSYCHE

In relating myth to the collective layers of the unconscious as he does, Zimmer makes it clear that he realizes that the spontaneous power of myth is derived from its position in the historical depths of the psyche. This is true no less for Celtic mythology than for the Indian. In fact, Zimmer gives as one of the reasons for his turning to the study of Celtic tales the fact that their symbols are deeply imbedded in the European unconscious and that therefore their contents must be more naturally meaningful to the European individual than the myths of an alien civilization.

[17] Ibid., pp. 40, 41.

His aim, he says, in recreating the Celtic myths "is simply to let the old symbolical personages and adventures again work upon and stimulate the living imagination, to revive them, and to awaken in ourselves the old ability to read with intuitive understanding this pictorial script that at one time was the bearer of the spiritual sustenance of our own ancestors. The answers to the riddle of existence that the tales incorporate—whether we are aware of the fact or not —are still shaping our lives." [18]

We can see, then, that Zimmer's conception of myth, his method of study, and the purposes behind his presentation, are all based on an historical conception of the psyche. While the universality of archetypes is a cardinal principle in his thinking (since it relates myths to psychic processes), Zimmer's historical point of view enables him to see that the figures and their symbolical meanings vary with the particular mythological system and its cultural situation. The symbol of the "forest," for example, has specific connotations in Celtic mythology which it does not necessarily have in other mythologies. It may be because of the role that the forest plays in the primeval conditions of European life that it signifies in Celtic myths, as Zimmer says, "the realm of the soul itself, which the soul may choose to know, to seek therein its most intimate adventure." For, "all that is dark and tempting in the world is to be found again in the enchanted forest, where it springs from our deepest wishes and the soul's most ancient dreams." [19] The forest does occur as a symbol in other mythologies, of course, especially in the mythos of the American Indians. Sometimes it has a

[18] *The King and the Corpse*, pp. 96, 97.
[19] Ibid., p. 193.

significance akin to the meaning of "desert" in the mythologies of people in arid lands. But the full meaning of the symbol does not derive from economic conditions—even though geography may provide the raw images and associations which are taken up and invested with symbolic significance. The connotations of the "enchanted forest" involve the whole spirit and fabric of Celtic mythology with all the nuances of its deeply-rooted sense of life.

Nietzsche has said—and Zimmer cites him to explain his own view—that "the myth itself is a kind or style of thinking." He means that the myth, coming from the lower levels of the unconscious, does its "thinking" according to the manner of the unconscious, that is, in an undifferentiated non-analytical way. "It imparts an idea of the universe," as Nietzsche says, and presents its conceptions not intellectually as consciousness does, but indirectly "in the sequence of events, actions, and sufferings." [20] The point can be made even more specific when seen from an historical point of view, since "the kind or style of thinking" is actually the particular essence of each system of myth and varies according to the underlying conception by which each civilization envisions its place in the universe. The "style of thinking," for example, in the Celtic myths is altogether different from the "style of thinking" in the Hindu myths, even though both express the same principles of psychic projection in their symbolism.

THE PSYCHOLOGY OF MYTHOLOGIC CHANGE

The great power of the archetypes in myths derives from the fact that they express what is primordial in the human

[20] Ibid., p. 310, fn. 1.

being. This is a fundamental principle in Jung's studies, and Zimmer accepts it wholly when he says, "Ages and attitudes of man that are long gone by still survive in the deeper un-conscious layers of our soul. The spiritual heritage of archaic man (the ritual and mythology that once visibly guided his conscious life) has vanished to a large extent from the surface of the tangible and conscious realm, yet survives and remains ever present in the subterranean layers of the uncon-scious. It is the part of our being that links us to a remote an-cestry and constitutes our involuntary kinship with archaic man and with ancient civilizations and traditions." [21] The theoretical foundation of such a statement is the conception of the universality of psychic processes and the continuity of the psyche within the race. Yet all the archetypal symbols are expressed in some historical form as part of some particular mythological system. The question that Zimmer is inter-ested in is what happens when one mythic system with one "style of thought" is superimposed on another system in which the symbols have quite other meanings. He offers a partial answer by referring to the situation of the ancient pre-Christian religions of Northern Europe. Christianity came with a mythologic system quite alien to the ancient paganisms, and while it won out as far as the conscious at-titudes were concerned, the old symbols maintained a some-what dimmer life for themselves by dropping down to the lower levels of the psyche. Zimmer is certainly historically correct when he says, "The Church did more than Ro-man culture to deprive the mythology of the Celts, the Teu-tons, and the pre-Celtic primitive population of the British Isles of the old creed in which it lived, moved, and had its

[21] Ibid., p. 310, fn. 2.

being. Nevertheless, it survived, without foundation or foothold, no longer a cult, and shorn of its ancient ritual. As elsewhere under similar circumstances, mythology became transformed into poetry and saga, became secularized, and lost its binding power; and since in this form there was nothing about it that the Church could attack, it continued to develop through the Middle Ages, supplying a rich nourishment for the soul, when the Church with its theology of salvation had nothing comparable to offer." [22]

The point, then, is that the ancient symbols of the pagan European, pressed out of consciousness by Christianity, continued to live surreptitiously in the unconscious. "Medieval man dreamed out his broken youth in the images and figures of Celtic and pre-Celtic myths and sagas; and it was these, in the form of the Grail and other romances of the Arthurian cycle, that became the popular novels of the knightly and courtly circles of the whole of Europe." [23] In other words, when one mythological system replaces another within the psyche of a people as a whole, it assumes a dominant position in consciousness and drives the displaced mythology into the submerged levels of the unconscious. The old figures and images which were once the daily speech of the people are then able to reach the surface of the psyche only when consciousness grows weak. The symbolism of an old mythology becomes the symbolism of dreams, sometimes of artistic creation, and of possessions in moods and inspirations. An example in Jung's work of the reassertion of historically repressed symbols is the re-expression of the Wotan mythology in the mass possessions of Nazism. In the western

[22] Ibid., p. 181.
[23] Ibid., p. 181.

European psyche the old Celtic myths reappear not only in cultural movements like Romanticism, but in the images of individual psychology; so also do the symbols of other pre-Christian mythologies—the Hebraic, the Etruscan, the Slavonic—come to the surface in various personal and social forms and break through the veneer of modern consciousness.

The problem of historical study, then, from the point of view of the continuity of the psyche is to understand the relation of the symbols of one mythology to the symbols of another resting above it in the psyche. Each mythological system is a manifestation in a particular form of archetypal elements in the psyche. Their foundation in each case is the universality of the processes of the psyche, but their specific defining characteristics are derived from their historical form. The perception of archetypes—isolating them and analyzing them as the hidden kernels of cultural systems—is just a first step. What is chiefly important after that is to follow the archetypes out into society and see the dynamic expression of old and new symbols in social movements and in the phenomena of individual personality. The most crucial requirement is to maintain a depth conception of the historical continuity of the psyche. Zimmer does have such a perspective, and his intention in his studies is to give expression to the variety of forms in which the archetypes are manifested; but that is also his limitation. The value of Zimmer's work remains largely on an appreciative and artistic level. In the final analysis he fails to provide the specific and discipline formulations which are necessary for a socio-historical understanding of the psyche.

THE VIEW OF CARL KERENYI

In very close relation to Zimmer, the work of Carl Kerenyi calls for special mention. Kerenyi has a point of view
that is particularly sensitive and valuable for the study of
culture. Like Zimmer, he is not a sociological thinker, and
his contribution, therefore, does not consist of an empirical
analysis of culture. His value in our present context, rather,
is that he draws attention to a dimension of society that is
fundamental if we would proceed in applying Jung's concepts
to the historical field. We mention Kerenyi's formulation of
the nature of society here because it articulates a view which
must ultimately be incorporated in our orientation to social
study if we would apply the depth conception of the psyche
fruitfully. Kerenyi's understanding of society is in terms of
the historical largeness of the psyche and is based on the underlying view that man's life in society must be studied as
an aspect of the operation of the cosmos as a whole.

Just as Zimmer's thought was profoundly influenced by his
studies of Hinduism, Kerenyi's specialization in Greek mythology is reflected in his basic outlook. His way of conceiving the nature of the universe is in the spirit of the great
philosophers of Greece like Empedocles and Heraclitus who,
living in the days before Socrates, phrased their concepts in
terms of the realities of myth. Kerenyi begins with the pre-
Socratic view that the world is, at bottom, a great flux, a
ceaseless ocean of change, in which individuality makes
merely a transitory, phenomenal appearance. He thinks of
the cosmos as a void, essentially undifferentiated, in which
particular forms are present mainly *in potentia*. The ques-

tion, then, of how the human individual comes into being involves for Kerenyi a cosmological process, a process of differentiation out of the formless flux of the world. He does not hold, however, that the individual emerges by himself, but rather that the process involves the emergence of groups as unities out of the cosmos, followed by a further process of differentiation by which the specific individual emerges from the collectivity. The latter process was formulated by Jung, as we described in the previous chapter. Kerenyi accepts the main trend—and certainly the spirit—of Jung's conception; but he wishes to go further into the question of the origin of society from the point of view of its ultimate source and the nature of its emergence from the cosmic flux. In addition, Kerenyi finds that the link between the cosmos and society is the myth—or the "mythologem" as he calls it—and he concludes that it is via the mythologem that the individual experiences himself as a part of society and places the significance of his life in the context of the cosmos.

In defining the relation between the cosmos and society, however, Kerenyi takes the unfortunate step of using the term "monad" in a very confusing way. He applies it, not with the Leibnizian meaning for which it has become famous in philosophy, but with a quite different definition. To avoid misconceptions, it would be better if another word had been adopted; but the term does have a certain aptness for the relationship that Kerenyi means to describe, as the reader will observe. It is necessary, however, to keep in mind that the word "monad" is used in a special sense that is far from its customary meaning. By "monads" Kerenyi means the elemental unities underlying each of the world's cultures and constituting the "structural principles" of the society's experience of life. In terms of this definition, the monad is the most fundamental essence of each culture expressed as an entity, so deeply rooted in the psychic lives of the members of the society that they cannot conceive of themselves as possibly thinking in terms other than those of their particular monad. Kerenyi's question, then, is how the monad comes about and what its significance is.

In relation to the cosmos conceived as a formless void, the monad is the unit by which form emerges out of the flux. "In order to define the ultimate basis of the monads," Kerenyi says, "we would have to say that it is the compulsion in man to produce something formed, formed in spirit just as only formed things are produced in the body. This compulsion is the origin—the first leap. But the next moment, in the leap itself, the monad, the spiritual plan is there. The plan is the first thing that is intelligible; here something original, experienced with all the immediacy of the origin, proves to be one with some aspect of the open world. If cosmos is understood in the Greek sense that everything spiritual and our compulsion towards the spiritual are an essential part of the cosmos, then here we have the cosmos meeting with itself." [24]

THE CULTURAL MONAD AND THE COSMOS

The emergence of the monad involves three main steps. The first is the general cosmic principle that the formless gives rise to form in a manner relative to each level of being; for man, it means that he contains within himself an urge to

[24] Jung and Kerenyi, *Essays on a Science of Mythology*, pp. 27, 28. Passages quoted from this book in this chapter were written by Kerenyi.

create form on his own level, that is, to create within the psychological or spiritual sphere. The second step, "the leap itself," involves the crude fact of the emergence of a form in a society; it means simply that a monad is in the process of coming into being. "At this stage," Kerenyi says, "everything is welling up, flowing, continually varying and changing shape, all variations within the same culture being determined by the same monad. Spiritual plans have now appeared in and bound up with the world, as ground-plans for unending development." [25] The third step involves the integration of the process by which the cultural monad is formed. In it the whole process, including its end product, is stabilized. The culture is "founded," perhaps by a law-giver or some other human representative of the divine, and it then is invested with specific historical and cultural form. Now the "leap" out of the formless cosmos has been completed. When the work of the founder—whom Kerenyi speaks of as a creative artist—is finished, "we find ourselves in the midst of a definite people—'people' being understood as a source of power and talent and also as a source of characteristics transcending the monadic." [26] The "people" then having been "founded"—virtually created by its founder—has a tradition, a basis for its existence, and is "possessed" by its monad, believing that life and the world can be understood in no other way.

This "possession" [27] takes place on an historical basis and

[25] Ibid., p. 29.
[26] Ibid., pp. 29, 30.
[27] Kerenyi points out that he is using the term "possession" in Frobenius' sense, i.e., to mean the domination of individual thought by the monadic pattern. His implication is that it does not necessarily have the same meaning as Jung's use of the phrase to convey the domination

grows stronger with the passage of time. It emerges in the primary act of establishing the monad, and it is based on the fact that in the specific situation in which the monad is formed, a definite constellation of qualities becomes fixed as the qualities of the people and becomes the identifying marks of the culture to the members themselves and to outsiders. "Each and every view of the world," Kerenyi remarks, "has its characteristic 'monadic' features." [28] They are set at the moment of "founding" when the monad of culture is formed. As time goes on, the various aspects of the act of "founding," formalized in traditions and customs, come to be ever more deeply imbedded in the nature of the "people" who have thus been "founded," and the qualities of the moment of founding become the pervading traits of the people.

Kerenyi's fundamental point is that the historical quality of the monad is underlain by its specific nature as a link between man and the cosmos. The reason that the term "monad" is so significant to him is that, from its philosophic background, it carries the sense of a unit of the universe which contains in itself the essence of the whole universe in the same way that a drop of the ocean contains all the qualities of the ocean. The monad is thus a piece of the world broken out of the flow of the cosmos, representing the world, and expressing it in all its aspects. When a society has been founded and its monad has emerged, the monad contains not only the essence of its society, but it is the unit which maintains contact with the deepest source of the society *via*

---

of the individual personality from within by an "autonomous partial system." Ultimately the monadic and psychic views of "possession" are not contradictory; they need merely to be integrated and synthesized.

[28] *Essays on a Science of Mythology*, p. 27.

its own source, which is the cosmos itself. The monad of a society is the embodiment of its creation, that is, of its having been founded as a culture and as a people. The essence of the monad is its having been created—that is, its having emerged from the formless flux as an entity—and the circumstances of this emergence are preserved and hallowed in myths which depict the source and origin of the society and of the sacred realities of its life.

Myths about the origin of a people tend to place themselves in a timeless primordial past. They may make their focus a specific historical situation, as, for example, the story of Moses, but this, in turn, is founded upon men of a distant mythic age: the Patriarchs, Noah, Adam. The basic unit of a system of mythology has a quality that cuts across time. The essentials of its meaning are present always; that is the basis of its constant significance. But the figures of the myth and the figures of its narrative always are placed in the dim past. They "are always set in a primordial time," Kerenyi says, and he observes, "This return to the origins and to primordiality is a basic feature of every mythology." It expresses a fundamental aspect of mythologic thinking. "The philosopher tries to pierce through the world of appearance in order to say what 'really is,' but the teller of myths steps back into primordiality in order to tell us what 'originally was.' Primordiality is the same thing for him as authenticity." [29] Reality for the myth consists in going down to the beginnings of being, finding there the essence of what happened when its monad first came into existence, and thereby expressing something that is thoroughly meaningful for all who partake of a given cultural monad as long as it remains in existence.

[29] Ibid., p. 10.

PRIMORDIALITY AND HISTORY

When a myth is constructed and given its primordial setting, it is invariably connected with a definite date, an actual moment of history in the past, and when it is recounted, this primordial past of the myth is invariably brought into relation with some specific historical situation. Despite this, the "primordiality" of a myth does not itself have an historical existence. It is merely expressing, in the form of a symbol, the emergence of its monad out of the cosmic flux and into existence. Just as the monad is an aspect of the cosmos and contains the cosmos in it, the symbols of the monad express an intuition of an element of the universe itself. In them "the world tells us what *is* in the world and what *is true* in the world. A 'symbol' is not an 'allegory,' not just another way of speaking. It is an image presented, or rather represented, by the world itself." And Kerenyi adds in a footnote, "Jung's theory of 'natural symbols' and of dreams as products of nature is in agreement with this." [30]

On the basis of this agreement with Jung on the nature of the "symbol," Kerenyi then carries the question further, from the historical point of view. The way in which the symbols of a monad are experienced varies according to the historical level on which they appear. When the monad is coming into being, it is formed out of the cosmos by virtue of a great struggle on the part of a people standing, in Kerenyi's words, "face to face with the absolute, that is, on the frontiers of the pre-monadic." It is, in other words, the actual work of bringing a people into cultural existence, in forming a monad, and living out a system of mythology.

[30] Ibid., p. 62.

This is the key thought. On the level at which the monad is created, its mythology is experienced directly, lived out in a primary way, its symbols understood and carried out, as it were, from within themselves. But the situation changes in time, and the symbols, even though they be "natural symbols," do not continue to be experienced in this intimate way. "When solidly constructed monads break down, as at the end of the antique era, or when their dissolution is already far advanced, as it is today, we find ourselves closer to various kinds of mysticism than to mythology." [31] That is to say, in the latter days of a culture, the approach to reality must be through philosophy and by intellectual means, since the myth is no longer real in itself. From a functional point of view, it is the same thing to speak of the breaking apart of "solidly constructed monads" as for Jung to speak of the failure of social symbols to continue to act as "libido analogues." From Jung's psychological point of view, the significance of such a failure is that the conscious forefront of personality, the Persona, can no longer be maintained in an acceptable and meaningful way so that there must be a period of psychic disharmony within the individual. Kerenyi places another emphasis which is altogether in the spirit of the larger aspect of Jung's work, and in fact expresses one of the main contributions of the Jungian approach. He points out that to understand our present social situation our focus must always be kept on the correct understanding of its mythology and especially on building the capacity to have a direct and lived experience of its symbols.

"To the religious-minded man of the Greek world," Kerenyi says, "his divinities had always appeared in classical

[31] Ibid., p. 30.

perfection since the time of Homer. And undoubtedly they appeared not as the fictions or creations of art but as living deities who could be believed in . . . As psychologists we may stress the fact that this truth is always a *psychic reality;* as historians we may add that the psychic reality of such a truth, as indeed of all truths, changes with time; as biologists we may call the alteration of the power that so moves us *natural decay,* but the essentially convincing inner structure of the classical Greek divinities remains unshakable for all time." [32]

The basis for this eternality, as Kerenyi understands it, is that it reaches into the universe itself by virtue of its expressing a monadic reality. Such symbols are primordial in the sense that they are developed and formalized at the very ancient date of the founding of a society; they are primordial also in the sense that the people who believe in them and live them do so because they feel that they are derived from dark archaic times so that they express a reality deep in the nature of life; and fundamentally they are primordial because they express in a "natural" symbol man's intimation of the cosmos from which he comes. Because they are a direct contact with the primary realities of Being, monadic symbols "can only be known by immediate revelation," that is, by immediate experience of their inner spiritual nature. Efforts to rationalize them into analytical terms cannot reach their essence. They can be grasped only in their own terms. And since these monadic symbols, expressed in mythologies and religions, are the basis of the fundamental systems of belief of all cultural units, it follows that the social scientist who wishes to get to the core of social beliefs must "be bold

[32] Ibid., p. 143.

enough to take the things of the spirit spiritually." [33] He must put aside his analytical methodology and learn to penetrate the cosmological depths of the myth. The first requirement is that he have a flexible method of interpretation so that the symbols will not be forced artificially into a system of fixed formulations. He must then maintain an attitude that is open and receptive to the myth in order that he may experience the force of its symbols in an intimate way on all their various levels. Kerenyi's very basic point, which is shared by Jung and Zimmer, is that the proper study of society requires a total participation in the images of the culture in order to find the categories of reality which the symbols carry for the people who live them. It requires a relation of intimate dialogue between the myth and the social student, especially so that the symbols will be free to speak their own language. In this speech the symbols reveal not only the underlying spirit of their world-view, but also what Jung has called their "natural" insights into life. The process of studying culture through myth is, then, a constantly deepening experience. Kerenyi's belief is that the most fruitful relationship comes when we take a completely open attitude and regard the monadic symbols as the "revelation of something *still unopened—like a bud.*" [34]

Ultimately, then, Kerenyi's approach to society culminates in something larger than a theory of culture. It involves not only an understanding of the fundamental symbols, but also a personal experiencing of their levels of meaning and of their psychic force. The kind of social study toward which Kerenyi points really is in the nature of an art. Even more,

[33] Ibid., p. 146.
[34] Ibid., p. 147 (Kerenyi's italics).

it has a religious quality, since one of its aims is to quicken the cosmological sense in the psyche. That it can have such a result grows from the distinctive nature of its concepts. The monad, conceived as the elemental structure of each culture's symbolic views of life, mediates between the universe and the human being. On the one hand, it is regarded as a "natural product" of the world, an emergence out of the formless flux; on the other hand, it is a phenomenon expressing the archaic layers of the psyche. The monad comes from the universe, and is manifested on an integrative scale in society; as it is then contained within the psyche of individuals, it comes forth from individuals in the multifarious forms of consciousness. In so far as an individual participates in his particular historical monad, his psyche has a kind of window on the universe: he is living out an historical manifestation of a "natural symbol," and it is through these natural social expressions of the cosmos in the individual that cultural symbols give the personality a glimpse, and a fleeting contact, with the ulterior meanings of life.

JUNG'S POSITION IN THE ANALYSIS OF CULTURE

Kerenyi's significance lies in the fact that he provides an orientation to the study of society through the experiencing of myths and symbols. What he gives, however, is essentially a point of view, an attitude toward the meaning of culture, and his work is keyed more to the artistic appreciation of symbols than to the factual analysis of cultural phenomena. In general, the Jung-Kerenyi approach to culture is still in this early stage, and the problem is now to follow it through and see its significance for the specific problems of the social sciences.

It is obvious, to begin with, that Jung's point of view does not fit with the approach currently popular in the social sciences. It comes from another direction and asks a different kind of question. Its purpose is not to solve the same kind of problems as a structural sociology, and it is not concerned with the statistical study of social phenomena. The aim of Jung's approach to culture is rather to grasp, from within, those principles of society which derive from the spiritual nature of man, which is to say, the psychological aspects of the human being's sense of cultural belonging and his need to experience the meaning of his life in relation to the universe. It thus has a different frame of reference from that taken by academic sociology. Its point of view is both humanistic and historical, and its special merit is that it derives through to grapple with the problem that must be the hub of every philosophical anthropology that aspires to be a unitary study of man; it cuts through the inhibiting traditions of positivistic social science to interpret the inter-relation in history of cosmos, society, and human personality.

There is a very long intellectual road between the positivistic (or pragmatic) approach to social science and that taken by Jung and Kerenyi. It is a journey that very few have completed, and yet it is a direction of thought which appears to be drawing increasing attention. It may very well be that Jung's significance for the intellectual history of our time rests on the fact that he has covered practically the whole distance, beginning with biology and reaching, finally, the conception of the psyche and of "natural" monadic symbols in society. This process of development involved a series of steps beyond his original psychiatric position, and in these steps we can trace the logical structure underlying his work.

At the beginning, the most important advance for Jung involved a change in methodology. He discarded the analytical approach to man in favor of a view that stressed the organic wholeness of personality. A further alteration then became necessary. Giving up the analytical orientation meant also dropping the reductive study of the individual in terms of so-called "causes," and adopting instead a teleological point of view. The emphasis was then placed on the evolution of the purposes of life within the human being and, correspondingly, the approach to therapy came to be no longer in terms of medical or biological types of cure, but in terms of the integration and harmonization of the personality.

Once Jung had changed his focus of study from the "causes" to the meanings of life, he necessarily moved from a biological to a social point of view. This step had great consequences in Jung's thinking, since, as a medical man, the foundations of his thought had been in biology. In recognizing that purpose in human life is essentially a social phenomenon, and that the meaning of the individual is derived from the group life, Jung took a much larger perspective than the biological organismic approach out of which psychoanalysis had grown. In the act of substituting the social for the biological, however, something very interesting happened: whereas the psyche had previously been biological, it now became inherently social, and for Jung, with his background in the thought of Burckhardt and Bachofen, it meant that the psyche now had to be understood in historical terms. Jung took this step, and asked the question: what are the historical roots from which the contents of the psyche are derived? As he drove the question back and back in the contexts of the histories of various peoples, he came to uni-

versal patterns which seemed to underlie the variety of historical manifestations of the psyche. What was the source of
these? Jung called them the "natural symbols"—as Kerenyi
called them "monads"—and he held that they arise out of
the deepest levels of the psyche, where the psyche is in contact with the "world itself." The "natural symbols"—or
archetypes—are not only the most fundamental elements of all
psychic phenomena, but they express a primary contact with
reality, and thereby they carry an intimation—partly clear,
partly clouded—of something that is real. It is at this point
that Jungian thought goes beyond Positivism and all relativ-
isms to deal with myth directly and to experience the full
consequences of its symbols.

We have already discussed in some detail the various levels
on which Jung interprets myth and symbol.[36] Fundamentally,
it is on these concepts that Jung's theory of society is based,
and we must therefore realize that, in large part, Jung's relevance for social thought depends on his analysis of myth.

Because of his identification with the theory of the unconscious, Jung is generally classified as one who interprets
society in terms of irrational forces. This would be true to
say of Freud, but it is misleading to think of Jung in these
terms. Freud's thinking, with its biological basis, constantly
maintains a dichotomy between the rational and the irrational in personality, with the irrational having by far the
greater importance. Jung also reiterates that "consciousness
comes from the unconscious," but, as we pointed out in an
earlier discussion, his purpose in delineating the lower levels

[35] *Myths and Symbols*, p. 195.
[36] See Chapter 7 regarding symbols in society and their relation
to myth in Jung's total theory.

of the psyche is not to extend the theory of the unconscious, but to set a deeper base on which to construct a theory of knowledge and personality as a whole. Jung's effort is to build a framework for studying the total process of cognition. The Objective Unconscious functions as the creative supplier of the materials of consciousness. It is the area of the psyche which acts as the dynamic source for the contents of personality. It provides the preconditions for consciousness; consequently, by its very nature it is much more than merely the negative side of consciousness and rationality.

We must stress this point in order to grasp clearly the significance of Jung's interpretation of myth. Since myth expresses the qualities of the unconscious, it must also be understood in terms of an affirmative and constructive role. The Jungian view is here at variance with other approaches because it grants myth an inherent psychological reality and does not treat it merely as a childish prelude to the development of reason. Particularly in those studies which have their roots in the rationalistic ways of thought of the nineteenth century, mythology is looked at from a negative point of view. We see this in Freud's work, where myths are described as mechanisms of neurosis and as "illusions"; in the French tradition, descending from Auguste Comte, mythology is viewed as an inferior mode of knowledge, although it is excused as being a necessary stage in the evolution toward philosophy and science. Even in the work of Ernst Cassirer, myth is placed in an inferior position as an early conception of the world, although it is admitted that each system of myth has its own logical structure and authentic insights.

CASSIRER AND RADIN: THE PROBLEM OF MYTHOLOGIC THOUGHT

The interpretations of culture developed by Cassirer are noteworthy both for their similarities with Jung's work and for their differences. Of all the current approaches to mythology, Cassirer's is certainly among the most intellectually imposing. His work is a philosophical anthropology in the fullest sense of being an effort to grasp the totality of cultural phenomena within the unifying context of a systematic philosophy. It is the grand intellectual structure of Cassirer's thought that makes his position so imposing, but this is also his weakness. His scope is severely limited by the fact that he builds upon a Neo-Kantian substructure.

Cassirer proceeds with the idea that man is essentially a symbol-making creature. It would be correct to say that Jung holds the same belief. The difference, however, is that Cassirer understands symbols as instruments which arise out of man's experience in his efforts to further his purposes in communicating with other men and in thinking more efficiently. The question of symbols has, essentially, an epistemological meaning to him. Jung, on the other hand, interprets symbols in terms of the inner functioning of the psyche. Symbols do not arise out of experience as a means of communication in society, but symbols arise out of the spontaneous creativity within the psyche. There is thus a basic difference in the conception of the ways in which symbols function. To Cassirer they are effective as means of knowledge in relation to outer experience; to Jung they are effective in the depths of personality as autonomous channelizers of psychic energy. Symbols operate on a more fundamental level for Jung. When they are understood only as means of communication, they are on the level of consciousness, which is the surface of the psyche; but as autonomous and spontaneous creations carrying large sums of energy, they operate in the unconscious and express basic psychic processes. They are thus much more dynamic factors than mere means of knowledge, and this difference has far reaching consequences in the two approaches to man.

One of the consequences of Cassirer's Kantian roots is a distinction which he makes between "substance" and "function." He holds that we are not able to understand the "substance" of man, that is, his essence, what man "really is"; but we can understand man only "functionally" in terms of his "works," that is, in terms of the visible activities and achievements of culture. In place of an effort to get at the "essence" of man in society, Cassirer urges an historical study. "The question of what language, myth, and religion 'are,'" he says, "cannot be answered without a penetrating study of their historical development." [37] Actually, what Cassirer offers both in his *Study of Man* and in the volume on mythical thought in his series on the *Philosophy of Symbolical Forms* is not really an historical study, but rather a description of some aspects of culture as they fit into his conceptual framework. Cassirer's use of the term "historical" —at least as he applies it in his studies—does not have the usual social meaning of historical studies, but has more the sense of "empirical" or "phenomenological." What he studies is not history as such but the "roots" and development

[37] Ernst Cassirer, *An Essay on Man*, Yale Univ. Press, New Haven, 1944, p. 68.

of the "symbolical forms" which are manifested in social life. Of these "symbolical forms," myth is one, together with religion, language, art, history, and science.

It is not too great a simplification to say that Cassirer's work on myth is an effort to make mythology stand to reason by fitting it into a large pattern of conceptual analysis. He interprets myth functionally, that is, in terms of the roles which its symbols play in the life of the culture as a whole. He points out that while the symbols and beliefs of a culture may seem strange and beyond understanding to an outsider, each system of myth has a rationale of its own. It has its own hidden assumptions, its own conception of the nature of things and of their potencies, and within this framework of preconceptions it maintains its own logic. This is the basis on which Cassirer refutes what he considers to have been Lévy-Bruhl's error in ascribing pre-logical thinking to the primitives. Primitive thought is as logical as modern thought, Cassirer says, when it is understood in terms of its own premises. He points out also that myth has its own "style" of thinking. "The world of myth is a dramatic world—a world of actions, of forces, of conflicting powers. Mythical perception is always impregnated with these emotional qualities. Whatever is seen or felt is surrounded by a special atmosphere —an atmosphere of joy or grief, of anguish or excitement, of exultation or depression." [38] The primitive invests the world of nature with his images and his conception of godlike and tribal potencies. He sees the world of nature as being alive, and that is the style of thinking that pervades his myths.

It is apparent that such an interpretation has much in common with Jung's analysis of myth and with those offered

[38] Ibid., pp. 76, 77.

by Zimmer and Kerenyi. All of them understand that the mythologic mind works within a system of its own conceptions and that the question of whether a line of thought in a primitive community is "logical" or not must be answered in terms of the assumptions on which it proceeds and also in relation to the customary habits of reasoning. A great deal depends on what a culture takes for granted. The Jungian writers are certainly also aware of the fact that myth has a dramatic pattern and a certain vivacity in its manner. The conception of the "style of thinking" in myth was developed by Nietzsche as well as by Bachofen, and the works of Jung, Zimmer, and Kerenyi are replete with articulate examples. On the descriptive level, then, Cassirer and Jung move in very similar terms, but the differences between them come from the fact that Cassirer does not have a psychic dimension with which to interpret the autonomous nature of symbol formation.

Like the Jungian studies of myth, Cassirer seeks to take an open point of view and to avoid any of the systems which interpret myth according to a rigid doctrinal principle. He rejects the Freudian view and also the aetiological view of James Fraser, and he concludes, "We cannot reduce myth to certain fixed, static elements; we must strive to grasp it in its inner life, in its mobility and versatility, in its dynamic principle." [39] Cassirer has in mind that each culture functions in terms of its own assumptions and categories, that these are natural to it, and that they are the only principles that can seem meaningful to the individual who lives in the culture. In this sense the system of mythology provides the frame of reference for individual activity, and its terms,

[39] Ibid., p. 76.

therefore, are the dynamic principles by which the community functions. This interpretation fits Jung's views because of its flexibility; the nature of its differences, however, will become clear from a brief comparison of Cassirer with the anthropological writings of Paul Radin.

In the United States, Radin's work stands out as the major exception to current academic anthropological views and the general lack of appreciation for Jung's concepts. As one of the first social scientists to realize the importance of Depth Psychology for the study of culture, he has been of the opinion since the early nineteen-thirties that, of all modern psychological work, "it is the application of the psychoanalytical theories of Jung that is most likely to have the most profound influence upon ethnology." [40] He reached this view when, after studying with the British anthropologist, W.H.R. Rivers, he came to the conclusion that Freud's concepts were focused in a non-sociological way which could only lead to misunderstanding when applied to the analysis of culture; he concluded, too, that Adler had oriented his studies altogether toward the treatment of individuals and did not have an historical point of view. Radin therefore rejected both Freud and Adler while maintaining the general conception of the unconscious, and from then on he applied aspects of Jung's perspective in his studies of aboriginal culture.

In accordance with the main interest of his life-work, Radin's studies of mythologic thought tend to focus on the problem of understanding primitive mentality. It is natural,

[40] Paul Radin, *Social Anthropology*, McGraw Hill, New York, 1932, p. 16. The same view is found in Radin's *The Method and Theory of Ethnology*, McGraw Hill, New York, 1933, pp. 265-267.

then, that he gives much attention to the work of Lévy-Bruhl, and Radin agrees with Jung as to the great theoretical significance of Lévy-Bruhl's analyses. In an effort, however, to balance the misconceptions created by Lévy-Bruhl's formulations, and to build an approach to primitive man more expressive of Jung's general position, Radin directs attention to some of Lévy-Bruhl's preconceptions. One of his principal targets is what Radin calls "the curious notion that everything possesses an evolutionary history." [41] He is referring to the nineteenth century tendency to carry over the principle of biological evolution to the study of culture and to assume that there are necessary stages in the social evolution of the human mind. Lévy-Bruhl has stated explicitly in his basic book, *Les Fonctions Mentales*, and in several subsequent writings that he believes that primitive peoples have the same mental and physical constitution as Europeans and that they do not by any means represent an inferior level of evolution. He has nevertheless maintained something of the conception of stages described in the positivistic social philosophy of Auguste Comte, and its overtones remain in his work so that, as in his term "pre-logical," he sometimes gives the impression that the thought of primitives is inferior by its very nature to the thought of modern times. Radin's well known book, *Primitive Man as Philosopher*, was intended to correct this view by stressing the other side of the question. He recounted some of the many instances of profound philosophical insights, abstraction, and poetic imagery found in primitive cultures, and then came to the conclusion that primitive thought in itself is no more and no less logical than

[41] Paul Radin, *Monotheism among Primitive Peoples*, Arthur Davis Memorial Lecture, April 27, 1924, Allen, Unwin, London, p. 66.

modern thought. Radin's view was essentially that the qualities of primitive mentality depend on two main factors: the
historical situation in which the tribe lives; and the personality type of the individual, who may either be satisfied
with the received doctrines or, if he has the temperament
and capacity, may seek a religious experience or a philosophical vision of his own. With this, the question takes on a
larger scope and comes to involve not only primitive mentality
but the nature and appearance of pre-logical thought in any
culture. It is at this point that Radin's position brings an
important clarification of Jung's setting of the problem.

In Cassirer's writings there is the same problem as that
which arises in Lévy-Bruhl's. On the one hand, he holds
that the question of whether thought is logical always depends on the context of beliefs in the particular culture; on
the other hand, he takes the category of "mythical thought"
as a distinct "symbolical form," as a separate and distinct
way of knowledge, inferior to the modern way of science.
Even while he criticizes Lévy-Bruhl's term "pre-logical,"
therefore, Cassirer implicitly falls back on the same schematic theory of stages in the evolution of thought. Actually,
there are points in Jung's formulations where he is subject
to the same criticism. When he speaks of "pre-conscious"
thought or of the presence of "participation mystique" in
primitive mentality, there is the implied belief in inferior
and superior levels of thought. As we tried to make clear in
interpreting Jung on this point earlier, however, the question
of a stage prior to the development of consciousness does
not involve a distinction between primitive and modern
thought as such, but rather a distinction as to the nature
and degree of differentiation of psychic contents. The levels

for Jung do not fundamentally involve types of culture but rather aspects of the change that occurs in the movement from the unconscious to consciousness. The processes of the psyche therefore become the hub of the question.

Radin's point, which is to stress that primitives are as logical, or at least no less logical, than modern men, is a deliberate overstress designed to make it clear that empirical anthropological studies do not permit a distinction between primitives and moderns on the basis of the degree of logic in their thought. The point could be stated from the opposite direction saying that moderns have as little logic as primitives. This would convey another side of Jung's meaning except that he would feel called upon to remark that very often primitives are more conscious—frequently more highly individuated with a more harmonious relation between consciousness and the unconscious—than moderns. When Lévy-Bruhl says, therefore, that his term "pre-logical means neither a-logical nor anti-logical," [42] but merely a logic that is different from ours, he is both right and wrong. The difference does exist and is very important to understand; but it cannot be put in terms of the two types of culture. It can be formulated psychologically only. Some readers of Jung have come away with the impression that he is interested in analyzing "the primitive in the modern," but we can see that this involves a slight misconception. Jung is interested in studying the relation between the images of the unconscious and their differentiation into consciousness in the psyche in any culture. To ask how consciousness and individuality emerge in primitive cultures, and how the unconscious and the collec-

[42] See Lucien Lévy-Bruhl, *La Mentalité Primitive*, Herbert Spencer Lecture at Oxford on May 29, 1931.

tive factors with their "participation mystique" remain in the modern are two sides of the same question. Both are underlain by the structure and processes of the psyche.

EVALUATING THE ARCHETYPE CONCEPT

The psychic processes provide the focus for understanding Jung's contribution to the analysis of culture. Set in terms of the psyche, all theories of culture-types or of social stages are fundamentally only attempts to interpret the surface manifestations in society of what are essentially psychic phenomena. The dynamics underlying the life of a culture are the psychic events that are taking place there. If one follows a functional approach to culture and studies the role that particular beliefs play in the total frame of reference of the society, there is always the further question of what are the inner experiences that implement these beliefs. In other words, a functional interpretation of culture leads directly to the need for the psychic dimension of the unconscious. This is essentially the difference between Cassirer and Jung. Cassirer analyzes the contents of culture by typologizing them and describing them under the headings of the various "symbolical forms." Jung traces symbols back into the psyche to find their psychic meaning.

All of Jung's interpretations of culture proceed on the basis of the idea that the nature and structure of the psyche are the same for all mankind. One gets an opposite impression from the writings of Lévy-Bruhl and Cassirer with their concepts of "pre-logical mentality" and "mythical thought" set in contrast to the modern, scientific point of view; but both these writers do fundamentally agree with Jung that the basic psychological equipment is the same for all the human species. In all anthropological work that carries over the idea of revolutionary stages, an overtone of invidious distinction inevitably creeps into the comparison between the primitive and the modern, and this is the reason that Radin has been so much at pains to stress the inherent dignity and intelligence of primitive man. Far from being "simple," primitive man experiences all the vicissitudes of life of his modern brothers, and he expresses all the psychic processes of personal development. Far from being static, also, primitive culture undergoes historical change sometimes at an intense rate, although this history is often revealed only by tracing changes in ritual and is obscured by the seemingly timeless tenor of primitive life. These two points, which Radin has emphasized, are very important in supporting Jung's point of view on the anthropological level. They indicate, firstly, that primitives partake on equal terms with other peoples in the universality of symbol formation; and secondly, that the contents of the primitive psyche, as of all others, are based on historical material. Radin himself has documented this last point by obtaining autobiographical material from the Winnebago Indians in which one can see very clearly the historical levels of symbols within the individual and their expression in the processes of personality.[43]

From the view that the basic processes of the psyche are the same in all peoples, it follows that these processes will be expressed in symbols with an underlying similarity. Jung's cardinal idea of the "archetypes" is, then, not an assump-

[43] See Paul Radin, "The Religious Experiences of an American Indian" in *Eranos-Jahrbuch*, Vol. XVIII, 1950, pp. 249-290. See also Radin's *Crashing Thunder, The Autobiography of an American Indian*, Appleton, New York, 1926.

tion of his, as it is sometimes thought to be, but a deduction made from the universal nature of the psyche in an effort to understand the varieties of symbol formation. The question of what the concept actually accomplishes has several levels: what it contributes to the understanding of personality; its value for the study of society, and especially for the historical aspects of the psyche; and what it signifies for the meaning of man's relation to the "world" as cosmos.

This last point is the most far-reaching of all because it involves the underlying point of view of Jung's position and his shifting of directions in modern thought. Fundamentally Jung's contribution centers around the fact that he has shown that the experiencing of the meaning of life is of crucial importance for the psychological life of the individual regardless of the culture in which he lives. The quotation from Jung which one most often encounters in the writings of contemporary authors has to do with Jung's discovery that the neurotic condition of those of his patients who were over thirty-five years of age was the result in every case of a confusion as to the meaning of their lives. The archetypes are important for their expression of the psychic processes of personality; but this is just the first part of their importance. Their main significance is that they represent in a form that is natural to the psychic life of the individual an experience of the cosmos and of its meaningfulness. This experience and its symbolic representation in some historical manifestation of the archetype are essential for the functioning of personality.

Since they involve the meanings of life, the archetypes extend to questions of a metaphysical nature. On this point, we should note that, even though caution is not Jung's dominant quality, he is anxious to avoid making any metaphysical assumption. It is not altogether apparent in his latest work, but a Kantian strain has been very important in the development of Jung's thought. Particularly at the time when he was thinking through his major conceptions as he developed them in the early 1920's in his books, on *psychological types and individuation*, Jung's analysis had a Kantian substructure. He accepted Kant's fundamental restriction that we cannot know things in themselves, and he concluded that the only reality we can study with confidence is *Esse in Anima*, Being in the Soul. It was in this book, too, that Jung developed his idea of the "psychologically real," from which there followed his most fundamental conception that the phenomena of the psyche constitute an area of reality which may be studied in their own terms. Even when Jung studies Oriental religions, as in *The Secret of the Golden Flower*, the reality he is dealing with is based altogether on the psyche. In fact, that is just why he finds spiritual disciplines like that of Tantric Yoga, Esoteric Taoism, and Zen Buddhism so significant. Their metaphysical starting point is limited to the human being and so they do not offend Jung's earlier Kantian predisposition. Even though the aim of these Oriental doctrines is to penetrate into the mysteries of existence itself, whatever they say about man's relation to the cosmos depends altogether on their psychic convictions and experiences. Even the gods are interpreted as emergences from the soul, and they are believed in—at least in the esoteric teachings—in psychological terms. In interpreting Jung's point of view, we must always remember the fact that all his doctrines about the "world" as cosmos are based, not on the world itself, but on the analysis of psychic contents. He has no metaphysical assumptions other than that reality is in the psyche; it is only from what he finds in the psyche that Jung derives his ideas about man's relation to the universe.

This is the philosophical context in which the doctrine of archetypes can best be appreciated. It is a means of dealing with ideas about the universe not metaphysically but psychologically; and yet it is not merely a psychological approach. The archetypes are a psychological but not a psychologizing concept. They are used not to explain away man's beliefs about reality, but to give a deeper insight into their symbolism as primordial intuitions of life.

Interpreting the archetypes in this way leads directly to one of the most provocative aspects of Jung's work. As "natural symbols" the archetypes are representations of the basic processes of the psyche. Their figures and images express not only a view of the world, but something of the very nature of the human being as such; they reflect man's elemental contact with the world. Just as the processes of the body are man's link to the animal kingdom, the psychic processes are his point of meeting with the primordial meanings of life. One of the aims of the study of archetypes is to penetrate to the Adamic past and so to recapture the intuitions contained in the first appearance of symbol formation. This is why there is a special significance in the interpretation of the mythology of the very early religions and of the symbol structure of the so-called primitives. In studying the primordial expressions of symbols underneath the overlays of history, we come in contact with the archetypes as primal aspects of the psyche at a point where they express man's primary intuitions of his relation to the world.

The archetypes are then to be studied with two purposes:

as a key to the psychic processes of individuals; and as an expression of fundamental intuitions of the meaning of life. The latter point involves the use of purely psychological data in a way that goes beyond psychology. On the one hand, it leads from individual psychology to the cosmos; and on the other hand—in fact just because it involves cosmological symbols—it moves into social theory. With regard to the first step, we should keep in mind that when Jung makes the statement that in a natural symbol the "world is speaking," his intention is not to build a cosmological theory, but rather to dramatize the largeness and variety of the sources of the individual's psychic contents. With regard to the second step—from psychology to society—we can easily see that since the archetypes involve the most fundamental meanings, they appear on a psychic level that is prior to individuality, and are expressed in the core of belief that underlies major cultural units. Taken abstractly, in their essential forms, the archetypes express an intuition of the world; but in their specific manifestations, they constitute the contents of the deepest layers of the unconscious. They appear in the individual psyche at its most fundamental levels, but always in the form given to them by some cultural system. Especially from the sociological point of view, the most important aspect of the archetypes is that they are universal psychic contents which appear in a variety of *historical* forms. Appearing as natural symbols, they comprise the core of what Kerenyi has called "monadic" systems of myth. The archetypes, then, are the basic material underlying the formation of the various social symbols in history; and, through these, they provide the figures and images which fill the collective level of the unconscious in the individual psyche.

In terms of these concepts, the archetypes provide extremely provocative possibilities for ethnological study. They are a means of finding the unity underlying the variety of cultural products. Works of art, poetry, and literature, social and political ideologies, as well as religious works, may be studied as expressions of basic patterns of psychic symbolism. Several fruitful studies of this type are to be found in the pages of the *Eranos Jahrbuch*. We have to note, however, that there is an underlying danger in indulging in analytical studies when their purpose is mainly to classify the various cultural products according to archetypal patterns. It can be very misleading to study the archetypes in a way that is only static and descriptive. They can really become fruitful concepts only when they are studied historically, since it is not abstractly but in their historical forms that they come forth in the ever-changing psychic contents of social life.

It hardly seems possible to study the archetypes historically without accepting Jung's historical conception of the psyche, at least as a working hypothesis. In the thinking of both Jung and Kerenyi, the fundamental and recurring pattern of each historical people is based on the monadic symbols of its culture. Out of the "Motifs" of its original founding myth, a people draws the images and figures which fill the lower levels of the unconscious of its members. In so far as the people is unified spiritually, its psychic contents have a common source. They come out of that myth which is most basic in a people's history. Jung holds that such mythologems are not only part of the world of nature for a people, but they are actually part of the human nature of the people themselves. Their symbols are seemingly unchangeable realities, like the mountains and rivers of their native land. This is one of the senses in which Jung speaks of such symbols as "natural." They *are* part of the world of nature for a people. If the images are firmly set at the collective level of the psyche, they are then a part of the people itself—as a group and as individuals—as much as the color of their hair or the shape of their skulls. In the course of history, as variations in beliefs and in social usages take place, the symbols change their dress, but their inner content remains the same. The motifs of the original founding myth of the people form the basis of a continuity in the psyche, a continuity which is a group phenomenon, but which nevertheless is expressed and experienced by the individual.

The inter-relationship between the psychic contents of individuals and the historical manifestation of the archetypes is one of the most provocative questions that emerges from Jungian work. Individuals are personifications of the images and figures found in the monadic myths of their people. That is one side of Jung's thought. On the other levels, the myth is understood as being within the group and also latently within the individuals in a way that goes through time. The questions of how specific traits of individuality are related to the historical form of the myth, and how, conversely, myths express themselves in the products of culture, require clearer analysis, but we can see the value of the concepts. The question of the archetypes and individuality is in one sense a paradox, and in another sense it is an anthropological statement of the eternal philosophical problem of the universal and the particular.

In interpreting the archetype concept, it is most important to regard it as essentially a tool of thought, a mode of formulating and organizing an exceedingly difficult and elusive subject matter. Its great value is as a focus for study in developing hypotheses regarding the creative and spontaneous manifestations of the psyche. Certainly, the worst mistake that can be made in interpreting Jung is to treat his work as though it were a final product rather than a brave expedition into a new realm of science. The value of his leading concepts—the archetypes, the collective unconscious, the historical conception of the psyche—lies mainly in the orientation they give to the study of man. They carry with them not so much a body of knowledge as an attitude toward the reality of the psychic life and the validity of the spiritual experiences of man in history. The depth conception of the psyche, focused as Jung's is toward social rather than toward biological questions, contains a perspective that is radically different from the current academic views. Its unorthodoxy is one of its great values if only for the stimulation of thought that it can bring to the social sciences. In its present state, however, the Jungian point of view still has left much undone. As we have presented Jung's thought bit by bit in the preceding pages, it must have occurred to the reader that here are concepts of tremendous originality and force which need yet to be more sharply focused if they are to be applied to social-historical questions with the best results. Our own conclusion is that Jung's concepts have a ground-breaking power for the social sciences, but that they will make their impact fully felt only when they have been reformulated and redefined with reference to the specific problems of social study. When this has been done, Jung's radical and profound penetration is bound to have a tremendous effect on the social study of man.

It has been well said that the penalty of taking the lead is to make errors. Since he is a pioneer, Jung has paid the penalty in the form of rough, unclear, and sometimes questionable formulations. It would not be fair if we were to judge him for his errors, however, for they are merely a sign of his having tried so much. Ultimately the test and justification of Jung's work will come when his depth conception of man will have filtered more thoroughly into the thought of our age. It will surely re-emerge transformed in new studies of man, and it is by these that time will judge Jung's seminal efforts.

EPILOGUE

Of all the major depth psychologists, Jung stands out as the only one who has interpreted the unconscious in terms of the spiritual nature of man. This, more than anything else, is the basis on which his influence is increasing and is due to continue to increase.

Since Bleuler first used the term "Depth Psychology," it has been adopted by thinkers who come from very different directions. They have all shared the one basic insight, however, that there is more to the mind than appears on the surface of consciousness. For a variety of historical reasons, the first part of the twentieth century was just the time when such a statement could seem to be a great revelation of truth. It was a time when a tremendous optimism based on a materialistic "progress" was collapsing with a force that destroyed not only material cultures but also the most deeply accepted meanings of life. The years after the first World War were an age of profound confusion, a time when people could see good reason for accepting a psychiatric diagnosis of their activities and for believing that Freud's "dirty" truths were the full truth. It takes away none of the credit of Freud's contribution when we point out that, after all, the uncovering of the unconscious was not an original discovery. That there are "depths" beneath consciousness was known by Erasmus and Montaigne and Balzac, not to mention St. Augustine and the ancient Hindus and Taoists. Freud's originality consisted mainly in the fact that he formulated the under-side of consciousness in the kind of psychiatric terms in which his fellow Europeans could see themselves reflected. When the whole structure of meanings had gone wrong, it was quite convenient to be able to say that their psychological problem was nothing but sex. It turned the attention away from the larger truth, much harder to bear, that the psychological problem involved nothing less than the totality of life in a culture that was going to pieces and was hell-bent on destroying itself.

Jung's diagnosis is much more adequate when it comes to understanding "the psychological problem of our time." He realized that all the special principles of the psychologists —sex with Freud, the power principles with Adler, and so on—were only outer manifestations of a more far-reaching breakdown, which involved the meaning of life itself. He saw that a psychiatrist could not solve the problems of people living in modern Western civilization unless he helped them find again the meaning of their lives. The issues which Jung raises in his approach to the individual, therefore, reach a basic historical need, a religious need. The reason that his work is gaining a progressively wider audience is simply that time is making it clear that there is a total spiritual problem where a mere personality problem had been thought to exist before.

In such a situation very little good can be done—regardless of all claims of "scientific" therapy—unless the individual finds a purposive direction for his life. Freud could never supply such an affirmative force; his own psychology prevented it. It is apparent to anyone who would really understand Freud as a human being that he had an essentially pessimistic view of life. Even while he made the Oedipus saga a cornerstone of his theories, it was not the sexual, but much more the tragic side of Oedipus that made the greatest impression on him. There is in Freud a pervading sense of the tragedy of life, and it constantly appears in his theoretical work. Just as the fates bring about Oedipus' inexorable destiny, so the biological instincts hold man to a course he cannot escape. That is why the "depths" of the unconscious are always dark and negative to Freud. They are depths in the sense of a dirty dungeon, in which, when all is said and done, man must remain enchained.

Quite a different approach is necessary if one would direct the modern man to a road that goes beyond his spiritual impasse. First, he must have a sense of freedom, or at least of the potentiality of freedom, as being within the bounds of human nature. Jung has articulated this very thoroughly and stressed it from several different angles in order to demonstrate the fact that the psyche is inherently creative. Man is caught in a trap only if he permits himself to be, for the very nature of the psyche is to integrate itself and to build a unity out of the disjointed segments of personality. Jung's conception of Individuation is essentially a road of freedom, pointing out that it is not only within man's power to find and experience the meaning of his life, but that his psychological health requires him to do so.

The second need is a sense of the largeness of the psyche and of its intimate relation to reality. One of the stultifying effects of the biological approach to psychology has been to close man off, cutting his direct contact with the world and permitting him only to have some necessary "illusions" to serve as beliefs. Here, Jung's great contribution has been to show that, of the many psychic contents, there are some whose essential nature is to give man a point of contact with the world as cosmos. These contents, which are the most deeply rooted, the most fundamental symbols in the unconscious, are an expression not only of psychic processes, but also of principles operating in the cosmos at large. What Jung calls archetypal images are a manifestation in man of these principles, and they constitute a link, a point of relationship, between the Self and the world beyond man's psychic nature. The psyche contains not only the repressed wishes and fears hidden in the dark depths of the unconscious; it contains also the experience of reality in man and man's psychic intimation of his place in the cosmos through a variety of symbols. The unconscious extends into the lower layers of man's animal nature, and it also reaches up, out and beyond the merely human toward a meaningful contact with the infinite aspects of life. We should then enlarge our concept and speak, not of the "depths" of the psyche, but of its "magnitude"—to take a phrase from Augustine—and this is the sense in which Jung has brought a new and necessary dimension to the old "depth" psychology.

The creativity of personality and the magnitude of the psyche are two pillars in Jung's thought. There is one more which is of the greatest importance, and that is his sense of time. This involves Jung's underlying idea that there is a principle of opposites operating in all things and that, to understand any subject, one must perceive its various phases in their proper position in its life-cycle. To look for the movement of opposites in time is, as we discussed earlier, more subtle than dialectics and profounder than a merely historical point of view. The appreciation of the principle of opposites at work beneath the surface of events gives a special perspective. It leads to an awareness of potentialities present in the midst of weakness and so focuses on the continuity in history underlying and transcending the decay of civilizations. It is of great value in attempting to gage what can emerge out of the modern psychological situation.

Fundamentally, Jung's diagnosis of the modern man is that he is suffering from a starvation of symbols, a spiritual malnutrition brought on by meanings that became too meagre to nourish the soul. Projections and images have been withdrawn from life, and as a result the world has ceased to seem alive. It is the deadening of images which once had a vital power that lies at the source of the confusions in modern consciousness. The question is whether the occidental peoples can continue to live as they now are with only a morgue of symbols to supply them with the meanings of life. From Jung's point of view, this is impossible; periodic confusion, paralysis of spirit, and ultimate breakdown are bound to result. That is the negative side, and on the affirmative side is the fact that as a result of the impoverishment of symbols, the psyche must, in time, out of the nature of its inherent creativity, bring forth new symbols from within itself. Eventually new faiths must arise and new meanings be born because the principle of opposites prevents a vacuum from lasting long. But how this will happen, at what time the now germinating symbols will come to fruition, and in what manner they will relate to the social and cultural crises through which Western civilization is now passing: these are questions on which Jung does not feel called upon to prophesy.

The solution of the psychological problem of our time, for our civilization and for the individual, lies in the emergence of strong, new, creative faiths; that much is clear. But the means by which they are to emerge is not so clear. It is one thing, of course, to say that it is psychologically of the greatest value to experience a symbol as a living reality; and it is quite another thing actually to have such an experience, or even to make one possible. There is a great gap here, and it is one of the abysses in Jung's, as well as in all advanced modern thought. As a psychologist, Jung is neutral, regardless of what people may sometimes read into him. He does not commit himself to belief in any particular symbol. When dealing with specific cases, he encourages the individual to follow the symbol that is most meaningful to him in terms of his own experience. Jung therefore considers it not at all inconsistent to endorse Catholicism for one person and Zen Buddhism for another, since he is mainly interested in the pragmatic value of the belief in leading his patient back to health. He knows, of course, that in giving a helpful direction to the relatively few individuals who are his patients, he is not solving the fundamental spiritual problems of our age in their profound historical sense; but that is not his task. Having gone this far, Jung then begs off. He sets his own limits. And yet one feels that more is necessary, that the line of thought which has thus been initiated will go on of its own momentum and culminate in a larger awareness, which finally will bring about the answer that is being awaited.

Some indications are here. The first, on the analytical level, is that now our spiritual situation is clear and understood. We know something now about the nature of symbols, the nature of faith, and the nature and consequence of the breakup of beliefs. We know something also about the sources and means by which new symbols can come into being, even if it is not within our power to create such symbols by an act of deliberate will. And, more important, we have learned about the limitations of the analytical point of view and now can see that it plays only an intermediary role in human knowledge. There is a step further, and the way is being prepared for it by the building of an open attitude, a non-reductive attitude, toward the meanings of myth and symbol. In an age which has witnessed the atrophy of its ability to experience images as living realities, it is no small thing just to realize that reality does speak through symbols. Knowing that it does speak so, we may in time learn how to listen.

Of all the signs, the greatest is the opening of the Western psyche to the symbolic visions and insights of the oriental, the ancient, and the primitive. It is an unconscious searching for an aliveness in imagery based on the feeling that what is dead in us may nevertheless be living in others. It will be an ever increasing experience in modern men to find that strange and distant symbols bring them into touch with reality in a way that is beyond the power of their traditional images. We shall have occasion during the coming generation to learn again the ancient truth that man must search far and wide in order to find the treasure buried within himself. It should not surprise us, therefore, to find that exotic cults will flourish in increasing numbers. Seen in the perspective of the history of the Western psyche, it will be a good sign.

It will mean that the soul is flexing its muscles, that it is reawakening and renewing its capacity to appreciate the vitality of images. And while the Western man practises with strange symbols the external forms of which are alien to him, he will be learning that there is a universality of meaning and a common intensity communicated throughout the diversity of human imagery. When the significance of this has dawned upon him, and the capacity to contact the power in imagery will have come vibrantly to life in him again, then the Western psyche will be ready for its next adventure. This is the time when new and lasting symbols will be born. This is the time when the shifting of spiritual directions begun by Jung on an intellectual level will reach its ultimate fulfillment.

INDEX

INDEX 299

Persona, 83, 106, 198, 227, 228
  Collapse of, 147
Personal Unconscious, 66, 92, 223
Possession, 16, 94, 173
  and Gods, 211
  in History, 205
Pragmatism, 73
Primal Crime, 43
Primitive Mentality, 168
Primordial Images, 69
Primordiality, 260
  and History, 261
Progression, of Libido, 63, 81
Projection, 88
Psyche, 57
  Layers of, 66
Psychic Energy, 58, 61, 64, 151
Psychic Processes and Archetypes, 72
Psychic Readiness, 199
Psychic Reality, 72
Psychoanalysis, 21

Radin, Paul, 270, 274
Rational Function, 101
Rebirth, 128
Reciprocal Relativity, 81, 204
Regression of Libido, 63, 81
Religion, 208
Repression, Freud's Theory of, 25
Res Cogitans, 164
Rivers, W. H. R., 274

St. Augustine, 128
Scapegoat, 88
Schelling, F., 30
Schopenhauer, A., 23, 27, 54, 167
Self, 151, 152
Semiotic, 184, 195
Sensation, 100
Sexual Trauma, 25
Shadow, 108
Shakti, 238
Shiva, 238
Signs, 184
Simmel, Georg, 37

Social Sciences, 13, 159
Splits, Psychic, 82
Sumner, William, 37
Switzerland, 21
Symbol
  and Dreams, 138
  and Religion, 208
  and Society, 181
  as Analogue, 183
  as Transformer of Energy, 181
  Definition of, 184
  in History, 197

Tao, 58
Therapy, 50
Thinking, 100
Tillich, Paul, 14, 15
Toynbee, Arnold, 12, 17, 51
Trauma, Sexual, 25
Types, Psychological, 98, 227

Unconscious, 10
  and Social Theory, 36
  Collective, 53, 66
  Freudian View, 40
  Personal, 66
  Repressed, 67
  to Hartmann, 24
  to Toynbee, 17

Veblen, Thorstein, 9, 36, 41

Weber, Max, 37
Whitehead, A. N., 233
Will
  in Hartmann, 24
  in Schopenhauer, 24
Will, 31
Will to Power, 131
Winnebago Indians, 279
Wise Old Man, 236
Wotan, 202, 253

Zarathustra, 31, 95
Zimmer, Heinrich, 234, 273

ABOUT THE AUTHOR

Since the early nineteen-fifties Ira Progoff has been exploring psychological methods for creativity and spiritual experience in their social applications. His doctoral dissertation was on the work of C. G. Jung and he subsequently studied privately with Dr. Jung in Switzerland as a Bollingen Fellow.

This work led to a reconstruction of depth psychology in terms of the later work of Freud, Adler, Jung and Rank in *The Death and Rebirth of Psychology* (1956) and a first statement of Holistic Depth Psychology in *Depth Psychology and Modern Man* (1959). In 1963 the method of Psyche-Evoking was articulated in *The Symbolic and the Real*.

Drawing on the principles described in these books, Dr. Progoff then developed in 1966 the *Intensive Journal* method of personal development. This is a nonanalytic, integrative system for evoking and interrelating the contents of an individual life. It is not limited to any one religious philosophy or psychological point of view and is now widely used. The two books that describe the method are: *At a Journal Workshop* (1975) and *The Practice of Process Meditation* (1980).

In 1983 *Life-Study* was published as a further step in the *Intensive Journal* educational program. It describes the application of the *Intensive Journal* process in experiencing the lives of significant persons from past generations. It is an approach that is increasingly utilized in programs of education for values in the conduct of life.

As the public use of the method increased, the National *Intensive Journal* Program was formed in 1977. It now supplies materials and leaders for the conduct of *Intensive Journal* workshops in the United States and other countries in cooperation with local sponsoring organizations.

Dr. Progoff is currently Director of the *Intensive Journal* program at its Dialogue House headquarters in New York City.